Each person's story is about all of us, and this book about David's story is told with ease, honesty and sincere generosity.

*— **Peter Block**,
Author of **Stewardship** and **The Answer to How Is Yes***

David has a great gift to write about authenticity in a truly authentic way. He does this by sharing his personal struggles to be authentic so that readers can relate and then by clearly pointing the direction to greater integration and wholeness. There are wonderful stories about his family that give his insights flesh and blood, thoughtful questions to aid readers in their own search for authenticity, a revealing way to face the shadow of one's personality as well as one's organization, and some stimulating ideas on how to develop one's own "Quality of Life Statement."

*— **Father Max Oliva, S.J.**,
Author of **The Masculine Spirit: Resources for Reflective Living***

To claim one's truest path and to live it is the only journey worth living. David Irvine has lived such a life and clearly shows the way to authenticity.

This journey is a practical, heartwarming, and inspiring guide to authentic living. It will help you remember who you are.

Wisdom only comes from fellow travelers and this one is a treasure. Irvine has lived the journey to authenticity and this book will help all of us claim our destiny.

*— **John Izzo**,
Author of **The Five Secrets You Must Discover Before You Die** and **Second Innocence***

David Irvine is sharing a compelling personal story about the journey to discover the authentic and true self. He opens his soul to readers in hope that it might serve as a guide in our journey of self-discovery.

*— **Kjersti Powell**,
Manager Human and Organizational Development, Syncrude*

David is a storyteller, and with his unique style he shares his journey and understanding of the meaning of life, spirituality, and calling. David's open and honest style will help you answer these questions for yourself. The end result will be more peace, contentment, and serenity… Isn't that what we all want?

David's book talks about the things that really matter: the meaning of life, spirituality, and calling. Anyone desiring personal growth in these areas will benefit greatly.

Would you like more peace, contentment, and serenity in your life? Join David as he shares his journey, in an open, authentic way, to achieve these states. David writes from the heart — the lessons learned and shared will help you on your journey.

— **Don Campbell**, *Rancher*

Most of us paint our lives by numbers. David's courageous and heart-warming book challenges us to rediscover our own authentic pallette and to paint large our own masterpiece. His generous spirit in sharing his very personal journey is a gift to those willing to accept it. David shows how ordinary day-to-day experiences can be transformed into extraordinary moments to cherish when viewed with authenticity.

— **Ian West**,
Administrator, Bethany Care Society

If this book is in your hand, it will soon be in your heart. You will be totally moved intellectually, emotionally, professionally, socially, and spiritually by the treasures of wisdom, the development of solid concepts, and the practical ideas you can use within minutes.

— **Dr. Lew Losoncy**,
Author of **If It Weren't for You, We Could Get Along!**
How to Stop Blaming and Start Living

Becoming Real

Journey to Authenticity

SECOND EDITION

Becoming Real

Journey to Authenticity

SECOND EDITION

By

David Irvine

PRESS

A Division of the Diogenes Consortium

SANFORD • FLORIDA

David Irvine
Box 358, Cochrane, Alberta, Canada T4C 1A6
Email: david@davidirvine.com
Website: www.davidirvine.com
www.newportinstitute.com

Published by DC Press
2445 River Tree Circle
Sanford, FL 32771
http://www.focusonethics.com

For orders other than individual consumers, DC Press grants discounts on purchases of 10 or more copies of single titles for bulk use, special markets, or premium use. For further details, contact:
Special Sales — DC Press
2445 River Tree Circle, Sanford, FL 32771
TEL: 866-602-1476

Book set in Adobe Caslon
Cover Design and Composition by Jonathan Pennell

Library of Congress Catalog Number: 2008922250
        Irvine. David,
Becoming Real: Journey to Authenticity, Second Edition
        ISBN: 978-1-932021-28-8

Second DC Press Edition
10   9   8   7   6   5   4   3   2   1
Printed in the United States of America

To Val, who came to me as a gift
and has walked beside me
on every step of the journey.

OTHER BOOKS OF INTEREST

Simple Living in a Complex World: Balancing Life's Achievements, by David Irvine

The Authentic Leader: It's About PRESENCE, Not Position, by David Irvine and Jim Reger

Accountability: Getting a Grip on Results, by Bruce Klatt, Shaun Murphy, and David Irvine

"What is real? ..."
"Real isn't how you are made. It's a thing that happens to you...
It doesn't happen all at once... You become... It takes a long time."

Margery Williams
The Velveteen Rabbit

Acknowledgments

Friends have I with the world before me,
Sun above and the wind behind me,
Life and laughter, double-blessed am I.
— **Brooks Tower**

WRITING A BOOK about authenticity is a lot like living an authentic life. It is an individual journey, while at the same time it cannot be done alone. I am indeed *double-blessed* by the people in my life. When I set out on this journey, my goal was to write a book so I could bring my voice to the world. The following are only a few of the many friends, colleagues and mentors whose support, criticism and perspective were essential in helping me find my voice and create this book:

Dennis McClellan, my publisher, without whose trust and encouragement this book would not exist. Authenticity is the heart and soul of DC Press. I am also grateful to Lew Losoncy, for his passion, trust, and support.

Father Max Oliva, who knows just when to show up in my life to release a logjam and get my spirit flowing again.

Don Campbell, a mentor and friend, who continues to support and encourage my spirit. Because of Don, I am a better person and this book is a better book.

Walter Brust, a rare and precious breakfast friend, who reminds me that life is an improvisation, not a strategic plan.

Jim Pender, whose clarity, wisdom, friendship, and belief in this project made it possible.

Janet Alford, who worked her usual magic and brought the manuscript to life. Ross Gilchrist, whose influence and perspective were invaluable.

Patty Kerfoot, whose insights and clarity were immensely valuable.

Brooks Tower, whose spirit and viewpoint were an inspiration.

Robert Terry, whose love and authentic presence touched the life of everyone he met. I wish he could have lived to see the completion of this book that he so deeply influenced with his affection and wisdom.

Bernie Novokowsky and Murray Hiebert, whose ongoing friendship and honesty and encouragement to be authentic in this venture have been invaluable. Bruce Klatt, whose continual friendship and support of this work remains important. John Izzo, whose perspective and encouragement to "keep your rear end on the seat" kept me going many times when I would rather have walked away from the computer. Mel Blitzer, whose perspective along the way was very helpful. Don Gray, who encouraged the early seeds of this book with the fresh and fertile soil of his acceptance, appreciation, and love. Jerry Weinberg, for his brutal honesty and congruence.

Ian West and John Charrette, whose authentic leadership and presence have been an inspiration and a source of courage to me along the way.

The lamplighter, Warren Harbeck, whose encouragement and support of this work kept my light going on many dark nights.

Kelly Rappuchi, whose clear and honest perspective and insights in the early stages of this undertaking helped immensely.

Carolyn Lea, whose patience, perseverance, and eye for detail gracefully brought this book through its final stages of production. Her skills, support, and commitment made this a better book.

Pat Copping, whose influence goes beyond words.

Susan Levin, whose impact on my life remains pivotal.

Jim Reger, whose support, friendship and authentic spirit in my life have been transformational to my work and life.

All of the participants in my workshops and presentations who courageously bring their authentic selves to their lives and continue to teach me.

Deep appreciation goes to my family, those closest to me: my parents, Joyce and Harland Irvine, whose influence lives on in my life. Kate Harling, my sister, whose authentic spirit continues to be a force in my life. Val, my wife and lifelong soul mate, who has stood beside me all the way. Her unfailing love, strength, wisdom, clear perspective, and gifted editing made it all possible. My daughters — Mellissa, Hayley, and Chandra — who gave their share of support as this project slowly came to fruition. This book would not be here today without you all.

A note about my daughters — much of this book tells about my own journey, illustrated with anecdotes from my experiences with those closest to me. Hayley's personality is similar to mine, so her observations and experiences often seem to reflect best what I desire to express in this book. As a result, Hayley's stories appear most often. But that doesn't diminish the unique influence that Chandra and Mellissa have on my life and on this book. Chandra, whose special gift is her gentle, easy-going, compassionate nature, and Mellissa, who is wise, loving and creative, both continue to enrich my writing and my life. My children are my mentors and my teachers.

Finally, to my Creator, who is the source of all that is within this book.

Table of Contents

Foreword

MY FRIEND AND HER HUSBAND were excited about their new little northern Idaho farm. In their first year, each day revealed another unexpected treasure. The little pond along the path from their front door to their driveway was pleasantly housing a few little fish dancing through life under the warm summer sky. One of their favorites was Charlie. Fall, then winter, blanketed the property with ice and snow. Janet and Bob, both city folk, would sometimes discuss their sadness at missing their little finned friends. Then one bright spring day while walking by the pond now teeming with life, there appeared Charlie, in the back of their reflection, in the small sea. Back to life!

Back to life! David Irvine's wisdom will quickly help you get over the hard, cold winter of your life and bring on springtime — again and again. You will come back to life without even moving from the spot in which you are reading this book. Your new world is simply a new mindset. There is so much information that moves deliberately to the center of yourself — your own private, precious real estate will be designed and decorated by you. Thomas Wolfe was wrong, you can go home again, and home is your own unique center, community, character, and calling. All yours. Why are you looking elsewhere? Where have you strayed? You are the best you and your best moments all combined — moments when you are congruent with who you truly are.

On solid ground, the author walks you through this journey to the center of yourself. Two millennia plus ago, Socrates asserted, "Know thyself." A century ago, the Christian existentialist Søren Kierkegaard concluded that the most common despair is to be in despair about not choosing, not willing to be oneself. The deepest form of despair, he said, was to choose to be other than oneself. "To thine own self be true!" preframes a theme you will discover consistently throughout this book of wisdom. And a half-century ago, Carl Rogers reframed neuroses not as a disease but a blocking of growth. The challenge is to grow and become the *one you* that you truly are and to counter the loss of center that occurs when one morphs into the "shoulds," "oughts," and "musts" of well-intentioned friends, role models, and authorities. In such cases, we again find ourselves frozen in winter with nowhere to move because we have nowhere to move from. We are lost in non-being. We are outer-directed.

If you and someone else are exactly alike, one of you becomes unnecessary!

We have to dress heavily for the winter, wearing a huge, heavy mask. Authenticity is the process of letting this burden down, moving lighter and brighter, and more cleanly. The tension of being discovered is removed. And your community begins sensing that you have it together. You are who you are. The answer is what this book is all about — the process of authenticity.

David Irvine's ideas are different because they are deeper. Many books teach surface change, such as how to change a behavior. This book will offer you gems to find your whole being. *Being change* is broader and deeper than *behavior change*. It's like finding your lost car — not just finding the carburetor. Plus, when you make a whole change, you change many behaviors as a result, don't you?

If this book is in your hand, it will soon be in your heart. You will be totally moved intellectually, emotionally, professionally, socially, and spiritually by the treasures of wisdom, the development of solid concepts, and the practical ideas you can use within minutes. Here you will find memorable quotes, compelling stories, and fireside-like chats of family experiences. There are so many stories and analogies that each one is like finding another toy inside the same Cracker Jack box!

All this, and yet curiously, there is an underlying written and unwritten message as you journey through the book to "relax." Just relax. You are going back to the one comfortable place in the universe where you truly belong. Back to the center of yourself!

Dr. Lew Losoncy
Author of If It Weren't for You, We Could Get Along!
How to Stop Blaming and Start Living

Preface to the
Second Edition

THE INSIGHTS OFFERED in this book have proven helpful to anyone committed to their own personal growth. In 2003, the first edition of *Becoming Real* was born from the leadership material I was researching. While interviewing people in a wide variety of organizations, I asked what they expected from their leaders. What I heard was, "We want our leaders to get past the gimmicks, the fads, the flavors of the month. We want our leaders to be honest. We want our leaders to be *real*." So I started to write a book about how to be a real leader. What I discovered is that before you can be a real leader, you first have to be a real human being. Then your leadership, your capacity to impact others, comes from the strength of that realness. It is about *presence*, not position. This book is about that journey to *becoming real*, the journey to authenticity.

Last week I spent a day with a longtime friend and colleague who has been battling cancer for the past eighteen months with a grinding mix of chemotherapy, radiation and all the other required oncology treatments. Though a few months ago his intensive PET-CT scan was clear (no cancer detected), and he is finished with "cancer camp" (as he calls it) for this season, he will continue to be monitored and tested by the cancer center periodically over the next several years. In the few hours we spent together, he articulated what the whole experience has meant to him:

"Ambitions for achievement in my business, my drive for financial success... well, let's just say they have been 'radiated' out of me. The only thing that seems to matter these days is love — for my life partner who has been beside me every step of this journey, for the beauty that surrounds me every waking moment, and for the people who matter most in my life."

Bernie continued, "I have also learned to value deeply the very small things in my life: being able to put my feet on the floor in the morning, to go for a walk in the sunlight, to be able to swallow. I am somehow strangely grateful for this experience of cancer. Not just grateful that I am alive today, but grateful for the deepening that this whole experience has given to the quality of my life. I'm a different person today. Although I would never wish this hell on anyone, today I *feel* more profoundly, I *suffer* more deeply, and I *love* more intensely. I have no idea how long I have left: two years or twenty years. I live each moment with a presence of mind that I have never had in my life. Coming so close to death, I have been awakened to life. I have become less tolerant of the stupid, trivial things people get upset with in our culture. The frivolous things of my life have been percolated out of me. I have been boiled down to a deep awareness of what really matters in this existence we call human."

Bernie is on a journey to authenticity. Through this experience, he has become more real. He is exploring and following the path of his heart in a culture that does not normally embrace this experience. Bernie recognized that the cancer and the enormous pain he experienced did not simply need to be eradicated; it actually needed to be *listened* to. His pain, he found out, was not the enemy, but a *messenger* that he had the courage to learn from. By examining the message of the pain and the illness, and by facing death, he deepened his connection to life.

I am not recommending cancer to move you to your authentic self, and I know that cancer and its pain offers no guarantee of achieving authenticity. This journey does, however, mean seeing oneself through new eyes; it means discovering and adhering to one's internal voice with consciousness, clarity, commitment, courage, and compassion. This is the path to one's true self, apart from the culture's demand for conformity.

Authenticity requires a dedication to seeking the truth about yourself, recognizing your destiny, and bringing more of that realness to what you do. It means realizing that life is not about proving oneself or measuring oneself by the standards of others, but is more about discovering and expressing one's truest nature. While the first half of our life is often about growing up, the authentic journey of the soul is more about growing down.

What fascinates me is the myriad of approaches for getting to the authentic self and the effect that taking the authentic path will have on your life and on the lives of people you live and work with. Having observed, studied, and focused my work on authenticity for more than twenty-five years, I have deep respect for the diversity of the human experience and the variety of ways that people enter this path: a life-threatening illness, the death of a loved one, a family crisis, a quiet and profound despair in the middle of the night, or a simple *knowing* that you need to make a change in your life. Each of these experiences, in their own unique way, can open the door to living with greater consciousness. For some, growth of the soul is sparked by a sudden event, a life-altering upheaval that causes a dramatic transformation. For others, this growth of the soul is a gradual evolution into a new, slowly developing awareness. By shifting from conforming to society's demands on the one hand to listening and responding to this quiet call of the soul on the other, a sustaining inner contentment emerges.

Becoming Real is an expression of my commitment to make a positive difference in the world, starting with you, the reader. I have written this book to support, inspire, and encourage you on your path to finding your authentic self in your own unique way. By having the courage to discover and express your voice, and by committing yourself to helping others find their voice, you make this a better world for all of us.

I offer no prescription for authenticity, for to do so would dishonor your own inner promptings and deep wisdom. Instead, I present my own experience in the hope that you will awaken to your own unique call to authenticity. In a world full of challenges, I have a dream. It is a dream that is deeply entrenched in my belief in the goodness and the resiliency of the human spirit, that one day we will open our compassionate hearts and realize that the sense of humanity within each one of us is the tie that binds us all. We will see that the path to a sustainable society lies in our appreciation for and connection to each other. I envision a world — in our homes, our communities, our organizations — where we can be real and honest, where we need not check who we are at the door, where we can grant ourselves the freedom to be who we are, rather than who we should be. I envision a world where we are respected and supported as we respect and support others.

We live in a time that demands listening to the call of authenticity in order to survive and grow as a species. We have moved beyond the industrial age to the information age and the age of the Internet, to a new and unexplored era of enlightenment. Technology, with all its advances, cannot take us there. Our challenge is to develop human beings with the awareness, the clarity, and the courage to be who they are meant to be and live the possibilities that lie within them. When we achieve that and connect with our personal power, we are in touch with our divinity, and in the process, are able to find meaning and contentment in our lives.

David Irvine
Cochrane, Alberta, Canada

Preface

As far as we can discern, the sole purpose of human existence is
to kindle a light in the darkness of mere being.
— *Carl G. Jung*

A FEW WEEKS AGO, I knelt by my nine-year-old daughter's bedside for our usual evening ritual of conversation about our day and a good-night kiss. On this particular evening, Hayley shared the challenges and conflicts she had faced that afternoon with her grade four friends — the usual stuff in the life of a nine-year-old — and then something in the room shifted. Hayley stopped talking and asked if I would stay a little longer and talk a little more. In the thin light, she suddenly looked up through moist, sad eyes and said, "I forgot to be myself today, Dad. I tried to be what my friends wanted me to be, and it just doesn't work."

I looked into her lovely eyes with awe and gratitude for her wisdom and openness, feeling her personal struggle to find and express her authentic self, the very thing that I am writing about in this book. I also knew that I could not take her pain away and thought, "How can I, as a father, affirm the strength and wonder and beauty of her spirit? How can I be fully present in this moment, so I can mirror back her splendor?"

Then I simply let the wonderment of the moment transform us and we hugged, experiencing a force that was beyond either of us. She relaxed back into the pillow and was soon asleep. I think at that moment she got a message that she is love and she is *loved* from a source well beyond me.

After leaving Hayley's room that night I reflected upon the brief and powerful connection that had taken place, not merely between a father and his nine-year-old daughter, but with a deeper, sustaining force that often gets buried beneath our roles and busy days. This force kindled a light in the darkness of that room and in my soul. It dawned on me that Hayley, in the sweet innocence of childhood, was able to tap into that deep well of the spirit and I was privileged to join with her in that experience. I have attempted to express in this book how connecting to this force within you and trusting yourself more deeply is the authentic journey. Authenticity is about opening to the experience of who you really are and courageously bringing that realness to the world.

Teaching about authenticity is akin to connecting with Hayley that night. Such a journey cannot be understood through words alone. So, rather than an explanation, I want to leave you with the *experience* of what it means to be embarking on the journey that will support, encourage and lead you to living a more authentic and fulfilling life, a life in alignment with who you are meant to be. More than being taught, the journey to authenticity probably will best be *caught*. The promise of living life without a facade and without pretense is sustained contentment and deep self-respect. Letting go of the need for prestige or approval from others will bring you freedom.

I have three reasons for writing this book. First, I offer it as a service to those who are committed to taking the courageous journey to authenticity and who can use some practical wisdom from a fellow traveler. Seeking perspective is an integral part of living authentically. As you travel along the path of living the life you are meant to live, you will find this book both personal and practical.

Second, writing has been a tool for my own development. My calling in life is to teach, an opportunity both to serve and to learn. When I put my thoughts to paper my philosophy can evolve through rich and life-giving dialogue with readers and participants in my programs. The line between the student and the teacher in this work grows ever dimmer over time. I invite conversation with you as you read this book and reflect upon its meaning in your own experience. This is how I learn and grow.

Third, I am writing this book because it is good for my soul. Working on this manuscript has helped me immensely along my own authentic journey. It has been said that what we are most capable of developing in others is what we are most in need of developing within ourselves. No truer statement could be made of my own path. Researching the topic, engaging in new levels of dialogue, excavating my voice, and telling the story of my own journey have awakened, strengthened and deepened my own authentic life. I learn by going where I need to go. I have learned enormously about my own path of authenticity by dedicating the past eighteen months of my life to writing about it.

In my work of writing and lecturing over the years, I used to see myself attempting to change the world. Today, I am less attached to changing the world and am learning to not take it personally when the world seems disinterested in changing. My work is simply to be myself and "show up" fully in the world, and to let the world change me.

David Irvine
Cochrane, Alberta, Canada

Introduction

to be nobody but yourself,
in a world which is doing its best, night and day
to make you just like everybody else,
means to fight the greatest battle there is to fight
and never stop fighting.
— e e cummings

THE GREAT SUFI MASTER Hazrat Inayat Khan, who introduced many important teachings to the West in the early twentieth century, offers an excellent metaphor for the development of the authentic journey. He compares the light of our spirit, our authentic self, to the light within a diamond. Just as the diamond must be cut to show its complete glow and brilliance, so must the authentic self be shaped to fully express its beauty. There are many insights, principles and philosophies that can be used as unique tools for cutting, shaping, and polishing your raw stone into the brilliance it is meant to be. Distilled from a variety of cultural, religious, and spiritual traditions and practices, along with storehouses of wisdom, the approaches to the authentic self that are described in the following chapters are insights and reflections to support you on your journey.

You will see, as you read my story, that my life is akin to the Buddhist proverb, "nanakorobi yaoki" — fall seven times, rise eight times. Truly, my life, which is my own greatest teacher, has been a tale of many ups and downs. I will share my experiences, my stumbling, and my falling and getting up again as it happened, in the hope that you may learn from my journey told in an authentic way.

Living the authentic life requires a dedication to seek, discern and move toward the truth about yourself, and in the process you become more comfortable with yourself. It requires a commitment to renewed consciousness, renewed connections, and renewed courage to act in the face of new awareness. But perhaps even more importantly, it requires gentleness and respect for being a more fully integrated human being and bringing that humanness to the world around us — to our workplaces, our communities, and to those closest to us. In the postmodern age, many live frantic and fragmented lives, often forgetting that we need love, companionship, internal unity, generosity, and time to read, reflect and take idle walks; we need time to be. The human spirit needs to be fed as much as the human body needs to be fed.

Living authentically asks the question, "What is really going on — both inside and outside of you — that prevents you from being yourself?" The path is about bringing more of who you are to what you do. Authenticity comes from within. Rather than living up to the standards and the mores of the culture, authenticity is much more about progress and honesty and realness. My goal in writing this book is to help release authenticity within you.

The promise of living life authentically is not freedom from pain or immunity from problems, but rather inner peace and self-respect in the midst of the external turmoil. As you liberate yourself by courageously letting go of the need to comply with how the world tells you that you *should* be, you begin to experience ordinary life as having value. You begin to live life from wisdom rather than from habits. You will experience freedom. You begin to feel the sustaining contentment that comes from knowing that you are a part of something larger than yourself. You embark on a journey of discovering "this is who I am" with a calm certainty, even amidst the chaos and uncertainty.

My oldest daughter, Mellissa, who is a potter, has taught me much while I watched her carefully mold a vase. Making pottery involves more than telling the clay what to become. The clay presses back on the potter's hands, telling her what it can and cannot do. She has to "feel with it," pay attention to it, and work *with* it, rather than work *on* it. And if she fails to listen, the outcome will be a disaster. Sculpting our interior lives is very much like this. It is the relationship with the clay that shapes us — as we shape it, it shapes us.

Before embarking with you on the journey to authenticity, I will begin with a few traveling tips. First, *respect yourself*. Your journey to authenticity requires that it be uniquely your own. No one can prescribe the shape your diamond is meant to be. Just as there is a multitude of ways to discover the God of your understanding, so, too, are there numerous roads to the growth and expression of the authentic self. I have chosen strategies that have been useful to me and are applicable on a daily basis. Everyone is unique, and our needs change over time. You may not relate to some of my experiences or you may be in a different life stage. Each of us has to do the work of releasing authenticity in our own unique way. The value of another's experience is to shine a light, not to tell us how or whether to proceed. Rather than driving yourself toward a goal as you read this book, I invite you to enjoy the pleasure of new awareness. Relax and enjoy the learning process, even in the moments when you might be uncomfortable with the new insights. If you miss something when reading the book for the first time, don't worry. Perhaps you'll pick it up the second or third or even the eighth time. Above all, take what fits, and leave the rest.

Second, *festina lente*. This advice from the Roman emperor Augustus means "make haste slowly." Be patient with yourself and those around you. Living life authentically requires perseverance and persistence. The journey of authenticity requires that we remember that anything worth doing is worth doing slowly, and that *direction* is more important than *velocity*. Aim for progress rather than perfection. Expect to succeed, but over the long haul. There are no quick fixes here. Be gentle with yourself. Small, steady, incremental steps are more important than huge leaps, especially when the leaps are followed by colossal crashes and disappointment in ourselves.

Third, as you read this book and reflect upon its application to your life, *keep an open mind*. Socrates said, "Wisdom begins with wonder." One of the qualities of authenticity is the willingness to be open or receptive. *Openness* is not necessarily the same as *agreement*. As a person who has conformed to others' wishes and wisdom considerably in my life, I often take on what others say too readily, only to find myself resentful afterwards, conforming to someone else's views that didn't fit my own. Be a student, but not a follower. Everything I say needs to be weighed and debated in your own mind, matched against your own experience and perceptions, then integrated with your own being before calling it your truth. Whatever desire or inquisitiveness brings you here, it is my hope that by reading about my experiences, you will connect more deeply with your own. This is what the authentic journey is about.

Fourth, remember to *sit while the credits roll*. Many people seem to be in such a hurry to get out of a theater after a touching movie. Maybe it is the discomfort of being in another world and coming back to reality or maybe they were not touched at all or perhaps they just had an appointment to get to. Regardless, I am learning to let life touch me and to sit with the stirrings. When my spirit has been moved in a dark theater, I sit while the credits roll and let the experience sink in. Give life the same opportunity to touch and shape you. Take time for the important events in your life to strike home, to affect you. Don't be in a hurry. If something stirs you or even irritates you as you read, sit with it. Write about it. Talk about it. Meditate or pray about it. Try to resist the temptation to run from it by shifting too quickly to your next experience. The journey to authentic living is through the heart. Learning to be still when discomfort surfaces can be a vital way to access your authentic self.

In a culture that reveres celebrities and materialism, I am writing to give some needed balance by recognizing the authentic value of every human being, not for what we *have* or even *do*, but most vitally for who we *are*. Some are called to extraordinary achievement. Most, however, are called to acknowledge extraordinary value simply in our humanness. The book begins with my own humanness, my own honest, authentic journey to authenticity. The four sections of the book that follow my story are intended to support and guide you in your journey. Each chapter outlines one of the four vital life-sustaining tasks that provide the framework for authentic living.

The *first* task on the authentic voyage is to find your *center* — to quiet yourself enough to listen to the voice of your heart, to listen to what you don't hear in the demands of your daily affairs. In my work as a psychotherapist, teacher and consultant for more than twenty years, I found that there can be no real peace or contentment without recognizing your spiritual nature. In the words of Teilhard de Chardin, "We are not human beings having a spiritual experience. We are, rather, spiritual beings having a human experience." Finding your center brings you to this awareness in your own unique way. Authenticity calls us to make the shift from being a thermometer, where we are simply an indicator of our outside environment, to finding an internal thermostat, where we can regulate the internal temperature, and thus find inner solace, strength, and wisdom, independent of the outer climate — of health or sickness, success or failure, a long life or a short life.

The *second* task of authenticity is to nourish *community*. The authentic journey is an individual one, but it can't be done alone. We need allies, confidants, mentors, and intimate relationships along the way. Connecting with a community means asking yourself, "Who supports me?" "Who am I accountable to?" "Who will hold me to my promises?" The price of community is some vulnerability, the risk of rejection, and possibly some frustration and pain that comes from deciding to be in relationship for the long haul. The promise of community is deep fulfillment and connection in belonging to something larger than yourself. You are not alone.

The *third* task on the journey of authenticity is to build strong *character*. Character is the outcome of living a life in accord with your deepest values and virtues. Strong character enables a person to make consistent choices under diverse situations based on principles rather than emotions. Character is about tapping into the strength of a well-developed conscience and thereby choosing courage over comfort.

The *fourth* task on the authentic voyage is to seek your *calling*. "Why are you here?" "What are you meant to do with your life?" These are the questions that shape and measure your authentic life. Calling connects you to your stewardship — the development and expression of your unique gifts in the service of others. Authenticity asks you to get to the heart of what your life is meant to be about.

At the conclusion of this book I have included an appendix entitled "Exercises for Further Reflection and Action." This section is for those interested in going further along the authentic journey in a more practical and concrete way. This section is meant as an extended workbook for those who wish to deepen their authenticity with some reflections and specific calls to action beyond the insights and inspiration.

Best wishes on your journey.

My Journey

THE DESTINY OF THE MIGHTY OAK TREE is inscribed in the tiny acorn, and like that acorn, we are all born as a seed of possibilities to fulfill in our lifetime. Life is a journey that awakens us to who we are uniquely destined to be, to a voice we are meant to bring to life. All of our life experiences are necessary for this awakening to occur. The call of authenticity is to be a gardener, cultivating and nourishing the soil of our soul, creating an environment that supports the unfolding of our unique potential.

Through authenticity we become conscious contributors in our own lives as we transform our experiences into a portal to our life's most vital work. We begin to see how we can learn and grow from each experience that comes to us. We acquire self-awareness resulting in new perceptions and new choices and shift from seeing ourselves as victims of our pain to co-creators of all our experiences. Every experience can be a blessing or a curse, depending on the meaning that you derive from it and the choices you make. Winning the lottery can, for example, send your life into ruin, while the death of a loved one can eventually bring you the blessing of a stronger character. We realize that pain, hardships and setbacks are not just obstacles to overcome but necessary experiences on the path of our innermost calling. One of the signs of the dawning of authenticity is the gradual extinguishing of blame and the subsequent emergence of the quiet acceptance of life's conditions as they occur, while making full use of what happens to you, both in the present and the past. Circumstances in this context do not determine us, but rather, they *reveal* and *shape* us.

Just as we are born as a unique seed of possibilities, so, too, are we born into an environment that has expectations, that tells us how we "should" be in order to fit in. Rather than growing in support of our seed, we often align ourselves with the terms, conditions and pressures of the culture and thus lose touch with our authentic self, the inner essence that we are put here on earth to fulfill. With the intent to survive in a culture that attempts to dictate our choices, we bring to the world a facade, a covering, while something else, something private, is growing underneath. The authentic journey is to reconnect with and awaken to what is hidden, to recognize the vital growth that is going on below the surface, and to bring who we are meant to be back into the world in a conscious and renewed way.

I used to think that in order to be authentic, you had to be inauthentic first. Looking at how I was living twenty years ago, I could easily judge myself and say, "How inauthentic I was then!" But now I am not so sure. The paradox is that as we recognize our past "inauthenticity," we realize that we were probably as authentic as our consciousness would allow us to be at the time. I now know that I *needed* to fit into the culture and lose touch with my interior life for a time, just as I now know that I can no longer travel on a road of incongruity. "Inauthenticity" at times in your life will save you. You had to go through what you went through to be where you are today. Choosing gratitude and curiosity about your past, rather than blame and resentment, will help you open the door to a new life.

The authentic journey — manifesting the person you are meant to be — is akin to the work of an artist. I think of Michelangelo, who was asked once how he carved and created such magnificence and beauty from a slab of cold marble. Michelangelo reportedly replied, "I didn't do anything. God put Pietà and David in the marble. They were already there. I only had to carve away the parts that kept you from seeing them!"

For me, carving away the parts that no longer fit, that blocked me from my truest self, came through a series of events, significant turning points in my life. These led me through seven stages in the development of authenticity, from survival to spiritual maturity: vulnerability, compliance, defiance, humility, integrity, contribution, and a return to vulnerability. Like a chisel striking marble, these stages were initiated by the hammer of "instructional moments of disillusionment." Although the experiences were painful and often traumatic at the time, they were actually necessary and profound teaching moments providing a passage to a deeper connection to my authentic self. At the time they seemed to be random occurrences that I coped with the best way I could and I didn't know that they were leading me to my destiny. I was unaware that there was a guiding, compelling force calling me to my authentic self. Below the surface of my "traumas," there was the power of a great sculptor, calling and preparing me to connect with a deeper essence that addressed the fundamental questions, "What is it, in my heart, in my soul, that I must do and be? Who am I, really?"

Like the work of an artist, there is no prescribed way to carve away the parts of your life that keep you from your destiny. The beauty of authenticity lies in your own unique expression of who you are meant to be. I have found that the seven stages can be used as guideposts in supporting you through your own distinctive excavation of your authentic self. I trust that my story will give you some perspective and sustenance on your journey.

The first stage of authenticity, vulnerability, begins in early childhood. The youngest of three siblings, I grew up in a home that was a blend of chaos and order, mental illness and love, unpredictability and respect, breakdowns and breakthroughs. In my upbringing, along with all the darkness, there was also enormous respect and love given to us by my parents and the community that surrounded us. As in all families, we had elements of both health and dysfunction. My parents were wonderful people, with good values, enduring wisdom, and loving hearts. They also had their dark sides, and I am grateful today that they exposed us openly to who they were. Even though there was pain and trauma, I know now that it was all part of my destiny to grow up in the home and community that I was born into. I could not be the person I am today, complete with all my flaws and my subsequent gifts, without the raw metals of my upbringing.

As a child, my innate nature was to nurture. It was part of the acorn I was born with. With my vulnerable and open heart I created a room that was filled with a wide collection of dolls. I loved and played with the dolls through my preschool years. Then, in grade one I eagerly and innocently took them to school for show and tell. After enduring the laughter and ridicule of my classmates, I did what I needed to do as a six-year-old to survive — I packed those dolls away in boxes, refusing to subject myself to such pain again. That day I closed a part of my heart.

This experience marked my first conscious memory of the end of vulnerability. The world no longer felt safe, and I learned to hide, to pretend and to comply in order to survive. The hammer of rejection came down hard on my exposed spirit, and the pain of betrayal ended my innocence and closed the door to vulnerability. Hiding my dolls was a form of anesthesia that protected me from both the uncertainty of a perceived judgmental world and simultaneously insulated me from my authentic nature. It was not only the doll collection that was disowned and hidden in boxes that day. I closed down and disowned and hid away a piece of who I was. In an attempt to protect myself and survive in the best way I knew how, I began to separate from that nurturing self, from that deeper, authentic part of me. It was as though my seed of possibility, my seed of nurturing potential, my gift of love, was buried like the treasures in King Tut's tomb. I made up my mind that day that there was little room for gentleness and sensitivity in my life. It was time to conform, to comply, to give the world what it wanted so I could be a part of humankind.

This experience marked the beginning of the next stage of my authentic path — the period of compliance, of conforming in order to fit in, of pleasing others in order to survive, of showing only a strong, competent side to match the world's demands, to present myself as "good" on the outside while I covered up and denied the soft, sensitive side on the interior. When I was around tough kids, I knew how to act tough. When I was around smart kids, I knew how to act smart. I learned how to "imitate" in order to "integrate," or at least I thought so at the time. I attempted to be a part of a world that I didn't feel I belonged in, yet wanted so desperately to be a part of.

In high school, wanting so very much to fit in led me to try out for the football team. I was a great football player lacking only two things: size and talent. I had no speed, no agility, no ability to catch or throw, and I weighed a hundred and fifty pounds. But because it was a small school, no one was cut. The coach really had no idea where to put me, so he assigned this scrawny fifteen-year-old to the offensive line. I think he was hoping I would get hurt so he could release me graciously. I ended up injuring myself after attempting to block a two hundred and twenty-five pound defensive tackle. While being carried off the field, I'm convinced that my friends back in the huddle could hear my quiet muttering, "Next time I am going to kill him!" I vowed that no one would ever see me cry, so not a tear was shed until I was alone in the emergency room.

During those elementary and adolescent years, unacknowledged depression surrounded me. Being depressed and not knowing it was, for me, like walking around unaware of high blood pressure. You don't know it is there, but all of a sudden, clinical depression engulfs you like a heart attack of the soul, which is what happened to me years later. By trying to fit in to the culture, I was shutting off from my authentic self. With a closed heart, I was not aware of what was going on around me. On the surface, I was cheerful and, for the most part, cooperative. I hid behind the cloak of politeness and achievement in school. In middle school I gained popularity as a leader in student council and I had a girlfriend that I clung to for nearly six years. I took up competitive running and became a nationally ranked long-distance runner. Running was a socially acceptable way to escape the aloneness buried deep inside. All of these activities had an element of goodness, of usefulness to the world and to myself. Yet no amount of distraction from my girlfriend, achievement, or external recognition could fill the unidentified hole within a lonely and depressed adolescent.

During this time period, I immersed myself in the religion of my family. The best my authentic self could muster at that time was to follow a code of moralistic ideals, values, and virtues that I took on as a part of the religious order in which I was raised. My goal then was to unquestionably conform to the expectations of others. Fundamentalism was my home. It offered me security, structure and clear solutions for dealing with an uncertain world and an insecure and unsettled inner spirit. Religion and its solutions along with my compliance gave me a much-needed road map for taking me into the tentative and uncertain world of adulthood. I walked blindly through life in those days with unquestionable obedience to the expectations of trusted, well-meaning, benevolent authority figures who were men of good standing and who role modeled their values. Unfortunately, I adopted a simple moralistic approach to life that reduced ethical living to making a list and checking it against an arbitrary image of perfectionism. I tried very hard in those days to be decent while carrying an illusion that someday I would actually be able to have a perfect checklist and get to the highest place in heaven.

After the "conforming adolescent" period that lasted until my mid-twenties, my independence began with the next stage of authentic expression — defiance. The instructional moment of dis-illusionment that inducted me into this stage came in the form of some significant growth experiences in my graduate education and through extensive study with the late renowned family therapist, Virginia Satir. My eyes were opened to new consciousness and at the age of twenty-four, I entered a seditious period and took the arm of rebellion with a vengeance. I escaped the shackles of conformity by running from all responsibility. "I want to be me!" I exclaimed. I then took my narcissism and left my marriage, a two-year-old daughter, and the security of the church — and in the process rejected any form of spirituality.

For the next fifteen years I lived with few virtues, values, or ideals except what gave me pleasure and relieved discomfort. It was during this time that I wrote my declaration of independence, pro-claiming my liberty from the shackles of the dictatorship of funda-mentalism. I did what I wanted when I wanted and with whom I wanted. I ran from relationships and responsibilities. When the going got tough, I got going — in another direction. I turned to external sources of gratification, obsessive achievement and worka-holism, to sustain and provide me with self-worth.

Looking back on this time, I realize now that in my attempt to break free of compliance, the ensuing defiance, although it was a necessary step away from conformity, actually swallowed my liber-ty. One's freedom is limited in the stance of either *compliance* or *defi-ance*. I was able to project an image of autonomy, but the truth was that I was angry, afraid, and insecure. By denying, escaping, and avoiding this reality, I was not a lot further along the journey to living an authentic life than when I was escaping under the oppression of compliance. It was the opposite side of the same counterfeit coin. Yet I was, somehow, still growing in my own limited way. At least this time I had turned the coin over and was exploring a new side of myself — the side that could be explicitly rebellious — and thus, another step along the way.

During those defiant years, the insecurity, instability and depression that were formerly hidden under a blanket of conformity surfaced with retribution. Without the structure and security of fundamentalism, I was lost. I had no one — nothing to answer to. I lived an illusion of freedom, running aimlessly through life with no anchor or rudder to hold me back from the open sea or to protect me from the tempests of life. I had no roots to keep me from breaking in the storms.

As an unsettled and restless person in desperate search of inner peace and fulfillment, I sought answers from external sources. I signed up for personal development workshops, bought a myriad of self-help books, and entered psychotherapy. I went to Buddhist retreats and practiced letting go of attachments, getting in touch with my "beingness." Then I would go to New Age workshops, listen to mystics, and request guidance from psychic readers and channels. I would listen to motivational speakers talk about the "Power of Positive Thinking" and "If it is to be, it is up to me!" They would remind me there was no limit to how successful I could be or how much money I could create for myself. I went on vision quests, extended fasts, and sat in sweat lodges. I am grateful for all of these experiences because they helped shape me and brought me to where I am today. They were a part of the mosaic of my life, necessary in the development of my authenticity, and while every one of them left me with a residue of growth, I longed for something more, something to sustain the inspiration, something to last longer than the few days following the high of a new insight.

Rather than being someone with personal integrity or self-respect during these years, I was a person with "situational values." My values emerged based on the situation in front of me. I gave the world what it wanted when I needed something back from the world. Moving still further away from my heart, I made my mark in the world through acquisition and admiration. I began a process, in my late twenties and thirties, of proving myself to the world, of portraying to the world my strength, of succeeding at business, of gaining self-worth by proving my importance in the world. I tried to fill my life with outside stuff. I bought a big house and filled it with things, but it didn't fill the emptiness inside.

This was a disintegrating time for me, for I was not able to consciously amalgamate much of my new awareness into sustained change. Fleeing from reality will inevitably take you into discouragement. I lacked the integrity that transpires from facing yourself and from keeping promises to yourself and others. Once the high of the weekend retreat or the latest book subsided, I reverted to my old lost and insecure self. I was listening to all the external teachers and was caught in the trap of trying to conform to all of them. Even when I was practicing as a psychotherapist, facilitating personal growth workshops, or making presentations, I learned all the right words, but I was not coming from a grounded, integrated place. I was seeking authenticity out of desperation rather than out of trust. What I was searching for was peace in my fragmented interior world. I struggled in intimate relationships. I got depleted and burned out practicing as a psychotherapist, trying desperately to be helpful to people, not knowing that my *helping* was really about *hiding* — hiding a deep sense of aloneness and insecurity — and was not the compassion and wisdom that emerges from self-respect and sustaining principles. I developed an insatiable desire for "more" — more recognition, more success, more materialism, more acquisition, even more answers. What I recognize now is that I was trying to fill, in the words of Pascal, the "God-sized hole in my heart," and no amount of recognition or acquisition would fill that emptiness in my soul. No sooner would I get the praise and affirmation from the world than I would look around and ask myself, "Is this all there is?" Then I would set another goal to fill the insatiable ambition for more. Behind the determination was a need to prove myself and seek approval from the world. This stemmed from insecurity, rather than a healthy desire to be a good steward of the gifts that had come to me. Although I was vocationally successful, I was continually in debt, both spiritually and financially, convincing myself that if I just had enough possessions or spiritual experiences or knowledge or status or recognition I would fill the emptiness inside. This was also a time when I was very difficult to live with. Just as I helped many in my work, I hurt many in my personal life.

My life had moved far from that seed of possibility. I was paying a price for being out of step with my true nature, with my destiny, and I was slowly and fervently being called to come back to myself. Both depression and manic busyness prevailed in my life. In 1986, my father died. The following year I ended a significant relationship and contemplated suicide. I checked myself in for psychiatric assessment and was diagnosed as having inherited my father's bipolar disorder, which, I was told, would progress, and I would probably need to be on medication for the remainder of my life. I resisted the diagnosis and left with a firm resolve to not be like my father — to *will* my way into a different life. I reverted to my highly driven, manic self, not allowing a place for vulnerability, dependence, surrender, or humility. I know now that with no humility, confidence is unattainable. I reverted to my old self of overworking, over-accumulating, over-exercising, over-eating and over-helping. I moved every year or two, thinking that a geographic cure would somehow bring a degree of contentment to the unsettled restlessness that persisted and progressed. I continued to escape from the discomfort of facing myself honestly. The mood swings worsened over time. The lows got lower; the highs got higher. The illness became bigger than my self-knowledge and self-will combined. I became further and further removed from a conscious connection to my authentic self, from my spiritual roots.

In the following years, I channeled my energies into socially acceptable endeavors. I met and married my lifelong partner, launched my speaking career, returned to the world of competitive running and continued to build my business into work that I loved. But the shadow side — the depressive and unmanageable manic tendencies — managed to creep into my life even though all appeared to be well on the surface. I found my endeavors both rewarding and insatiable. There was always another challenge to overcome, another goal to achieve, another race to run. I was always in search of better accomplishments. By *needing* my business for my worth, I allowed it to *own* me and was gone from my family more than two hundred days a year. Indeed, I had a rich standard of living and a poor quality of life. To the world I was a success. But there was incongruity between what I was teaching and how I was living. Each day I got up with resolve to do better, and so I stayed busy, always fearful of letting down the mask. But I didn't have the awareness or tools to know how to stop the masquerade and be comfortable with what was underneath. Like the Cheshire Cat in Lewis Carroll's *Alice in Wonderland*, I was following the path of "any road will get you there" if you don't know where you're going.

I was inducted into the next stage on the authentic journey — humility — through a series of inner nudges, inviting me to move forward on the path. These started with small wake-up calls — falling asleep at the wheel of my car and hitting an embankment late one night, anxiety attacks, bouts of depression, and inner desolation that swept over me like a black cloud in the middle of the night — but I have learned that if you push the snooze button, if you don't listen to the early warnings, the universe has a way of increasing the intensity until you wake up. My "instructional moment of disillusionment," that moment of awakening when I knew I needed to make some important changes in my life, came when I was working out of town and missed my daughter's birth. Hayley was born early, and despite what I thought were adequate precautions, I was simply too busy working — achieving — to be realistic and make it to Val's side in time. The irony of this painful situation is that Hayley was born while I was away leading a retreat on how to build a meaning-ful life beyond success, with enduring and lasting connections. This was when it began to dawn on me that my life was growing increas-ingly incongruent, disengaged from, and out of alignment with my inner values, with what mattered most to my authentic self. In my frantic and ambitious pursuit of wealth, I had succumbed to the poverty of spiritual isolation.

It was at this time, in my early forties, after sleepless nights, bouts of anxiety, and lengthy periods of despondency, that I began to realize I was living separate from my authentic self, my spiritual center, and those closest to me. I hit a spiritual bottom that opened the door to humility — the deep realization that self-reliance alone will only take you so far, that self-will alone will eventually take you to a wall that you will never be able to climb alone. Entering into the stage of humility means to begin the search for the truth about yourself, to seek an understanding of what is going on within you and around you, and to surrender to a power beyond yourself. For me, the door of humility opened to reliance on the God of my understanding as my source of direction and strength. Recognizing the limits of self-will paradoxically brings strength. Discovering and turning to a power beyond self-reliance brings spiritual maturity as you turn to a divine center as the source of worth that sustains you beyond anything imaginable within the physical realm. I could not live any longer without faith and without a reliance on a power beyond myself. Without faith and the humility that is required to trust, I was at sea without a rudder or an anchor, drifting on the ocean of life. By surrendering to a power greater than myself and trusting that power, I gained the strength to face whatever comes.

Living life from this spiritual source is no longer a search for happiness. Sustained contentment is independent of the fleeting emotions of happiness or unhappiness.

I know now that my need for recognition, power, and social acceptance was fueled by a profound sense of insecurity that stemmed from a disconnection to my spiritual roots. There was much incongruity between what my soul was yearning for and what the world was furnishing, for the world could not possibly fill my spiritual emptiness. I was on the journey to "find myself" and was, instead, lost in the darkness of self-will and self-centeredness. I began to fear again for my sanity. I felt things closing in the inner chamber of my life. I had real difficulty explaining to the people around me what was going on in my soul, behind the confident mask I showed to the world. But my family knew, as did the deepest part of me when I took the time to look in the mirror at night.

The rehabilitation of my authentic self through the process of humility began with truthfulness with myself. I began facing my compulsive and addictive tendencies. I started to face myself with honesty, open-mindedness, and a deep desire to change. I stopped running from my broken self and started looking at what was fueling my insatiable human hungers. I started to reach out for support from individuals who began to hold me accountable for living a life of *character*, rather than a life of *comfort*, for accepting and facing the weaknesses and darker aspects of myself. I began to create a structure for accountability to keep promises to myself and to others and for living a life of order and moderation. As I clarified what mattered most and aligned my choices in a very real way with my core virtues and values, my spirit was awakened. I started building a solid and sustaining spiritual foundation on which to build my life and rest my soul. With the rehabilitation of my authentic self, I learned that I need structure in my life — a community to support me and hold me accountable, a daily practice of connecting with a higher power, a structure for healing my past, adequate rest, good nutrition, and a daily commitment to overcome self-centeredness.

The awakening of my spiritual source and the reliance on a strength beyond myself ignited the restoration of my integrity — the next stage on the journey. Integrity — the inner union that emerges from keeping promises to yourself and others — is about integration. Integration can only come as we open ourselves to the entire spectrum of our inner life and create an accountable structure to hold our humanity in a socially responsible way. This kind of structure gives me an inner peace and my spirit is awakened as I am learning to see the world through a new set of lenses. My depressive nature and bipolar and addictive tendencies are always present, but by being honest with myself and mindful of these darker sides of my nature, I am learning to manage my mood swings in a socially responsible way. I have learned that my depression is the result of an imbalance in my approach to life — an imbalance that gives rise to chemical changes in the brain and central nervous system — and these chemical changes create and perpetuate the depression. Managing with depression begins with listening to it, not as a pathology to "cure," but rather as an instructive indicator of imbalance. Healing depression then becomes a matter of restoring balance to the brain chemistry. I am able to achieve this through the use of nutrition, consistent and balanced exercise, new ways of thinking, ongoing support, and behavior changes.

As old tendencies no longer own me or control my life, I am able to feel some freedom. I am learning to face and talk openly about the fears, doubts, and insecurity that underlie the symptoms of overwork, frantic busyness, over-eating, addictive exercise, obsessive approval seeking, over-spending, and over-attachment to relationships. In this daily practice I am finding a degree of freedom and am on a healing journey of self-acceptance.

Gradually, the journey took me through the door to the next stage of authenticity — contribution. The darker aspects of my nature are gradually being transformed into useful gifts that serve a useful purpose as I learn to bring them into my community. Authenticity must be given away in order to be kept. We must give in order to live. We must serve in order to sustain ourselves. Civilization would cease if all of us existed only for ourselves. As our gifts are awakened, particularly at midlife, we must shine a light on these newly discovered talents and bring them into our community. If the unique and powerful life force within us is suppressed, it will be lost from the world, and our spiritual, mental, and physical health will suffer. Authentic contribution comes not from our positions, but from the *presence* we bring to whatever roles we hold. Contribution moves us to a place where we cease to define a good day by one in which everything goes our way, but rather when, through some small act of ours, we were able to make the day better for someone else.

As I enter my second adulthood, and take root in the stages of integration and contribution, a variety of emotions surface. I have a sense of being more settled, both within and around me, and have less of a need to prove myself. I still like nice things around me — a nice car, a comfortable home — but materialism is now becoming my servant rather than my master.

Today I am less driven and more reflective. I am more comfortable with myself. I am more content. I have less of a need to *make* things happen, and more trust to *let* things happen. I am less interested in the approval of others and know that what others think of me is none of my business. I am less interested in getting my own way and more interested in getting *out* of my own way. Having gone through periods of betrayal and anguish, I am now finding myself returning to the mindset and wonderment of a child, only with the eyes of a more spiritually mature and less self-centered adult. I have less of a need to write in order to sell books, and more of a yearning to write — and live — from my heart. I will never retire, if retirement means sitting still too long. I see myself forever contributing, learning, serving, and giving back what I have so generously been given, and as I move into the next leg of my journey I will work, contribute and serve in a new way. I will probably always work hard. It is a part of me, but I am learning to do so in a new, more relaxed way.

As I enter the second half of my life, I sense the promise of authentic living — a deep and sustaining inner peace, but I am also aware of moving into a new period of vulnerability. I am being initiated into an era of loss. I am losing some hair, some strength and flexibility, some eyesight, and some sexual potency. I take action daily to counter the natural effects of aging through renewed relationships, regular exercise, stimulating conversations and learning opportunities, but I am becoming increasingly aware of my own mortality and the frailty of life. I cannot deny the losses I am simultaneously experiencing. My hope is that I can walk gracefully through the next fifty years of my life and face death with the same sense of curiosity, wonderment, gratitude and acceptance that I am learning to live with. This is a good time to be alive, and I would not have been able to say that had it not been for the grace of a power beyond me that helps me face what comes one day at a time.

This unfolding of my spiritual self and my authentic life is not based on external manipulation or strategies, but is like a seed that is growing in ways that cannot be fully comprehended by the rational mind. Authentic expression is like beauty: it is easier to *experience* rather than describe, to *recognize* rather than analyze. The authentic life is much more of a work of art than an endeavor of strategy. Just as the work of an artist is never complete, so, too, the work of painting or sculpting or crafting an authentic life will go on for a lifetime. By slowing down, listening carefully to our inner voice, allowing the pain, discomfort, and uneasiness of life to touch us and shape us, then emerging with courage to follow through on our calling, we tap into the deep spiritual roots from which meaningful living emerges.

I clearly recall how the evening summer sun was glowing through the trees as we turned into the cemetery and followed the road that led to the sunken headstones. Although my four-year-old daughter and I had spoken many times of her grandpa Harlie, this was Hayley's first trip to his gravesite, three hours from where we lived. My father died seven years before her birth, so she never knew the gift of his loving arms around her as she sat on his lap or the feel of his whiskers on her tender cheeks.

As we stepped out of the car, Hayley ran ahead looking for her grandfather's name amidst the rows of granite stones. It didn't take her long to find his gravestone. Wilfrid Harland Irvine, 1918–1986 — "A New Beginning" is inscribed on the bottom of the headstone and two seagulls are carved in the top corner, just as two gulls are on every one of Dad's paintings.

I stood beside my father's grave, holding Hayley's little hand in mine. Tears welled in my eyes as I sought words to tell Hayley what a great man her grandfather was, how proud he would have been of his beautiful granddaughter, and how much he would have loved her. At that moment, Hayley ever so tenderly surrounded both sides of my open hand with her tiny fingers and gently brought my palm to her heart.

I will never forget her words: "Don't be afraid, Dad. Grandpa Harlie is still alive. He is a spirit. He is an angel. He lives right here in my heart."

Hayley did not *learn* this. We had never had conversations about God or religion or angels or spirituality. Hayley *knew* this. It was a deep knowing that she brought with her to this world. It was the wisdom of innocence we are born with. The challenge for all who seek the authentic journey is to develop the capacity to embody this wisdom and to manifest it in the world. We do this, in part, by see-ing the world through lenses that allow us to take the experiences of life — a painful upbringing, the loss of a loved one, a hard-earned achievement, a troubled relationship, or an immense joy — all of the grief and the bliss, and let them shape us into an authentic self. Rather than a destination, authenticity is a method of travel. It is a way of being in the world. It is a way of relating to yourself, relat-ing to others, and relating to life, forever growing, changing, shap-ing, and becoming real.

* * * *

CHAPTER 1

&

Finding Center

Dwell as near as possible to the channel in which your life flows.
— **Henry David Thoreau**

* * * *

FOR FOUR YEARS, I TRAVELED with an accountant, a lawyer, and a financial planner in a single-engine Cessna 180, leading succession planning workshops for family businesses throughout Alberta. Because the pilot was instrument rated, I got used to flying through unpleasant weather where visibility was nonexistent. One afternoon Brock turned the yolk over to me when we became engulfed by a severe storm. We couldn't see anything. It was as if a white blanket covered the windshield. Suddenly the engine began to sound louder. I noticed, as I read the instruments on the panel in front of me, that we were dropping altitude and flying to the right. However, it felt to me as if we were flying straight and level. I shared my concern with the pilot, who was patiently watching me go through this experience. He then gave me a lesson about disorientation when flying by instruments without sight and how I needed to trust the instruments and not my feelings or impulses. I pulled back on the yolk and turned to the left to straighten out the plane. Now the instruments indicated that we were flying straight and level, but I felt as if we were flying up and to the left. My feelings said we were flying upward too steeply, which could potentially stall and crash the plane, but the instruments said we were fine. I had to fly with that fear for several minutes before the feeling that we were flying off course went away.

Finding a center is akin to having an internal gyroscope to rely on during the journey — and inevitable storms — of life. Finding a trustworthy center that lies beneath your feelings and your impulses, and relying on this center for guidance and strength and wisdom, is similar to trusting the flight instruments. It is the difference between believing in a higher power and *trusting* in that higher power. But just what is this "internal gyroscope" — and how do we find it?

A former client in his early fifties is battling with a diagnosis of MS, and in a recent conversation he made a very simple and profound statement. "You know, if I was really honest with myself, all my life my work has been the only thing that really mattered to me. When my kids were young I was too busy working to pay any attention to them. Now I have this disabling illness and they are too busy working to pay any attention to me. One of the mistakes I have made in my life is that I confused *means* with *ends*. I was focusing on the wrong things and missing the big picture. My work was supposed to be a means to an end, a *tool* for creating what was most important to me. What it became, instead, was the totality of who I was. It became, mistakenly, an end in itself."

This man is at a stage in his life where he is struggling to find his center. You can tell where your center is by asking yourself five questions: Where do you get your sense of worth? Where do you get your sense of security? Where do you go when times get tough? What sustains you? Where is your home?

I have met many people in my lifetime whose center is their work. They define themselves by their jobs, their sense of security is in their career, and they deal with life by going to work. I have met parents whose center is their children, where their sense of worth comes from being a parent. I have met people who are centered in their possessions, who define and value themselves by what surrounds them. People who are possession-centered feel secure after they have gone shopping and enclose themselves with more "stuff." Some people are centered in their marriage, where their sense of worth and security comes from their life partner. People often get centered in their roles, where they define themselves by what they do. As long as they have a job they are secure and have worth. This was true for me for many years when I practiced as a psychotherapist. Blinded by my own insecurity, I found my refuge and worth in being needed. Many are centered on their achievements, on being the best. Many are centered on materialism.

People can be centered in their body, where their worth and security comes from being fit, from the striving for a "perfect" body. We all know the preponderance of self-centeredness in our culture, where we center our lives on what feels good, what brings us pleasure and what provides us comfort.

As you reflect on where your center is, recognize that part of the human journey is to attach ourselves to a variety of external centers that evolve and change over time. It is only human to define ourselves by these external measures. It is also important to see the positive intent behind each of them. For example, it is next to impossible to start up a business and be successful at it without, for a time, being centered in your work. It is wonderful when you have young children and can center your life on them in the early formative years. It is rewarding in the beginning stages of a significant relationship to center your lives on each other. It is worthy and commendable to set a goal and reach a pinnacle in your accomplishments or to be disciplined in the development of your physical fitness.

Yet there is a trap that comes with too much attachment to any of these external forms of worth and security. They are all temporary. Eventually, all of them will be gone. What happens when you are laid off or retire? What happens when your children become independent and leave home? What happens when your life partner dies? What happens if you lose your capacity to achieve a certain goal or you have an injury or illness that prevents you from maintaining your fitness discipline? What happens if you are no longer needed in your roles in the same way? Remember, "You aren't what you do, because if you are what you do, then when you don't, you aren't!"

Authenticity calls us to be connected or engaged with our work, our children, our goals and achievements, our roles and our fitness, but not attached. We must be careful that these aspects of life do not become the totality of who we are. When we define ourselves by our work, we rob ourselves of the wider spectrum of authentic expression and become vulnerable when the work is not there. We also set ourselves up for workaholism and neglect of the other important areas and responsibilities in life. Soon our work runs our life, rather than our life running our work.

When we get our security and worth through our children, we unknowingly put unreasonable pressure on them as they grow older. They are expected to conform to our standards, not necessarily for the inherent value of a job well done, but for the worth that it conveys to you as a parent. You will see how attached parents are to the achievement of their children by watching a minor league hockey or baseball game. Parents who are centered on their children need their children to make choices in line with the parents' expectations, and adolescents will run as far as they can from this pressure. The work of a parent is to step back as your children grow and allow them the room to be their authentic selves. Remember, you are not stepping back from your love, but from your attachment to them. One indication that you have successfully achieved this is when they reach adulthood and leave home, and you have a good cry to simultaneously celebrate their adulthood and your newfound freedom! You will have great interest in staying connected to them and little interest in having them remain dependent on you in their adulthood.

Centering means following the counsel St. Paul gave to the Romans when he said, "Do not conform to this world, but instead be transformed by the renewal of your mind." This ability to step back and take hold of something more solid and lasting than the reflexive emotional reactions to life's trials, tribulations, and traumas is the work of centering. If you have been busy all your working life and upon retirement begin to find discomfort in being with yourself, it is easy to revert to your old way of staying busy and distracted. As a parent, when your children are grown, if you have not cultivated any other interests besides parenting, you may want your children to move back in while you become not just a grandparent but also another *parent*. Of course, these familiar choices may be better than the despair or even death that frequently occurs during the early years of retirement when this transition period gets blocked. But an alternative is to respond to the authentic call along the way, the appeal for a connection to a lasting center that will sustain you through each of the cycles of life. When you lose a job, a position, a role, a possession, a relationship, or even your health, something deeper and more sustaining than all these can be accessed.

In the marvelous music production *Les Misérables*, adapted from Victor Hugo's great novel, the theme deals with struggles of the soul, the balance of good and evil in human beings, and the continual challenge to conscience. In a touching scene, Jean Valjean has just been given a new lease on life by the very bishop from whom he stole. Valjean is overwhelmed by the forgiveness of the bishop. No one has given him a break before. "He told me that I have a soul. How does he know?"

Authenticity invites you to see the difference between your *soul* and your *role*. Most of us are not very good at this. We are so busy in our various roles that we don't take time to find that peaceful place from which we can view our own lives. Jean Valjean spent his life in the role of a thief. The bishop inspired his awakening and helped him realize that he was more than his role. It is a moment of authentic presence when we awaken to this awareness.

When you meet someone for the first time, the conversational question inevitably emerges, "What do you *do?*" Politeness necessitates that we answer the question based on our role. We respond with, "I am an author. I am an engineer. I am a teacher. I am a stay-at-home parent. I am chairman of the board," etc. These are all civil and reliable ways that we describe ourselves in public. All of these descriptions of ourselves are in relation to our roles. It is not possible to live life without roles.

The trap occurs when you lose your capacity to see yourself as separate from the roles you play. You lose your sense of authenticity when you become blind to the "I" that is expressing the role of husband, mother, engineer or boss. Freedom comes when you can detach yourself from your roles and live your life without being owned or controlled by your functions. Then you can see the roles in your life for what they are: an *expression* of your authentic self, rather than a *definition* of who you are. One of the things I have learned is that you have made it as a parent when your kid slams the door in your face and you don't take it personally.

By over-identifying with our roles, we center our lives in the expectations and values of others. When our worth and energy come from what we do, when our roles give us our primary source of stability and fulfillment, there is a voracious thirst for more. We end up overworking, over-helping, over-spending, over-doing, and never feeling at peace with ourselves. For many years, my work was the center of my life. My job defined me and, consequently, it owned me. The problem was that I found work insatiable. There was always something more to pursue. As I was finding my place in the world, I soon discovered that the world was finding its place in me. I was ambitious, and I was not content. I had no foundation, no anchor that was larger than my work. No matter how much I had, it was never enough, and thus, *I* was never enough. The implicit rationale was that the next achievement, the next book, the next purchase would yield the happiness I was seeking. I learned the elusive power of this seductive force.

The path of authenticity asks not that we renounce our roles, but that we see them for what they are and connect with them in a new way. By centering our lives on an inner foundation, rather than being anchored to social mirrors and expectations from others, we can detach from our roles. We all need to be reminded that we are more than our paychecks and our positions and our job descriptions. Authenticity requires us to remember who we are and come back to ourselves. I have found great strength and solace in finding a deeply secure place within — aside from my roles — so I know that no matter what happens to me on the surface, it will all pass and I will be okay. Your authentic self is bigger and deeper than the roles you fulfill.

When a Zen master who had a great serenity and peace about him no matter what pressures he faced was asked, "How do you maintain serenity and peace?" he replied, "I never leave my place of meditation." He meditated early in the morning and for the remainder of the day brought the peace of those moments with him in his mind and heart.

The greatest storms of life we will face are the hurricanes within our own soul. Finding a meaningful, lasting center within us, and drawing strength and renewal from that source, is like having a solid rock on which to stand firmly during those daily tempests. We can know a deep and residing inner peace amidst the pain, happiness, success, failure and anguish that might surround us. Finding your center means knowing deeply who you are and what you are about. A nourishing connection can reside within you so you can be in solitude, but know you are never alone. From that centered place will naturally flow public triumph, where your gifts and unique abilities and talents will be used for utmost good in the world.

There is no formula for finding this center. Each journey to that authentic center is unique. Here are some ideas to facilitate the journey.

* * * *

OPENING THE DOOR THAT LEADS IN

I shut my eyes in order to see.

— *Paul Gauguin, artist*

The key to accessing inner wisdom and authenticity is to s-l-o-w d-o-w-n and be in silence, taking time to attend to the voice within. As we make time for daily solitude to listen to the sounds of silence, we begin hearing the voice within that calls us to authenticity. We can begin to feel and sense and observe what emerges; we open ourselves to receptivity and reach a deeper knowing.

Our five senses, however, can potentially suffocate the inner voice. My friend, Ross Watson, blind from the age of eleven and now a successful community activist, adventurer, and speaker, recently gave me a lesson on how to listen. "Sight," he contends, "is such a powerful sense that it blinds us to so much of what is happening in the world."

Another barrier in our culture that "blinds" us to connecting with our inner life is the constant bombardment of noise. Silence has become elusive. I remember having a friend from Los Angeles stay with us. One morning I took her for a walk along the river trail behind our home. As we walked, I was teaching her about some of our local wildlife and how to recognize the finches, blackbirds and waxwings by the sounds they make. I kept asking, "Do you hear that?" and "Listen to that," but she didn't hear anything. It took days before she started to tune in to sounds that she didn't hear earlier.

Under the reign of horns blowing in traffic, stereos blasting in restaurants, and TV-sprinkled lounges, silence has become so rare that the human ear — and mind — can't seem to deal with it. Although many people say they yearn for peace and quiet, in practice many dread it. Many live with the television on for background noise, the car stereo constantly blaring, and exercise done to the strains of MP3-headphone concertos. Even some cemeteries are now piping in music.

Silence hasn't always been so disquieting. Monks once flocked to deserts searching for it. Musicians wrote pieces immersed in it. (Beethoven inserted forty crucial pauses in the first movement of his *Fifth Symphony*.) Scientists and philosophers analyzed it.

Today, silence is practically unheard of. In this postmodern age, we seem to have lost the art of being quiet. We are so unused to silence that we make constant conversation. Silence at a cocktail party, for example, evokes uneasiness and agitation.

Maybe our reluctance to be with silence is because it forces us to be with ourselves. Silence invites the question, "How comfortable am I with myself?" The answer comes from your inner life, the very essence of what you want to connect with in the silence. The benefits of silence include wisdom, relaxation, and contentment. I speculate that silence holds the key to mental as well as spiritual well-being.

However, these benefits are increasingly hard to come by now that all of life seems to have its own soundtrack. From elevator music pumped into restrooms to waiting on hold on the telephone, the musical assault alone has become almost impossible to escape. The audio onslaught is so pervasive that one can even find oneself regaled with light popular music while strapped to an MRI machine. Radio stations have a device that automatically slices out dead air time from pre-recorded music and conversation and inserts more music. We go to see movies on the big screen, in part because of the loudness. Everything is cranked up these days. I have to constantly remind my kids to turn down the television and their iPods.

By turning down the volume and turning off the noise in our lives, we can "hear" the silence, and by slowing down, we make room to listen to our inner self. In our busyness and constant activity, we have lost the art of the idle moment. Just what is so urgent?

I recently attended a concert and sat behind the press row. During the last number, cell phones were put to ears. The press couldn't wait for the music to end to call in a review.

We now notice beepers going off during the benediction or cell phones ringing during a play. I've even seen a person with a laptop turned on at the movies!

Is all this really so pressing that none of it can wait?

In the multitasking culture that has required us to become increasingly mentally ambidextrous, we are left somehow disjointed, wondering what has happened to the art of enjoying idle moments. I once looked across at a woman in her car as we edged our way along in a traffic jam. She was talking on the cell phone, putting on her makeup and adjusting the car stereo, all at the same time. Quite comical, really, until you stop and realize that this person was driving — and next to you at that!

When was the last time you just sat and stared into nothingness — with no newspaper, cell phone, MP3 player, or television? When was the last time you just lingered, or wandered, not asking for the correct time or tapping your foot? When was the last time you just let your brain take a cool-down lap, allowing time to unwind?

Indeed, reveling in idle time is now an art somehow forgotten. Even our kids have picked up the activity virus as many of them over-program their time, not allowing themselves the time to be kids, to be idle, to just be. And rather than cutting back, the answer for many is to get better at charting activities on Excel spreadsheets!

Activity has been a barrier in my own journey. It is easy to throw stones, to pass judgment on others. I know all too well how difficult it has been to make room for idle time. Contemplative time has not come easy for me. I have been guilty of exercising too much, of working too hard, of filling every minute with plans and activities and appointments. It has been hard for me to learn to sit and just be with myself because, like shutting off the noise, initially it is uncomfortable. Keeping busy, keeping active, is a socially rewarded habit that is reinforced by how "productive" and "organized" you can be. But in the quiet, sleepless nights, as you begin to wake up to yourself, you may feel that you are not even a part of life, but a hurried bystander, rapidly watching life pass by. Instead of living in the "here-and-now," I have often been in the "when-and-if."

As I consciously step forward in this journey to authenticity, I have begun to slow down, turn off the noise, and go within. What I discovered is that my excessive busyness and attachment to noise were really distractions to cover up an emptiness in my life. Not an emptiness of stuff, for there was plenty of that, but rather a lack of intimacy or connectedness — an unarticulated inner hunger. For years it was easier to go for a run than it was to stop and be with myself long enough to recognize the emptiness in me. I tried for years to fill this emptiness with noise, activity or food, but that only further removed me from my authentic self, from the person I was meant to be.

I am now discovering the wisdom of the saints, monks and philosophers, who taught that the human spirit needs solitude, silence and stillness, just as the body needs oxygen. To try to pretend otherwise will suffocate a deeper life within us. The rests in a musical number are as vital as the notes, just as the pauses in a theatrical performance are as imperative as the words. Our authentic self asks us to slow down and make room for silence and stillness; and in the discomfort and anxiety, inner wisdom, trust and creativity will emerge.

I am not inferring that we smother the desire for activity or for noise, for these do have a place. But we can be more mindful. I agree with Aristotle when he said, "Wisdom is in the wise balance, not in the extremes." Some may sell their televisions and their MP3 players and retreat to monasteries to find balance. Others may wish to simply shut off their radios and computers a little more often and make room for silence and contemplation. Just be more mindful of the choices you make with the intent to bring more balance to your life. "There is a time for everything," says the book of Ecclesiastes, "a time to speak and a time to be silent."

As a musician, I like to think of the authentic journey in musical terms, as symmetry of silence and sound. For Beethoven, an exactly measured sound and silence and the interaction of the two was what constituted rhythm. Wisdom, indeed, especially considering that his knowing this came from the sound of his deafness.

* * * *

SANCTUARIES IN TIME AND SPACE

Abstinence and quiet cure many diseases.

— Hippocrates

When Socrates described himself, he drew a crucial distinction between wisdom and the passion for wisdom. Having a passion for wisdom surpassed the attainment of wisdom. Curiosity was a virtue. Indeed, he considered only a life of ongoing examination worth living. The voice of authenticity is a whisper from within. If you wish to hear that whisper you must turn off the noise of culture and create an environment, a sanctuary, a place where you can attune to that still, small voice. Authenticity asks us to slow down and make room for contemplation, reflection and ongoing examination. Authenticity will not take root in the depleted soil of frantic busyness. The habit of daily quiet time begins the practice of going within.

To keep any relationship alive, one needs to listen and tune in. I was trained as a psychotherapist. One of the first lessons I learned in my schooling was how to listen, and after six years of training I spent another ten years developing the skill of empathizing, clarifying, and reaching a deep level of understanding before attempting to be understood. Listening in a relationship is life-giving. Relationships begin dying when people stop listening to each other. It takes continual practice to be an open, reflective, empathic listener, and fully be there for someone without evaluating, advising, judging, interpreting or jumping to solutions too quickly. As the saying goes, "The best present we can give anyone is to be fully present in the present."

Several years ago I began to consciously apply the principles of empathic listening to my inner navigator. As with any relationship, a relationship with your soul takes time, patience, and the capacity to listen. I began taking one half hour each day for quiet time. We all need a safe harbor to settle into while we unload the day's consignment. I find that the more I have to do, the heavier my load, the more important it is to take extra quiet time because then I am able to face the day's demands with a renewed mind, body and spirit. When I am frantic or overwhelmed, the only answer is to go within. Calm is critical for forward and productive energy.

Silence is a second language. It requires an intentional focus if you want to learn it. Even though I am an introverted, contemplative person by nature, setting aside quiet times for prayer, meditation and reflection has not come naturally to me. Like authenticity itself, making time for contemplation guarantees neither comfort nor being trouble-free. It takes some discipline, a willingness to be uncomfortable at times, and occasional anxiety, frustration, and boredom.

When I speak to audiences about setting aside time daily for quiet time, I usually get a couple of questions. First, "Where do you find the time to be still for thirty minutes?" and second, "What do you do for thirty minutes while you are just sitting there?"

Both of these questions were ones I, too, have asked. They are born in a culture of *doing*, a society that is out of balance and has lost the art of sitting still and *being*. My answer to the first question is, "How important is your authentic, spiritual life?" I believe we make time for that which matters most. Be honest about your willingness to make this a priority. My daily quiet time is now the most important time of the day to me. It is one of those "important" but not "urgent" activities. In the beginning it didn't feel important and I felt restless, irritable, and frustrated. Plus, the benefit of daily quiet time is not necessarily immediate. But after six years, I can see the added depth to my life. I am more relaxed, I trust myself more, and have more genuine inner peace. I know that these results have been in part due to my commitment to daily reflection and quiet time.

The second question — "What do you do for thirty minutes while you are just sitting there?" — is very personal. Each must find his or her own way. I generally have a balance between meditating (quieting and focusing my mind while relaxing my body) and praying (listening to the still, small voice of God guiding me and supporting me).

I know many people, on the other hand, who find strength in daily quiet time and yet don't have a belief in God. They may simply meditate, relax, empty their mind, or sit quietly and attune to their breath. At first, you may not need a full half-hour or you may need more than half an hour. You may simply want to reach inside and get a sense of yourself outside of your roles. Regardless of what you find as a meaningful way to get more in touch with your deeper, authentic self, resist the human temptation to think you are too busy for quiet time. It was reported once that Mahatma Gandhi was asked how he kept himself centered. His reply, which seems humorous, is probably closer to the truth that any of us may realize. He reportedly replied, "I take two hours of quiet time each day, unless I am really busy. Then I take four hours."

Like any relationship, your relationship with your authentic self or with the God of your understanding will have days that are disturbing or boring or exhilarating. You will have days when you may feel it was a complete waste of time to sit and "do nothing" for thirty minutes. Practice letting go of the results, let go of natural emotions that will surface, and just keep at it. It will make a significant difference in your life.

Writing or journaling, combined with this daily quiet time, is also a good tool for helping you reflect and go inward. Many authentic people I know have the habit of daily journaling along with their prayer and meditation time. When combined with a clear quality of life or mission statement, journaling can serve as a daily report card. Through journaling, you can ask yourself: "How did I measure up today? What events or patterns got me off track? How might I do better next time?" Journaling can help you be more mindful of being the person you are meant to be. When combined with imagery, it can be a useful tool for positive change in your life.

Listening to a deeper voice within you requires a place where you can hear it. Many voices have access to us today: advertisers, customers, well-meaning friends, solicitors, extended family members, clients, children, bosses, community members, and the media to name just a few. In this age of hurried and easily accessible information, I am hard pressed to go through thirty minutes in any given day without someone trying to sell me something or wanting something or offering a solution to a problem I didn't even know I had. When living amidst so many voices demanding our attention, we can easily lose our own voice. We need to preserve a place — a sanctuary — where we can turn off technology and be alone to hear ourselves think; a place to retreat from the world's demands, where we find solace, serenity and much needed space to listen to the whisper of our own voice.

A sanctuary is defined formally as a sacred place, the holiest part of a temple; the part of the chancel containing the altar; an area where wild birds and animals are protected; a refuge. In practice, sanctuaries are very personal. A sanctuary is a haven, a place you can go to step away from the demands of the world, a designated place to contemplate, relax, and just *be*. Claiming sanctuary is part of our nature — it is both innate and necessary for us to want to retreat regularly. It is vital to give yourself permission to seek sanctuary. Trust your instinct to create and use sanctuaries. By consciously developing both external and internal sanctuaries, you reach untapped resources.

For some people sanctuary is a religious place, a formal institution. For others it could be a kitchen table or a jogging trail or a special bench you sit on by a quiet river or under beautiful trees. In our own home we have a designated quiet room — the library. When people are in this room and the door is closed, it means they are in need of some quiet time, a refuge.

I have a favorite story about sanctuary. After one of my presentations on sanctuaries a woman came up and was beaming. "I got some insight during your presentation as to why I have been angry at my husband for the past three years!" she exclaimed. "He has been renovating our bathroom!" You can imagine where this woman's sanctuary was. Turns out she hadn't had a hot bath since the renovations began three years before. She responded excitedly, "I'm going home to complete the construction myself!"

A man standing beside us and listening in on the conversation laughed. "Guess where her husband's sanctuary has been for the past three years? I understand why he was not in a hurry!"

In my travels, I have found solace in the sanctuary of airport chapels. Every major airport has one. They are rarely used, and they are wonderful places to find peace in the demanding and stressful world of travel. Churches, synagogues, and mosques in cities across the country are opening their doors at the noon hour. I have met business executives who take their lunch across the street and sit quietly for an hour in a church. They are drawn there, not necessarily because they are religious, but because it provides them with a quiet place to go within.

I have even found chapels in some of the larger shopping malls. If there is no chapel, I create my own. I bring spiritual literature with me when I travel and will often create my own little chapel right in my hotel room, where the big armchair is more comfortable than the pews. Of course, a hot bath helps. Creating a sanctuary calls us to be mindful — mindful of what our body, mind, and spirit needs in order to retreat from the world. Be mindful of the difference between nurturing your spirit and feeding your ego, between doing what is soothing to you and what is escaping, and between self-care and selfishness. These are not always easy distinctions. They are not always clear. We must stay with the questions in order to create sanctuary.

When we create a haven of serenity — whether in a quiet room or by means of a walk in the park between home and work — we make room for spirit. My authentic self insists that life is more than dashing from one thing to the next.

One of my employees at the time, after reading my thoughts on creating a sanctuary, sent me an email with this note: "Interesting thought on sanctuary. I remember long ago, when I was selling advertising for a regional newspaper... people would laugh because there was a window into my office and I could be caught a few times a week with the lights off, my sunglasses on, and my feet up on the desk. I think I have lost that technique of 'coming down' in the last few years, and I do think it is still vital to my sanity and my sales success. This was a good reminder for me! I have been remembering my 'sunglasses break' during the past few weeks and just assumed it was a memory — not a possible sign!"

Regardless of the form, sanctuaries are like a warm cabin at the end of a day of cross-country skiing in the Canadian Rockies. There is nothing like coming in from minus twenty degrees after spending hours on the trails and curling up in front of a warm fireplace. In a world that moves so fast, it is good to create a place where we can slow down and listen to the sound of silence. As we rediscover our own rhythm, we can bring it back to life.

* * * *

RITUALS AND OTHER SOURCES OF INSPIRATION

Authenticity will only grow in fertile soil. Those embarking on this journey will find value in surrounding themselves in an environment where the seed of authenticity can take root. In part, this includes the people we associate with who support our authentic journey. But also, we need to spend time in *places* that support our authenticity. As you travel this path more mindfully, you become aware of what nurtures your authentic self and what erodes it. For example, walking along the river behind our home nurtures me more than sitting in front of a television watching superficial sitcoms. I find most shows are intrusive and invasive to my inner life, and I am carefully and gradually helping my daughters to be more discerning about this. We talk about what is nourishing and what is diminishing to their mind and their spirit. As they attune to their own inner light, they are able to make these decisions for themselves, and for the most part, they too, leave the television off.

Rituals bring you back to yourself. They help you remember who you are and lessen the grip that the world has on you. Attending church, partaking in a sacrament service, and singing hymns are faith-based centering rituals. Rituals of the major religions — for example, the ritual of confession in the Roman Catholic faith — can act as a centering practice. Repentance and seeking forgiveness are integral parts of the process of purification and illumination in most religious traditions. The purpose of these rituals is to turn the mind away from the worldly and toward the spiritual life.

There are also daily practices that bring you back to yourself, especially when you are making a transition from one role into another part of your life. For example, taking a bath, changing clothes, stopping in the park on the way home from work, meditating, going for a walk or doing some enjoyable, relaxing exercise, praying, taking some quiet time, or just lying on the floor while you listen to music that makes your heart sing are all examples of *transitional rituals* that help you shift gears, regroup, and reenter new environments with your authenticity intact. Transitional rituals can be done in between work and home or at the end of the day if your evening is full of various roles. Anything that helps you come back to yourself will help you to find inner contentment while loosening the grip your roles have in giving you security and worth. These rituals will open the door to a more lasting, sustaining spiritual center.

Prayerful meditation and quiet time, combined with spiritual reading, help take me through the transition from sleep into my various daily roles. I find value in connecting with God and my soul — centering myself — in the morning before I pick up the newspaper and start responding to the world's demands. Similarly, the transition at night from work to time with my family can be a challenge that creates some anxiety. This is a time when many people head to the bar for a drink, but that can extinguish the authentic flame within. I will take some extra quiet time before coming home or get home a little early and play the piano. Playing a piece by Beethoven or Enya is a way to bring me back to myself, especially if I have had a day of mundane work that was not particularly stimulating to my spirit. These transitional rituals separate me from the world of roles. They bring me back to that lasting center, to my spiritual self. My kids are also useful for the transition at the end of the day. They love me, and I them, for who we are, not for what we do. Rolling on the floor, wrestling together or reading stories to them are activities that help ground me and bring me back to myself.

A good friend sent me an email recently expressing the meaning that the principles of transitional rituals had for her. "When I was a single parent, the kids knew I would spend the first ten minutes at home each day after work rocking in my rocking chair. It was a real chore to let go of all the numbers and the pressures and the people and technology where I worked and come back to the person underneath all the demands. Little did I know it was a good transitional thing. It saved my kids from me, and it saved me from my work. Now I think my fourteen-year-old son is doing the transitional thing: skateboarding after school before he even comes home! He says it delays the questions: 'How was school? What do you have for homework?' etc."

I notice my daughters create their own transitional rituals. It seems part of their very makeup. They will come home after school and become absorbed with their stuffed toys and blocks. Pretty soon you will see them acting out all the challenges they faced during the day with teachers and friends.

My daughter, Hayley, and I have developed a transitional ritual at her bedtime. We take five minutes at the end of our reading time to talk about our day. We talk about the best part of our day and the worst part of our day. Then we hold hands, close our eyes, have a few minutes of quiet time, and share on our experience. What did we hear? What did we notice? What did God say to you tonight? We ask and answer these questions together. Some of the most amazing insights come out of these moments together from a place that is beyond either of our knowing. One night when I opened my eyes I found Hayley lying peacefully with a smile on her face. "I saw white swans tonight, Dad," she shared. "They told me that I am here to be the tune in God's song." Another evening after our quiet time together, she reported, "I saw God and Mother Nature getting married. They had four children and named them Spring, Summer, Autumn, and Winter." On another night she asked me, "Dad, what is the bravest thing you have ever done?" What an intriguing and challenging question for anyone to wrestle with, especially after surfacing so spontaneously from a nine-year-old. These are precious moments and indeed sacred transitional rituals. We merely create the opening, allowing a power greater than Hayley or me to move through us both.

Nature is very soothing to me. I am nourished by the gentle and unending force of the Bow River behind our home and by the steadfastness of the Rocky Mountains just west of us. Trees give me sustaining strength and wild animals help connect me to my yearning for a little more wildness in my life. I love the spirit and energy of dogs and horses. Being in their presence grounds me and connects me to a deeper side of myself. I get irritable, restless, and discontented when I haven't spent enough time in nature or with horses or other animals I am drawn to. What's good for my soul is also good for my moods. Being in the sunlight, putting my feet on the ground, being around animals that inspire and nurture me, and getting off the main route are ways to keep my authentic self alive.

When beginning the process of writing this book, it was my good fortune to connect with a Boston-based editor named Kelly Rappuchi. As a writing coach, Kelly actually put me through an intensive personal development workshop as we worked together for a week, formulating what I really wanted to write about. My first assignment was to go out and buy a journal. On the left side of the page I was to write about what I noticed. On the right side of the page I wrote about *why* I noticed what I did and what was happening to me when I noticed. What was my voice in the story that I would write about? I was to go to places that would help awaken my voice and open my heart. I spent a week in the marvelous museums and bookstores on the Harvard University campus, so rich in authentic expression. I began noticing what I was noticing. I took time to awaken my musical side and listened to CDs I had never heard before. I spent time in the parks surrounding this beautiful campus.

That week I learned that being my own authentic self was my most powerful resource for becoming a change agent. I also learned the strength, power and awakening that comes from being in places that support the authentic self when my mind and heart were receptive. I went forth on "outings of noticing" with no agenda, no preset plan, just simply being open to where I was led. One afternoon I visited the Virgin Child room in the Fog Museum, looking at the display of the Men of Suffering. Something about the quality of the expression of these artists and sculptures from centuries past made me weep as I moved on to the nineteenth-century Sensuality room. I was profoundly impacted by the relationship between suffering and sensuality. It seems to be all the same at the level of the soul. Spending time in such culturally rich environments and the parks surrounding them served to feed my spirit and awaken my creativity.

Authenticity calls us to notice what depletes us and what nourishes us and then to act in accordance with this. I find inspiration in art galleries and museums, but I also need my feet to touch the ground every day. Concrete is insufficient. I need a daily practice of being in nature. We need to surround ourselves with that which nourishes us. I am intentional about getting our daughters into nature, attempting to inspire them with the wonders that the Creator has given us, but I am competing with malls filled with consumer items, computer games, and surfing the Net. How easy it is to be lured into the seductive force of a human-created world that celebrates the inventiveness and productivity of human beings. But there is no way that human ingenuity can match the incredible wonder, magnificence, and inspiration of the natural world billions of years in the making.

In addition to nature, I find inspiration from connecting with wise people. As a child, my parents surrounded me with individuals of various backgrounds and divergent points of view. Mom and Dad were continually bringing people into our lives who brought new perspectives and wisdom. My parents would often have people visit and I was allowed to be part of the heated and thought-provoking discussions on the meaning of life. Dad and I listened to Earl Nightingale every Sunday morning on our way to church and the resulting discussions made a lasting impression on me. A great gift from my parents was the exposure to stimulating individuals and their philosophies. The habit of seeking inspiration from the wisdom of others stays with me today.

* * * *

CONNECT WITH YOUR ROOTS

About five years before her death, my mother was able to return, for the first time, to her homeland of Ireland. She spent several months touring, visiting, and reconnecting with her roots. She was so alive when she came back and spoke of her experience. "Growing up, I used to think, along with all our neighbors, that my father was crazy," she told me soon after her return to Canada. "But after spending months in Ireland, I now realize he wasn't crazy. He was *Irish!*"

Finding and reconnecting with your roots can mean many things to many people. Connecting with your genealogical roots is a way to return to where you came from. It is a way to come home to yourself with new eyes. As I get older, an interest in my ancestors is roused. More and more, I love to visit my aunts and uncles and hear the stories about my parents and their early struggles. My father was an active genealogist and had some lines traced back to the fourteenth century. As I age, my yearning for a connection to my roots grows. I now recognize that those binders full of the records he tenaciously filled are not just paper with names written on them, but a repository of my ancestral roots. They represent who I am today. Authenticity is about unity; it pushes against the societal call for separation, for discarding our past. In a transient society where people are so used to change and moving and separating, there is disconnection from our roots. The time has come for me — and I suspect for others — to appreciate wholeness and value our deeper heritage. It is all part of the journey to grip something more substantive than the fleeting offerings of our current culture.

Where on earth are your spiritual roots? Besides our genealogical roots and the connection with our authentic self beyond our own generation, there are spiritual roots that may need visiting. I speak with many people in their thirties and forties who are returning to the church of their origin. A friend who was raised in the Mormon Church had never been back to Nauvoo, Illinois, the birthplace of the church, until one summer when he took their six children back for a visit. He cried when he spoke of the meaning and significance this had for him when picturing the early pioneers laying stake to a new religion in the early nineteenth century. "You know," he said, "visiting the birthplace of my spiritual roots was one of the most meaningful holidays we have ever given our family. We enjoyed Disneyland, but you won't find your spiritual roots there."

Getting in touch with the sacred landscapes in one's generational path is a useful step into authenticity. Recently our family traveled through the Maritimes, the provinces along the eastern coast of Canada, where many of my ancestors are buried. As we explored some of the countryside, we found old churches and gravesites surrounded by immense hedges. Entering these old sacred burial places felt like walking into another world. It is a reflective experience to walk through a hundred-year-old burial ground and, as you read the names on the headstones, to imagine stories of the lives of the people buried below.

Sitting outside St. Dunstan's Basilica in Charlottetown, Prince Edward Island, on the very street that birthed Canada, I reflected upon the history of this quaint and beautiful province, on this land, and on my life. It was a different moment on our vacation, away from the amusement parks and the traffic and the tourist attractions.

"Life is so fleeting," I thought as I sat quietly beside my wife Val and my two young daughters. "It passes by all too quickly. What is the thread that runs through all things? What really sustains us? What is the larger context in which we are building our lives?"

Connecting with your roots can come in the form of a physical space, such as a gravesite, historic church or birthplace. It can also come in a conversation. Authenticity asks us to put on a new set of lenses, to be continually seeking a new view of the world. As we see our parents from an adult point of view, we can appreciate, understand and accept them and in the process, appreciate, understand and accept ourselves. Knowing is loving.

Visiting, studying, and connecting with your ancestral and spiritual roots can shed light on your authentic self. Going back to your roots, whatever those might be or however they might be explored, brings a sense of clarity to the mystery and wonder of it all and is another step into authenticity.

* * * *

GUIDANCE RECEIVED: THE AERIAL VIEW, INTUITION AND SYNCHRONICITY

Coincidence: God's way of remaining anonymous.

One of the promises of centering is the awareness that you are not alone. You realize, on this journey, that you do not have to rely solely upon yourself or even on others for guidance. As you center and connect with your authentic self, you simultaneously begin to know and trust that there is a force continually available to you from which you can seek guidance, support and perspective, a universal force that is always moving us toward growth, wholeness, and completeness. In the process of trusting this life force, you will discover a spectrum of inner resources that you never knew were there, which will strengthen your capacity to know and trust yourself.

Learning to listen to and access your inner guide requires a respect for and development of your sixth sense. Most people think of intuition as a hunch that occurs now and then, like déja vu — the random acts of feeling a connection to the mysterious side of life. But it is really much more than that. Intuition, or inspired living, is a very sophisticated language that connects us to the sacred in life.

It is really a system for helping you find your way by paying attention to what is happening within you.

This is different from what most of us have learned. We are, after all, a *five-sensory culture*. Depending on your five senses requires you to pay attention to what is going on around you — on the outside. For example, we are used to learning by *touching* a hot stove, *hearing* the advice of others, *seeing* a solution on the blackboard, *smelling* spoiled food, or *tasting* something worth eating again. We are also used to making decisions based on feelings or thoughts gathered from external sources.

Relying on resources outside of ourselves can certainly be useful at times, but with too much dependence on external teachers we can rob ourselves of finding the source of authentic truth — within. Our five senses, and even our feelings and thoughts, are not always accurately aligned with our authentic self. I may, for example, feel pain in a relationship and want to leave, but a deeper voice tells me that it is important to use the pain, and the right thing is to stay and work it through. Alternatively, I may be devoid of feelings and miss the inner guidance I need to get away from a particular relationship. Intuition requires that we pay attention to what is happening inside of us, which is the opposite of what we are used to. When we speak of "trusting our gut," we are embarking on an endeavor that lies beyond our five senses, our feelings, and our thoughts.

In a culture that puts little value on the interior life, the simplest yet most elusive lesson for us is to learn to listen to and trust that guiding voice, while distinguishing it from feeling, thinking or sensing from the outside. This quest comes with at least four requirements. First, bring a willingness to be curious. Bring with you the spirit of an open, willing student as you embark on learning to live a new way. Second, bring a forgiving heart. I recall a feeling that caught me once as I drove away from visiting a friend. It was a kind of sadness. I realized that this inner knowing had told me to say something, and I did not pay attention to it. With some regret I thought back to other times when I heard that voice and ignored it. I am learning to respond to it more and more, yet the times still come when I miss some extraordinary experience because I failed to catch the message fast enough. It is vital at such moments to forgive ourselves and to recognize that the awakened state means being ready to listen and respond, something that no one can do perfectly all the time. Like any new skill, this takes time. Progress, not perfection, is the goal.

Third, bring some courage. Inspired living means not just passively hearing the voice, but acting on it. The outpourings of intuition consist of a continuous and rapid flow of choices and more choices. When we act with our whole heart on this guiding voice, the choices come so rapidly that we often have little time to be scared and retreat from what intuition is telling us. Practice riding the flow and have some fun.

Finally, be patient. It takes time to distinguish passing feelings and short-lived impulses from our real inner voice. As you are developing the art and skill of listening to a voice from below the surface of your mind, it is easy to confuse emotions or impulsive thoughts with intuition. You may, for example, be going through a period in your life when you are feeling some general discontentment, but do not know precisely what is at the root of it. After spending a few minutes in meditation or prayer, you suddenly get a feeling that all of your problems are caused by your stressful job or difficult boss and that you should immediately quit and find a new career. Although this scenario is undoubtedly an extreme example, it illustrates that going within and listening for deeper truth is very distinct from allowing fleeting whims and impulsive emotions to direct our decisions. Wisdom from within does not usually come in a momentary blinding burst, but rather in a gradual awakening brought about by the practice of daily prayer and meditation.

The other day when driving into the city, I ran into a huge traffic jam caused by a multi-vehicle accident. I had to wait about thirty minutes while traffic was rerouted. While I sat, I noticed a traffic helicopter above me and turned on the radio. The announcer, speaking from within the helicopter, was warning traffic many miles back, before they even knew there was an accident ahead, to stay away from the intersection where I was sitting. The helicopter, high above the earth, could see a much larger picture. It had the *aerial perspective*.

If you had a radio in your car and could tune in to a traffic broadcast from a helicopter you could avoid the traffic jam. And even better, if you could communicate with that helicopter, you could potentially learn about better routes, gain information about more scenic roads, or even get advice on how to get where you are going. The key, of course, is to be able to tune in to the right station at the right time. If your radio isn't turned on or if you are listening to a different station, you won't hear the broadcast or even know it is on, even though the signal is always available.

Intuition is like a car radio. It is an instrument, a tool, for receiving information from your spiritual source. There is a continual broadcast within you, and a larger perspective — the aerial view — is available to broaden your limited view and perception. A whole new world can be opened up to you, simply by shifting your attention. Attending to this larger perspective is the work of centering or tuning in to the aerial view.

While driving through the Rocky Mountains on a gorgeous fall afternoon only weeks after the death of my mother, I pulled the car over and stared almost breathlessly at the vast array of autumn colors scattered across the valley in front of me. I had driven through this pass hundreds of times, but that day bereavement was heightening my awareness like a new pair of glasses. I noticed colors and sunlight and ridges and the sparkling river below as I never had before. I was feeling peaceful and serene when the thought came to me, "You need to go visit your uncle. You haven't seen him for a long time."

At eighty-four, Jack and his wife Ev were living a full life. It was hard to get in to see Jack. You had to make an appointment. I called and asked if he was up for a visit.

"Sure, I can squeeze you in," he replied. "I've got a lunch meeting on Saturday and then church at five o'clock, but why don't you drop by about two o'clock?"

Uncle Jack loves genealogy. So my daughter Mellissa and I brought a box of old family photos and family history documents and arrived shortly before 2 p.m. Spry as ever, he greeted us at the door with his usual warmth and spirit. We then spent a stimulating hour or so talking about family history.

Suddenly Jack turned pale and said he was feeling faint. Ev was out shopping, but after some coaxing, he consented to letting us take him to the hospital. Within seconds of wheeling him into the emergency room, Jack suffered a major heart attack. But because he was there with all of the medical staff and equipment at his service, he survived. After an extended recovery, Jack lives on and is getting back to his old spunky self.

As Mellissa and I sat quietly in the waiting room after Ev arrived and Jack was admitted, we felt the impact of being wandering messengers who had helped save a life. That we would choose that particular day to visit and be there to deliver Jack to the hospital *before* his heart attack seemed more than coincidence. I sense there was a deeper force guiding us, almost carrying us.

Even though the receiver has been shut off for much of my life, this unseen force seems to guide me whether I am listening or not. As I expand my capacity to tune in to this navigational guide, I am learning to relax, trust the process, and enjoy the journey. The great helicopter pilot within me is forever waiting to guide me. There is a force that is close at hand waiting for those who will listen, who tune in to the signal, the heartbeat of the spirit. I have come to know that there is a force for good in the universe, and that if we will tune in or link up with this force, we are carried onward to a new awareness and will be guided to where we are meant to go.

The process of writing about this has heightened my awareness of the presence of this force in my life. When my youngest daughter, Chandra, was in kindergarten, we would often have a game of cards after lunch. One day she stayed around briefly after I came home and then disappeared. I didn't think much of this at first, until about five minutes later when a voice within me said, "Where is Chandra? You need to go and find her." I went downstairs and Chandra was swinging on a swing bolted into beams on our back porch. "Watch how high I can go, Dad!" she exclaimed with passion. As I looked up at the top of the rope, my heart started pounding. The bolt that was securing the swing was within half a turn, an eighth of an inch, of coming out of the beam it was bolted to. I am certain that if I had arrived five minutes later the bolt would have broken free and Chandra would have been thrown to the cedar platform below.

There is no single way to tune into the signal of intuition. It is different for everyone. Just as every human being is unique, so, too, no two human beings experience intuition in the same way. Some people have hunches while others get ideas. Some people see pictures; others hear music. Some get sensations; others hear conversations. For some it is a combination of these. For me, intuition comes in the form of a feeling or deep sensing. There are no right or wrong ways.

You can develop your intuition by creating space in your day to slow down. Pay attention to what is happening inside you. Listen to your body. This is the biggest difference between five-sensory awareness and multi-sensory awareness. The five senses require you to pay attention to what is outside of you. Intuition requires the opposite — that you pay attention to what is happening inside of you. Once you practice and learn to keep your own unique intuitive radio turned on, events like the ones I have experienced will become commonplace as you trust that a force much stronger than you is guiding and carrying you, and moving you toward growth.

These experiences of connection between a thought or feeling and an outer event, or "meaningful coincidence," are what Carl Jung called *synchronicity*. On my car radio there is a tiny red light that comes on when my radio is tuned in to a station. It is the indicator that I have a strong connection — that I am "tuned in." Synchronicity is like the light on the radio of intuition. It is an indicator, a useful gauge to remind me, "You've got the station you need" or "You are on the right track."

My own efforts to describe and communicate the phenomenon of synchronicity have not always been met with the greatest success, in part because of the elusive nature of the concept. How do I describe something that has been such a guiding force in the emergence of my authentic self when the idea is so difficult to put into words, and the concept runs completely counter to logical and rational thought processes? Perhaps the best way is to share my experience with it and not attempt to justify it with any degree of logical explanation, letting you decide if it has validity for you on your journey. Have you ever been thinking about someone just when the phone rang and, sure enough, there they were?

One night, Chandra, who is so tuned in to this wider frequency, started crying for what seemed to be no reason at all. As I went to comfort her, I noticed she had gathered up a number of the gifts given to her by her grandmother in the years before her death two years earlier. I held her close and as the sobs subsided, I asked gently, "What's wrong, Honey?"

We lay on the bed and began to relate a few short stories about Grandma Joyce. Soon Chandra drifted gently into sleep with a smile on her face. Val came into the room following this experience. Unknown to both Chandra and me, at the time of Chandra's sudden flow of emotion, Val had been in another room "coincidentally" editing a story I had written about Grandma Joyce.

As I left Chandra's room I felt a strong sense of wonder and connection to her, to Val, to my mother Joyce, and to God. I felt comforted in my own grief. The logical, left-brain part of me wanted to simply dismiss this experience, chalking it up to a random act, a chance occurrence that Val would be reading about Grandma and Chandra would be touched by her spirit in different rooms simultaneously. Yet, another deeper part of me felt the significance of this small moment, and I was both consoled and filled with grace.

In writing about the power of the aerial view, intuition, and synchronicity, I am aware of being called and subsequently carried in a new direction — not a new direction in my career or my life, but in the way that I *live* my life and my career. And I cannot stop the process. I am in it for the ride. I am becoming aware in the subtle voice of my authentic life that there is an inner yearning for more spontaneity and playfulness in my life, and this is what I have been praying for.

Soon after this inner sense came, Val and I attended a production at Loose Moose Theatre, an internationally known improvisational theater in Calgary. Afterwards I found a brochure on a course offered at the theater on improvisation. My schedule and the offering were completely in sync — another indication of synchronicity! I couldn't *not* go. There is a creative, playful, spontaneous part of me that is emerging, and I cannot stop it. My authentic self is pulling me down this river of spontaneous expression. Signing up for the workshop, I now recognized that improvisation is "intuition in action."

Living spontaneously is living with more trust in the universe, in the life force, and in myself — *letting* life happen rather than following my old tendency of *making* it happen. I am noticing that my office is a little messier than it used to be, that some mornings I sleep in a little more often than I did in the past, that I am more prone after a hard day at work to get the super-soakers out and have a water fight with my kids on a hot summer's afternoon, that I play more piano than I ever have, that I am appreciating poetry more than I used to, and that I am a little gentler on myself and others. I am noticing when I give my public presentations that, even though I come prepared, I am more likely to set aside some of those plans and relate, in the present, to the people in the room. It is fascinating to me that the information about spontaneity, creativity, and playfulness has been around much longer than I have been. But I was not ready to tune in to the frequency. Now that I am ready to embrace it, the floodgates are open.

I remember clearly the week of my father's funeral, when I went to a quiet place in the park behind his home where he loved to spend time. In my grief, I sat quietly and wished that I could have some sign that his life was continuing. At that time of anguish, my faith was treacherous and tenuous. As I sat in reflective prayer, I saw two Canadian geese fly overhead. They circled above me and stayed in sight long enough for me to remember that Dad put two birds in one of the top corners of each of his paintings.

As the geese flew out of my view, I felt some reassurance and a sense of wonder. I knew these birds lived on beyond the horizon, even if they were out of my sight, like the wind whose effect can be felt, even if beyond view. The logical, analytical part of me wanted to discount this experience as an indiscriminate occurrence. Yet another deeper part of me felt my father's presence and a humbling connection to him. I felt both consoled and blessed as I sat in the company of grace.

The lesson in my stories is to be receptive to where your heart wants to take you. When you tune in, the clarity will come and the doors will open. Being open to synchronicity allows you to connect to this life force and experience its power in your life. Things don't just happen. There is a guiding force. The final story of synchronicity is a favorite of mine.

A poor Scottish farmer named Fleming heard a cry for help coming from a nearby bog. Dropping his tools, he ran to the swamp and found a terrified boy, screaming and struggling to free himself from the black muck. Farmer Fleming saved the lad from what could have been a slow and terrifying death.

The next day, a fancy carriage pulled up to the Scotsman's home. An elegantly dressed nobleman stepped out and introduced himself as the father of the boy Farmer Fleming had saved. "I want to repay you," said the nobleman. "You saved my son's life."

"No, I can't accept payment for what I did," the Scottish farmer replied, waving off the offer. At that moment, the farmer's own son came to the door of the family hovel.

"Is this your son?" the nobleman asked.

"Yes," the farmer replied proudly.

"I'll make you a deal. Let me give him a good education. If the lad is anything like his father, he'll grow to be a man you can be proud of."

And that he did.

In time, Farmer Fleming's son graduated from St. Mary's Hospital Medical School in London and went on to become known throughout the world as the noted Sir Alexander Fleming, the discoverer of penicillin. Years afterward, the nobleman's son was stricken with pneumonia. What saved him? Penicillin. The name of the nobleman? Lord Randolph Churchill. His son was Sir Winston Churchill.

* * * *

LISTEN TO YOUR BODY

The body knows.

I was a competitive long-distance runner for more than twenty years. At university in the seventies I trained under one of the finest U.S. college track coaches, Sherald James, who mentored many Olympic athletes. He taught me to listen to my body: "Your body knows what it needs. If you will learn to listen to it, it will teach you what to eat to give you the sustaining energy you require. It will teach you how to rest *before* you are tired. It will teach when it is ready for a hard workout, and when to back off." Before each training session, we had ten to fifteen minutes of relaxation and meditation, listening for the internal navigator to instruct us as to the kind of workout our body needed on that particular day. Still today, listening to my body and designing my workouts based on my energy level and physical readiness rather than on ambition requires daily discipline and practice. Other superb coaches I have worked with — Rod Constable (who coached me during the eighties) and Grant Molyneux (who prepared me for my first marathon when I was forty) and, in recent years, Pat Copping, my massage therapist and yoga teacher — have each, in their own way, reinforced the age-old wisdom of learning the finely tuned art and science of listening to and trusting the messages that come from our bodies.

I have to admit, however, that I didn't always pay attention to this insight and practice. My obsession to compete and succeed often blinded my own inner wisdom. Invariably injuries and illness resulted from disregarding the internal guide. I remember once getting an overuse injury on the bottom of my foot — plantar fasciitis. I went through a series of medical advisors, including a sports medicine specialist, physiotherapists, a chiropractor, and a podiatrist. As helpful as all these competent professionals were, I realize now that I could have saved a great deal of money and time if I had put my ego aside and simply listened to my body. It was telling me to slow down, rest more, and run less.

Although I could train for four to five hours without tiring, my body was telling me that I needed to learn to sit and be *still*. I was getting a clear message to *connect* with life rather than to run through it. I took up yoga and found it to be more conducive to the changing rhythm and nature of my body. I still run, but my body is asking me to do it more slowly, to rest more, and to run less. Letting go of my ego and the competitive compulsive side of exercise was not easy. Soon after taking up yoga I was heading downstairs to begin the Sun Salutation — a favorite series of stretches to start the day slowly and gently. In my haste to slow down, I broke a toe by walking into a couch. My body continues to send me the messages I need: "Don't turn your yoga practice into another competition. Slow down." I must always remind myself of the importance of listening to my body or paying the price when I don't. The body will teach you everything you need to know, just not everything you want to hear.

Listening to your body is an integral part of the authentic journey. Readily accessible pain relief medication often prevents the body from instructing us. We take a painkiller instead of listening to what a headache is trying to tell us. We take an antacid for heartburn instead of listening to what our stomach is communicating. We take medicine for back pain instead of listening to what the back is trying to say. We take a sleeping pill instead of listening to what our insomnia is telling us. We take an anti-depressant instead of listening to depression as a voice speaking from our soul. We work too hard in a job that is disrespectful to our spirit and go to a doctor, expecting a pill to improve our energy. I am not saying any of these practices are wrong and I do not envision a world without some pain-relief. I am merely suggesting that medications are simply tools which are sometimes useful. However, the real responsibility and message lies within. Wisdom and authentic knowing are found in our own bodies, if and when we take time to go inside.

We often find ourselves on cruise control, acting habitually and being so swept up in the momentum of our daily lives that we don't take the time to check where we are or where we are headed. Our bodies are powerful navigators. We pay a price for not listening as the "nudges" get increasingly more intense and severe. People with a catastrophic diagnosis have often had symptoms that were ignored for years. In a technological culture where we rely on machines, we can be out of touch with our bodies, detached from what they are trying to tell us, and soon we lose the ability to pay attention to the nudges along the way.

A vital component of listening to your body is learning to rest *before* you are tired. There are two important components to keep in mind when clarifying the nature of the rest that is right for you. One is to recognize your need for rest and relaxation on a day-to-day basis, which asks you to look at rest within your twenty-four-hour cycle. How much sleep is right for you? How do you relax within your day? How do you shift gears between your commitments and your roles? How do you separate from your usual work? How do you find renewal each day? If you find yourself more irritable or less able to concentrate, these can be symptoms of sleep deprivation. Pay attention to your body's unique needs for rest and relaxation and make decisions accordingly. It will support your authentic journey as well as your health.

The second component is the amount of rest and relaxation you require while within the cycle of a year. Rest is a season as much as it is a daily requirement. All of nature respects the cycle of life, the balance between effort and rest. Living authentically allows us to attune to the cycle of nature. A two-week season of rest, called an annual vacation, does not, for me, adequately respect my inner life cycle during the year. Our culture, in its obsession for efficiency, does little to respect the soul's need for a season of rest. Although it may not be practical for you to take a three-month rest season every year, there is some real value in extended sabbaticals, whether they be regularly scheduled long weekends or even extended periods of relaxation, reflection, and renewal.

At the beginning of each year, when I go away for a weekend to review and update my quality of life statement with those close to me, I ask myself, "How many 'days off' am I going to take this year? How many days am I going to take to completely disengage from work? What do I need this year on the effort/rest continuum?" Val and I discuss this together, and we schedule our days off. I put them in my Day-Planner just as I would schedule a meeting with a client. We talk about it as a family and decide together how many days off each year we need.

Rest today is not a luxury. It is a necessity on the journey of authenticity. The amount of rest we need varies from person to person, and the amount of rest we need changes over time. Authenticity calls you to know yourself, to listen to yourself and those close to you, and to make decisions in line with what is right for you. In the early 1990s, when I was building my speaking and consulting business, I took few days off. Looking back, I know my business and personal life would have benefited from more time away from the demands of my work, but time off would still have been less than it is today. Each year, the number of days off I take grows as I become more clearly focused, less driven, and more trusting of my life and work unfolding.

* * * *

MANAGE YOUR HUMAN HUNGERS

Everybody has a hungry heart.

— *Bruce Springsteen*

Nature gave us certain basic instincts for a reason. Without them we would not survive as human beings. The desire for control, power, security, recognition, ambition, and comfort or the wish to be needed or to be close to another human being, for example, are hungers necessary for our existence. But when these natural desires are not managed, they can exceed their appropriate purpose and turn into an addiction — an insatiable desire that creates unmanageability in your life and insulates you from your authentic self.

The key is to be aware of what you are hungry for and not to go looking for it in the wrong places. Often our spiritual hunger is expressed through unquenchable hungers of the body. The insatiable hunger for food, possessions, alcohol, sex, power, prestige or relationships is often an indicator of a deeper spiritual yearning. Until this spiritual yearning is acknowledged and sought after, the thirsts will remain forever unquenched. If we fall prey to the illusion that filling the thirst will fill our longings, everything we find will be unsatisfactory because what we truly long for lies below the surface of all these symptoms. Lacking authenticity, we attempt to gather these alluring satisfactions in great masses, thinking that quantity will make up for lack of quality.

Much more subtly, human hungers can take over and destroy your life. Without clear boundaries, conscience, or accountability for the expression of these hungers, devastation will result. Unbridled ambition, for example, can tear apart health and relationships. The unbridled need for power can create an abusive egomaniac with an inferiority complex. In fact, when you stop to think about it, most of the harm done in this world is due to people with an insatiable need to feel important.

The keys to prevent destruction and to use hunger as a positive force in your life are balance and manageability. These come from self-awareness, a willingness to face some of the dark aspects of yourself that you may be running from and then having the courage to live a life dictated by your conscience, not your ego. Managing human hungers is the foundation of a sustaining center and subsequent authenticity.

Back in the 1980s when I had a private practice as a psychotherapist, I worked alone, counseling troubled families, hour after hour. It was not unusual for me to work sixty-hour weeks and to see more than thirty families over a six-day period. Ironically, I was also regularly facilitating workshops on burnout to social service and health care professionals. In reality, I was blind to my own burnout, in part because I was blind to the underlying motive or hunger below the surface of my helping. Instead of serving from an authentic place of overflow, helping got heavy. I did not realize then that the force that was driving my desire to help went beyond authentic self-expression or a simple willingness to serve. I was, instead, *driven* to help from an unacknowledged and thus unmanaged hunger to be needed. My self-worth was dependent on it. I over-identified with my role as helper. I defined myself by how helpful I could be. The need for self-importance went beyond the normal human need for significance and self-respect.

What I understand now is that we each need to feel important in our lives. Everybody wants to feel that they matter. But when people like me come to the work of helping through unacknowledged pain and get plugged into a situation where people are desperate to be helped, soon they are conducting high voltage emotional current. Being blind to my unmanaged hunger left no room to recognize my limits, forgive myself for bouts of impatience or guilt, have compassion for myself, or acknowledge my own needs in the work of helping. Toward the end of my work as a therapist in the late 1980s, I suffered from all of the symptoms that I was trying to resolve in others: irritability, insomnia, a lack of patience, a reliance on rules, an inability to concentrate, excessive anxiety, and cynicism. I was depleted and started thinking, "Everybody is looking to me to have the answers and solve their problems." Helping, instead of serving, became a burden when people kept expecting me to pull the next rabbit out of the hat. In the guise of service, I began to impose my values on others and became exhausted, trying to be a better and better magician. Eventually I fell from the pedestal I had built for myself. My health suffered, my spirit suffered, and my overall mental stability crumbled. I was clinging to my role as a helper to fill an unmanaged human hunger.

Since being away from the psychotherapy profession for several years, and having gained new awareness about my life, I now have a fresh perspective on my burnout. I understand that the impetus and skill to enter the helping profession came from my previous experience of being wounded. The resulting sensitivity was a necessary skill and strength for a therapist. But left unconscious and unmanaged, this hunger eventually became the downfall both to myself and to those I was helping. In the end, the unacknowledged and unmanaged hunger of being needed and important almost destroyed me.

I see a similar phenomenon in leaders of communities, governments and companies, as well as in some of my colleagues in the field of consulting and speaking. In these cases, there is hunger for control and power. Like being needed in a helping relationship, everybody needs to feel some sense of power. Being powerless is not a feeling most of us embrace. But when this need for control is unacknowledged and unmanaged — by remaining blind to one's vulnerable, insecure side — natural instinct goes awry, resulting in destruction and unhappiness. When people who are vulnerable and desperate for the restoration of order (especially in times of chaos) are put together with a leader who promises to reinstate order, another high voltage emotional current occurs.

Consider the hunger for ambition. Like the appetite for feeling important and having a sense of control and power over one's life, the desire to achieve, to better oneself, to live a dream and to create a vision are also authentic human needs. But if the driving force behind the ambition is an unacknowledged need for power, recognition and prestige, and that energy goes unbridled, it will create another form of high voltage current that has the potential to destroy. I have met some very ambitious and successful people in my life — athletes, CEOs, adventurers, entrepreneurs, etc. I celebrate their successes, and I know first-hand those times in one's life when balance is impossible due to the building of a dream. For example, to devote a decade of one's life to train for the Olympics is truly a remarkable celebration of the human spirit. Yet what about when the Olympics are over and the same drive continues into an entrepreneurial venture? What happens when crisis strikes as a message to slow down, but the ambition goes blindly forward? What happens if this human hunger for "more" goes unacknowledged and unmanaged? Unbridled ambition, like the unmanaged hunger for power, can be a destructive force. Many successful men and women, who may be revered by the world's standards of success, are killing their personal relationships, their health, their own sense of contentment, and even their soul with uncontrolled aspirations. Many broken homes are the result of this misaligned instinct of ambition as parents work long hours in pursuit of their career aspirations. Carried to the extreme, unmanaged ambition creates the glorification of greed and consumption, causing a "disconnect" with our conscience and disengagement between the interests of the few and the well-being of the many. Failure can play a role here. While falling down is hard, success can lock you into something far more dangerous. It can keep you on a treadmill of "more" so that you don't stop long enough to listen to the voice within. Failure, even a small one, can stop you in your tracks and invite you to go inside.

Like being obsessed with helping, being driven to achieve and not allowing any time for connection, balance, sitting still or *being* are almost always symptoms of running away from something. Whenever you meet someone who is gripped by, hungry for, and owned by the need for achievement, you soon learn that there is something within them that they are trying to escape from: pain, fear, doubt, insecurity, loss, uncertainty, etc. Because so much of society celebrates achievement, it reinforces the illusion that if you just *achieve* enough, you'll *be* enough. This belief, we soon learn, is only a mirage.

Another human hunger is for money and materialism. When John D. Rockefeller, Sr. was asked how much money it takes to make a man happy, he gave the reply, "Just a little bit more." Socrates believed that the wise person would instinctively lead a frugal life, and he even went so far as to refuse to wear shoes. Yet he constantly fell under the spell of the marketplace and would go there often to look at the great variety and magnificence of the wares on display. A friend once asked him why he was so intrigued with the allures of the market. "I love to go there," Socrates replied, "to discover how many things I am perfectly happy without."

Throughout history the most widespread and recognized difficulty with money is that its pursuit is insatiable. The desire for money can become an unquenchable thirst. The hunger for money usually represents a deeper starvation for intimacy, power, protection, approval or a connection to our spiritual nature. I know that when I am having a down day, the malls can look appealing. The illusion is that money, and the things money can buy, will satisfy us. The lesson is that money cannot buy our deepest desires. Money never purchases that which matters most: love, inner peace, character, self-respect or contentment. Recent research on the long-term effects of winning the lottery shows what we already know but forget as we wait in line for the next lottery ticket. It reminds us that money will buy options, but it won't buy a new person. If you are a miserable person to begin with, winning ten million dollars will only make you a rich miserable person. What people are looking for and what they get in the end are often very different. If you are an unhappy person who believes that happiness comes from what you have around you, you will enjoy the windfall for a while, but soon you will be broke and unhappy once again. If you are expecting the lottery winning to change your life, it may mean that you need to make changes in your life now. Authenticity calls us to stop and examine more deeply our hunger for more money, or our thirst for what we think money will buy. We certainly can enjoy what money can buy, but we must seek a different path for what it cannot. "Nothing gained" is the final lesson of insatiability.

Let's take a look at the hunger for sex. Everyone has a need for intimacy. The desire to feel connected, to be held, and to be close to other human beings is a natural part of our survival. Like feeling important, powerful, and successful, we all need to feel connected to people. Yet, if this desire is left unchecked, unacknowledged and unmanaged, we end up with another high voltage current that can potentially destroy everything we stand for. Leaders in a position of authority are particularly vulnerable. When you are the containing vessel of a large social system and you are holding that system together, it amplifies the need to be held. So powerful can be the craving, that extraordinary people sometimes engage in very self-destructive behavior because they are besieged by their own hunger to be held. Many examples of political, business, and religious leaders in recent history demonstrate this fall from grace.

Not every leader seems to feel this sexual hunger, and not only those in a position of power or authority are vulnerable to it. But for many people, whether in positions of leadership or not, this hunger is very real. The illusion is that the craving we desire for closeness can be satisfied through sex. Like an addict for whom one shot is too many and a thousand hits are never enough, the inevitability of this lie is eventually revealed. Why else would those who allow themselves to be owned by this hunger continue to fall for it over and over again? Faced honestly and contained with clear boundaries and support, sexual instinct or natural desire has the power to deepen the intimacy in your life. Left unharnessed, it will destroy any authenticity and character you are building, along with your close relationships.

The final hunger discussed here is the hunger to escape. We all have a need to withdraw, from time to time, from the stress and strain of living. Escaping is another natural survival mechanism. Think back to times in your life when you have had challenges, setbacks or stress. Ask yourself, "What do I use for escape? Where do I go when times get tough? What do I do when I am depleted or challenged?" We all need to be able to step back, relax and disconnect from the demands of daily living. We all have our own way of withdrawing from the world, ranging from gardening to television, from taking an extra nap to going to a cocktail party, from meditating in our sanctuary to sharing with a close friend, from connecting to consuming. Research shows that societies with the most compulsive work habits watch the most television. We all have ways to escape. The escape method I am most prone to use is busyness. "Just keep busy," I say to myself; "I don't have to experience the discomfort of sitting still and facing myself." I continually have to remember to make room to stop, to s-l-o-w d-o-w-n, to watch the sunset, to talk about the rainbow with my children, to make time to sit still and just be. Frantic busyness is an escape from connection — from my authentic self as well as from my loved ones.

Remember, there is a difference between *escaping* and *replenishing*, between *running away* from life and *restoring* your authentic self. Many of the strategies outlined in this book help you replenish your mind, your body, and your spirit and give you support to nurture yourself in wholesome, life-giving ways. There is nothing wrong with a little escape. The hunger to escape, however, like the hunger for importance, power, ambition, and connection, can destroy you like a 10,000-volt current, if left unacknowledged and unchecked. Unmanaged escape can lead to alcoholism, drug addiction, gambling, over-eating, over-spending, over-exercising, too much television, excessive time on the computer, or any other unbridled hunger. Building life on the short-term pleasures of over-consumption eventually leads to collapse. Sand-filled foundations are simply not sustainable.

The key, of course, to all these human hungers is balance and manageability. This comes through awareness and integrity — keeping promises to yourself and others. Being willing to face these darker, more shadowy aspects of your nature and having the courage and the commitment to contain them in socially responsible ways, according to the dictates of your own conscience, builds character and authenticity.

* * * *

INTEGRATE BEING WITH DOING
AND WELCOME PEACE

Find the joy in the moment and, if it can't be found, be in the moment and the joy will find you.

— *Bill Morris*

If you have started a spiritual practice, you are no doubt familiar with this scenario: you have just had a peaceful quiet time, connecting with your authentic, spiritual nature. You feel centered, balanced, and in touch with your authentic self and vow not to let this feeling slip away as the day progresses. Then, within the first half-hour of your workday, you become stressed by the demands of urgent emails, imperative requests by your clients or customers, and intruding deadlines. In the words of Stephen Covey, you are completely lost in "the thick of thin things" and have misplaced the connection and composure you had less than an hour before. Even more disturbing is that you have no idea how to get it back. It's as if the urgency has closed the door to a deeper dimension, to a place of balance, flow, and trust. By the end of the day, you are frazzled and stressed, and you can't wait to get home to your transitional ritual.

This scenario reminds me of the hopeful prayer: "So far, today, God, I've done all right. I haven't been grumpy, greedy, nasty, selfish, or overindulgent. I'm very thankful for that… But in a few minutes, God, I'm going to need your help. In fact, I'm going to need a lot of help… Because pretty soon, I am going to be getting out of bed!"

Despite our recurring vows to remain balanced in all situations, our loyalties are often divided between our authentic, spiritual aspirations and the fleeting satisfaction of achievements, solving problems, or urgent demands. This division leaves us wondering, "Why and how do I get knocked off my center?"

I am often off center when I polarize *being* and *doing*. Many times I have decided to *do* all day and then come home at night and try to *be*. What I am learning is that doing and being are not mutually exclusive. They can be integrated. We often miss recognizing the being in the midst of doing. Many of us mistake being for the familiar feeling of tranquility, relaxation or pleasantness that we achieve in our quiet time. Then we try to "reconnect with the being" by recapturing the previous serenity. But feelings have an exasperating habit of coming and going and resisting our attempts to control or reproduce them. Being is much more immediate than that. It is the pause between thoughts, the space in which everything comes and goes, and the stillness underlying all activity. In music, authenticity is an integration of the rests and the notes with the way you play. Connecting to your authentic self can happen right now. It is not something you *make* happen as much as something you *allow* to happen. But it is so subtle and empty of content that the mind may overlook it. Breathe, pray, close your eyes, and you can connect now with your authentic self. Don't wait until after the song.

No matter how still you try to become, *doing* is always happening: the heart is beating, the lungs are breathing, blood is flowing, and internal organs are functioning. No moment will pass without performing actions. In the end, any attempt to *be* will be another form of doing. The question, then, is no longer "Are you doing or being?" but rather "How do you relate to your actions?" You can learn to *do* and *be* simultaneously. If you are floating down a river, you are just being, yet you are moving downstream. However, until you experience this stillness of being in the moment, regardless of your activity or lack of activity, you won't realize the union of being and doing.

To *do* and *be* simultaneously requires the willingness to be *mindful*, which simply means that we commit to be present in each moment. Is mindfulness spiritual? If we look up the word "spirit" in a dictionary, we will find that it comes from the Latin, *spirar*, meaning "to breathe." The in-breath is inspiration; the out-breath is expiration. With the breath of life come all the gifts of the spirit: vital energy, consciousness, and aliveness. In the most sincere sense, breath itself is the ultimate gift of the authentic self. But, as we have seen, we can be blinded to the strength and breadth of this spirit as long as our attention is engaged somewhere else. The work of mindfulness is to awaken to vitality in every moment that we have. In wakefulness, everything arouses us.

I was in a restaurant the other day and saw a sign in front of the till for all staff as a reminder before going about their respective duties. This little poster encapsulated, in three words, this entire notion. It read, simply, "Be here now." The thought came to me that if the staff would practice this prompt, it was probably the only guiding principle they needed to run a successful business.

It takes practice to be mindful, to be present in the moment. Feelings that are authentically experienced in the present take time to emerge. The only way to kick the habit of living both in the future and the past is to awaken your essential nature. Being aware of the now, experiencing it, connects us to authenticity. We join the flow of time.

Jon Kabat-Zinn writes, "When you are immersed in doing without being centered, it feels like being away from home. And when you reconnect with your (authentic) being, even for a few minutes, you know it immediately. You feel you are at home no matter where you are and no matter what problems you face."

Not long ago Chandra climbed on my lap, curled into the crook of my arm while I was reading a book, looked up into my eyes, and said softly, "I love you, Daddy."

"I love you, too," I replied.

After several minutes of sitting embracing each other, her gentle voice broke the silence with, "This is peace, isn't it?" I agreed that it was indeed.

"I like peace," she said.

"I like peace, too," I replied.

Authenticity calls us to slow down enough to notice that the small moments in life are the big ones. In fact, that's all we really have: moments in which to be present. Being open to the present makes us a channel for peace, for I am only stressed when I start living in the future or when I start thinking about the past. It's hard to be open to the present and be a channel for peace when we are on the run so much of the time, in too great a hurry to shape and savor meaningful interactions — both with ourselves and with those closest to us. These connections bridge us to our authentic life. Only by stopping long enough to observe our inner life can we bring clarity and meaning to our lives and make the small adjustments needed to stay on our authentic course. And making room for peace within opens the channel for peace to flourish outside.

If there is light in the soul,
There will be beauty in the person.
If there is beauty in the person,
There will be harmony in the house.
If there is harmony in the house,
There will be order in the nation.
If there is order in the nation,
There will be peace in the world.

What I have learned is that peace is a perspective. I recently heard a story that reportedly took place over enemy lines in Europe during World War I. For a twelve-hour period, German and Allied soldiers stopped their battle long enough to sing Christmas carols together. I can only imagine what went through their minds as they momentarily stopped their battle to be open for peace. What if, each day, we could be open for such a miracle?

St. Francis of Assisi, the patron saint of animals and ecology, wrote a prayer eight hundred years ago that speaks to this notion. As he came through his own painful experiences of ill health and ridicule from the world, this prayer expressed his personal desire:

Lord, make me a channel of Thy peace — that where there is hatred, I may bring love — that where there is wrong, I may bring the spirit of forgiveness — that where there is discord, I may bring harmony — that where there is error, I may bring truth — that where there is doubt, I may bring faith — that where there is despair, I may bring hope — that where there are shadows, I may bring light — that where there is sadness, I may bring joy.

Lord, grant that I may seek rather to comfort than to be comforted — to understand, than to be understood — to love, than to be loved.

For it is by self-forgetting that one finds. It is by forgiving that one is forgiven. It is by dying that one awakens to Eternal Life. Amen.

In light of the challenges we all face these days, the Serenity Prayer written by Reinhold Niehbuhr seems particularly relevant:

*God grant me the serenity to accept the things I cannot change,
the courage to change the things I can,
and the wisdom to know the difference.*

Said another way, you can keep your soul alive and your authentic spirit strong if you remember three rules:

1. Change the changeable.

2. Accept the unchangeable.

3. Remove yourself from the unacceptable.

The promise of the Serenity Prayer is an inner peace that is available to all of us. Today you can find peace and poise amidst the extreme uncertainty that we have come to live with. Learning to be here now, in the present, and trusting the life force that grants us serenity is perhaps our greatest challenge. For yesterday is history; tomorrow is a mystery. Today is the present that invites us to be present.

* * * *

PRACTICE GRATITUDE AND GENEROSITY

A grateful heart is a peaceful heart.

— *Veggie Tales*

Gratitude is the sweetest of all practices for living an authentic life. It is the most easily carried out, and it requires the least amount of sacrifice for what is gained in return.

It is easy to forget just how blessed we are to live in this culture. So many of my own challenges are luxury problems. If we compare our conditions to what goes on in most of the world, few of us know real pain. We have become so accustomed to a comfortable standard of living that it seems natural to take it for granted and look for what is *not* here.

Several years ago, I co-facilitated a bereavement group with a woman who was living her life in a wheelchair. She had lost her legs, a child, and her life partner when hit by a drunk driver fifteen years earlier. She knew real pain. What I was so touched by in the months when I worked with Emily was her amazing capacity, in spite of her inconceivable grief, to bring gratitude to her life every day. She was grateful to be alive. She was grateful to be able to breathe. She was grateful for the gift of sight. She often spoke of the marvelous fall colors in the trees that *I* failed to notice. "Always make gratitude greater than your abundance, because you are always more abundant than you perceive yourself to be," Emily would say.

The grateful heart that Emily radiated was genuine. It was not superficial, submissive thankfulness. It was, instead, authentic gratitude that took years to excavate amidst the rubble of anguish, anger, and inordinate grief. This kind of gratitude is not an excuse for being passive in the face of injustice, saying, "Yes, these things are wrong and unfair, but I should be grateful for what I have," or "At least we have this," or "Compared to these people, look how much better off we are." There was, instead, rigorous spiritual work behind Emily's gratitude. Years of tears, torment, and rage were part of the emergence of a grateful heart that was authentically hers. It was anything but passive or submissive, nor was it equated with obligation or the denial of life's difficulties. Out of real appreciation for the blessings that remained in her life came the promise fulfilled by gratitude: healing and freedom.

The practice of gratitude is useful because it turns the mind in such a way that it enables us to participate in life and all it entails. Having access to a small piece of joy while we are suffering helps us to face life and death with an open heart. Gratitude keeps us from being lost in the pain. When I get locked into depressive tendencies, self-pity, or self-defeating thinking, gratitude helps me step back and realize that there is a larger context in which my story is unfolding. Being relieved of the endless wants and worries of life, even momentarily, is liberating. It is freeing to be able to say, "I am angry at this moment, *and* I am grateful for...." Cultivating thankfulness for being a part of life blossoms into a feeling of generosity which creates further joy. Gratitude softens the heart that has become too guarded and too spoiled, and nourishes the soil for authenticity to grow.

In my first book, *Simple Living in a Complex World*, I tell the old Sufi story about a man whose son captured a strong, beautiful, wild horse. All his neighbors told the man how fortunate he was. The man patiently replied, "We will see." One day the horse threw the son, breaking the son's leg. All the neighbors told the man how cursed he was that the son had found the horse in the first place. Again, the man answered, "We will see." Soon after the son's leg was broken, soldiers came to the village and took away all the able-bodied young men, but the son was spared. When the man's neighbors told him how fortunate his son was to have a broken leg, the man would only reply, "We will see." At last, the people were no longer confused.

The story teaches us that every blessing is a potential disaster, and every disaster a potential blessing. We can never fully predict the fortune or misfortune that change and chaos may bring to our lives. Events that appear to be misfortunes may ultimately present hidden opportunities. Each of us must discover how to face the unknown in the world. Gratitude for participating in the mystery of life is also like this. *We will see.* Indeed, there is always something more going on than we know.

When we take this accepting outlook toward time, seeing every event as part of a continuous whole, both understanding and trust become possible. With this perspective, every moment is capable of being redeemed from tragedy and deep suffering and sculpted into something meaningful. Experience is a teacher. Herein lies the heart of wisdom.

Gratitude, in this case, opens the window to a larger world. Problems and pain that we are so afraid to bring into the light can be seen with respect and acceptance, knowing we are all in this together, and that no one is immune from problems, regardless of the masks we wear. Suffering can be a teacher of sorts, a defining and universal condition of life that brings us the unwrapped gift of deeper meaning and perspective while wearing the appearance of pain.

I have gained both comfort and strength in my own darkest hours from the Sufi poet Rumi and particularly from this poem called "The Guest House":

> *This being human is a guest house.*
> *Every morning, a new arrival.*
> *A joy, a depression, a meanness,*
> *some momentary awareness comes as an unexpected visitor.*
> *Welcome and entertain them all!*
> *Even if they're a crowd of sorrows, who violently sweep your house*
> *and empty it of its furniture,*
> *still, treat each guest honorably.*
> *He may be clearing you out for some new delight.*
> *The dark thought, the shame, the malice,*
> *meet them at the door laughing, and invite them in.*
> *Be grateful for whoever comes,*
> *because each has been sent as a guide from beyond.*

Gratitude practiced in this manner can bring delight, balance out the tendency to focus on the negative, and lift a dark mood.

In the book *The Hiding Place*, Corrie Ten Boom tells the riveting story of her experience as a Dutch watchmaker and how she became a heroine of the Resistance, a survivor of Hitler's concentration camps, and a remarkable evangelist of the twentieth century. This book is full of timeless virtues cultivated in the haven of a gentle watchmaker's shop and then tested in the horrors of Nazi Germany. Corrie writes, "Every experience God gives us, every person He puts in our lives, is the perfect preparation for the future only He can see."

Corrie's sister, Betsie, was a constant companion and inspiration to her through their horrific experience in the camps. Each morning they would secretly read from the Bible together. One morning, they read from First Thessalonians. In the feeble light they turned the pages, "Comfort the frightened, help the weak, be patient with everyone. See that none of you repays evil for evil, but always seek to do good to one another and to all... and give thanks in all circumstances." Corrie writes eloquently about how the practice of gratitude carried her through years of torture. She practiced being grateful for the crowded barracks, so that many more would hear the secret readings. She sustained a grateful heart, always seeking for what they still had. At one point, she even practiced gratitude for the fleas, for they were a part of all circumstances. As you read her story in a larger context than I can do justice to here, you know that Corrie and Betsie were not martyrs, but courageous women who brought to life that precious perspective of seeking the gift in everything.

In 1989, I gave up my family therapy practice to shift into the field of organizational development. For nearly two years I interviewed consulting firms in Calgary, searching for a group that supported my values, from which I could learn and with which I could create synergy. On this journey I met Murray Hiebert, a consultant who was teaching internal consulting skills to companies around the world.

When I expressed my desire to learn about consulting, Murray handed me his binder that represented nearly twenty years of development.

"What do you want in return for this?" I asked.

"Nothing right now," he responded. "But perhaps after you get to know my work, our connection could evolve into a relationship of mutual value."

Murray trusted me because he trusted himself, and later that year, along with two other colleagues, we formed a consulting consortium. Murray is a person of strong character, and my respect and admiration for this mentor has grown substantially over the years. What Murray taught me in our first meeting was the *abundance mentality* — the belief that there is enough for all of us. The abundance mentality is a philosophy that leads to a continual commitment to win-win relationships. It shifts one's approach from competition out of fear to cooperation out of faith.

During downturns in the economy and difficult psychological times, there is a natural tendency to hoard and withdraw, to keep work for ourselves, to go into fear, and to think scarcity. But it is during challenging times that we need each other and the spirit of abundance more than ever. To counter this natural tendency to hoard and withdraw, we need to remember that when times are tough, the best way to overcome obstacles is with partners, alliances, and gratitude, with the mindset of abundance.

* * * *

CONCLUSION

Margaret Mead, the distinguished anthropologist and author, talked about her grandmother as a person who impacted her deeply. She described her grandmother as one of a rare breed of women who understood the nature of change and the need to be prepared for the unknown. She said, "This generation must discover how to raise children in the unknown world, how to bring them up without absolutes. My grandmother taught me to *nest in the gale*, which is why I am still around." A great principle we can teach our children is to nest in the gale. Like the sea birds that nest high in the storm-battered cliffs, we need to be able to build a rock-solid place in the midst of the massive turmoil and winds that rock our world. The sea birds have a secure and basic foundation to weather the storms so their young can fly out at last to build their own nests. Storms will always come in life; the key is to have a solid nest that provides a foundation.

A sustaining center is a nest in the gale. It takes us beyond the spectrum of health or sickness, wealth or poverty, success or failure, a long life or a short one, roles or no roles, happiness or unhappiness. Centering allows us to let go of the desire for refurbished circumstances, realizing that true strength and serenity are independent of external conditions. The journey to finding a lasting center is a very personal one. For some, their center is God. For others, it is a quiet place within, where they go to find solace. For some, their center is a spiritual practice of emptying the mind and relaxing the body. For others, center is not so much a *noun*, as in a place to arrive at, but a *verb*, the practice of simply detaching themselves from the importance of the world and its demands and bringing themselves back to themselves. For still others, it is the practice of being *in* the world without being *of* the world. For some, it is a combination of these. Regardless of your path to center, make it a habit of going within. For in the storms of life, we must have a solid nest to withstand the battering force of the wind.

I conclude this section on Finding Center with a story that illustrates both the challenge — and the barrier — to going within. According to an old Hindu legend, there was a time when all human beings were gods, but they so abused their divinity that Brahma, the chief god, decided to take divinity away from people and hide it where they would never find it again. Where to find divinity became the big question.

When the lesser gods were called together in council to consider this question, they said, "We will bury humankind's divinity deep in the earth."

But Brahma said, "No, that will not do, for man will dig deep down into the earth and find it."

They replied, "Well, then, we will sink their divinity into the deepest ocean."

But again Brahma responded, "No, not there, for people will learn to dive into the deepest waters, will search out the ocean bed, and will find it."

Then the lesser gods said, "We will take it to the top of the highest mountain and there hide it."

Brahma replied, "No, for people will eventually climb every high mountain on earth. They will be sure someday to find it and take it up again for themselves."

Then the lesser gods gave up and concluded, "We do not know where to hide it, for it seems there is no place on earth or in the sea that human beings will not eventually reach."

Then Brahma said, "Here is what we will do with humankind's divinity. We will hide it deep down in the people themselves, for they will never think to look for it there."

Ever since then, the legend concludes, humans have been going up and down the earth, climbing, digging, diving, exploring, and searching for something that is already within them.

* * * *

CHAPTER 2

Nourishing Community

*The day will come when, after harnessing the winds, the tides,
and gravitation, we shall harness for God the energies of love.
And on that day, for the second time in the history of the world,
man will have discovered fire.*
— Pierre Teilhard de Chardin

* * * *

MANY CENTURIES AGO, a Persian king approached the legendary religious teacher, Zarathustra, seeking the mysteries of life. Without a word, Zarathustra gave him a grain of wheat. The king thought that Zarathustra was making fun of him and, in a huff, took the grain of wheat and walked back to his palace. He didn't know what to do with it, but after some reflection, began thinking that perhaps there was a lesson in the grain of wheat for him. So he had a gold box made and put the wheat inside it.

Every few days the king would go to look at the grain of wheat in the gold box. Each time he discovered that no change had taken place. Disappointed, he finally went to an Indian wise person, told him about the dried, withered wheat grain in the gold box, and asked him to explain the mystery of life.

The wise person told him, "That is the mystery of life — unless that grain of wheat is put into its environment and comes in contact with all the different elements of life — moisture, soil, nutrients, sunlight — it cannot grow. It cannot be what it is meant to be. If you keep it buried in this box, it will remain a shriveled and lifeless piece of wheat. Nothing will happen to it."

We are like that tiny grain of wheat. As individuals, we cannot grow if we stay isolated in our golden boxes. We need to be in communities — surrounded and nourished by our relationships within meaningful groups — in order to be who we are meant to be.

In 1835, the Frenchman, Alexis de Tocqueville, traveled through the young United States and published what is still considered a classical work on the American makeup. In his *Democracy in America*, de Tocqueville described "habits of the heart" that gave citizens of the United States a distinctive culture. The one personality characteristic that impressed him most about the United States was individualism. Tocqueville admired this character trait immensely. He then strongly warned that unless this individualism was continually balanced by other habits, it would inevitably lead to the fragmentation of American society and the social isolation of its citizens.

As I consider our culture, I bear witness to some of the isolation and fragmentation that is prevalent in today's world. We are a society of individual members that, for the most part, keep to ourselves, watch increasing amounts of television, and lack methods of coming together in meaningful ways. Relationships are becoming automated. Email has replaced handwritten letters and conversation. By touching a key, we have computers that will transmit a message to everyone on our mailing list. This advancement is driven by commerce. People are being converted from human beings to consumers, a target market, a need to be satisfied. All of this is the reality of our culture — it will not fade away and it carries with it many benefits. However, in the face of all of this, there is a need to be reminded of our own humanity and to resist the enticement to live life invisibly.

I personally know of this isolation and aloneness in a culture of millions of people. My own loneliness has been covered up by the things I do to seek recognition and success. Many times in my life I have overachieved, performed, and driven myself to do things that are seen by others as valuable; but at the end of the day I still feel isolated and alone. I have come to know that loneliness is part of being human. It can only be masked and will never actually go away because there is nothing in the external world that can completely fulfill the needs of the human heart. Loneliness is essential to our humanity and can act as a force for human good, but where in our lives can we share that loneliness? Loneliness without community means emptiness, anguish and despair. We simply cannot create a cohesive society based on rugged individualism. We have to understand that we are all interdependent and interconnected.

For all but the last small percentage of recorded history, we have lived tribally in communities, with everyone dependent on each other. Around the time of the Renaissance, tribal existence began to break down in our culture. Individual rights and freedoms took priority over obligations to the community. This, in part, resulted in the release of great creative energy and brought about extensive artistic and scientific advances, but it came at a price — the possibility of ultimate loneliness. Finding balance between individuation and connection, between the inner life — the internal community — and external community, is perhaps the great story of life itself. (Individuation is a process of developing one's sense of autonomy.) In our culture, individualism is winning the battle, and loneliness is becoming an epidemic.

Many who struggle in relationships find themselves deprived of intimacy and thus feel lonely. This aloneness is really a symptom of a fragmented inner life, but is projected onto a relationship as expectations. As a result, many cut free of intimacy altogether and hold firm to the one person they know won't stand them up, let them down, or fail to come home for dinner: themselves. Although these instinctual tendencies to recoil in the face of anguish may be necessary from time to time during the course of a well-lived life, sustained healing will never come from separateness, nor will it come from the demands placed on another.

We can be grateful that there is no war between autonomy and community. Both are needed for the full expression of the authentic self. It is not balance in the polarity that we are after, but rather an integration of both. Paradoxically, we must both stand alone from as well as be a part of. We must connect both with our inner lives and with the community that surrounds us. Rather than dichotomizing individuation and connection, let's explore how we can — and need to — integrate community into the authentic journey.

I have a strong introverted side that, by nature, makes me want to detach myself from the world's expectations. I also have a strong tendency toward perfectionism, which pushes me to perform, prove and achieve. If I don't meet my high expectations, then I will create an image of being more perfect than I really am. This is the part of me that is afraid of — and thus frustrated with — my own weaknesses. When I am in this place of inner contempt of my humanness, I am disturbed by the cry of a child, judgmental of my mistakes and those of others, intolerant with those who are sick (including myself), and overly demanding of others in an attempt to seek control. If I always want to be strong and powerful, I deny a part of my being and create an illusion that I am further along the journey than I am, and, in the process, I avoid vulnerability. Not until my late thirties did I accept emotionally that insecurity, fear, and self-doubt were acceptable feelings for me. I became aware, at that time, that I was riddled with anxiety. It was only through opening up, slowly and surely, within a community that I recognized my need for emotional, physical and spiritual support. Now, in my fifties, I am in continuous contact with members of my community and most of my anxiety has subsided, but I am still in the process of learning how to ask for help, to share my fears, and to show my dependent side when appropriate.

Learning to be "in community" is learning to accept who I am with all my weaknesses and strengths, as well as accepting and loving others as they are, not as I think they should be. To be a part of a community means bonding together, each with our weakness and each with our strengths, because we need each other. Authenticity calls me to slowly break the shell of individualism that both protects and isolates me. More strongly than ever, my soul yearns to fulfill that fundamental human need — a sense of belonging.

Before going further, stop and take a moment to reflect on what community means to you and how it relates to the growth of your authentic self. Who in your life supports you on your authentic journey? Who guides you to your own voice? Who knows you? Who cares about you? Who looks beyond your possessions and your roles and your failures and successes to who you really are and loves you anyway? Who matters to you? Who do you serve? Who holds you accountable?

You simply will not stay on your authentic journey without community. Authenticity calls us beyond individualism to acknowledge our need for interdependence and to connect with each other in significant ways. We are all part of a larger whole, and we need to find sensible ways to make meaningful connections. If we commit ourselves to the making of a culture in which we are concerned only with our own rights, then that society becomes more closed in to itself. Feeling responsibility to the greater whole calls us to work harmoniously toward the common good as we simultaneously receive support on the journey. Maturity, centering, listening and responding to the call of authenticity comes through working with others, through dialogue and through a sense of belonging and searching together.

I have given to and received strength from so many others in my lifetime. Not long ago I was speaking to a group, and a longtime friend, Peter, was in the audience. Our connection transcends the superficiality of competition and small talk. During this particular presentation, Peter wrote me a letter:

"How is it that you walk into my life when I need to see you and hear you and just be with you... I love to hear what you are doing, how you are doing it, how you are struggling, but persisting, and I value the importance of you sharing about that 'Higher Being.'"

Peter then went on to share his gratitude for knowing my mother and what that relationship meant to him and his family. This is how he concluded:

"David, know that your friendship has been, and is, a critical part of my life. What you have written about your talents and your need to share them... is right on... Dave, I love you. I value our friendship. Thanks for being there, for being you. Peter"

I am indeed blessed by the friends in my life.

Community comes with many faces, all carrying unique expressions of human connection. There are work-based communities, religious communities, recovery communities, informal communities, monastic communities, family, learning communities, political activist communities, and neighborhoods. Among this wide range of manifestations, a sustaining community breaks through superficial exchange to an authentic connection that can be distilled down to seven key elements. Community is about: friendship, people you simply enjoy being with; confidants, those closest to you, who you can empty your heart out to at the end of a day and who will stand beside you through the storms; mentors, people who have walked before you and can pass on their perspective, their wisdom, and their vision; fellowship, those with whom you share a common spiritual path; citizenship, working for the greater good; service, an opportunity to give back what you have been given; and accountability, a connection with those who keep you on track. Rarely does one community consist of all of these, yet some element of each is contained in most lasting communities. Many people in your community will serve in more than one of these elements. Community gives witness to what matters most to you. It provides structure and resources to enhance your authentic path. Perhaps, above all, community gets you out of the house.

I was raised in a church environment that provided a superb container for community. There were many opportunities to participate in family church activities, and through them I became firmly rooted in the values of community. In addition to church events, my family had other ways of building community, and my father and I found one through a rather unique contest. With no central heating, we used a potbelly stove to heat our home for many years. As a teenager, it was my job to light the wood in the stove in the evening, and my father's job to do the same in the morning. We used to compete to see who could get the room the hottest. Do you know that you can heat a potbelly stove so hot that it glows? I won the heat competition — at 117 degrees, until my mother put a stop to it. We almost burned that old log cabin down. But there was something authentic, connecting and important in cutting wood together, preparing the fire, and burning the coal to keep the family warm.

Today most of us no longer gather around the central fire. The vivid flame and the roaring glow that gathered groups together have been replaced with television sets and computer screens that portray two-dimensional images and stories that do little to knit us together as a people. Through these media, treasured values and beliefs can be diminished to sagas of self-indulgence and lust, sound bytes and canned laughter, and advertisements promising a better life with a new shampoo.

The most lost and dangerous people in this world are those who are not emotionally bonded to family, community and humanity and who have acquired personal power without being initiated to a sense of the source of that power. The collapse of traditional cultures and the loss of shared myths and rituals that bond the individual into the group are producing generations of unbounded children and adults who are not initiated into the purpose and meaning of their own lives.

In many tribal cultures, it was said that if the boys were not initiated into manhood or shaped by the love and skills of the elders, they would destroy the culture. In the words of Michael Meade, if "the fires that innately burn inside youths are not intentionally and lovingly added to the hearth of community, they will burn down the structures of the culture just to feel the warmth." No proliferation of laws, no adjustment of the curriculum of early education, and no social action will remove the threat of the destruction of our culture until we regain our respect for elders and children, until we stop depending on consumption to sustain us, and until we can help each other see into our souls. This can be done with a return to community. Only when enough people gather and weave the authentic threads of their lives together so that the patterns of both the old and the young can be expressed can there be the promise of healing.

I like my alone time. But beyond my nature to prefer isolation, I also realize that I have been afraid — afraid that being in a community meant living life with the painful, fearful part of my upbringing; afraid of being out of control; and afraid that vulnerability would cost me my autonomy. Even the friends I have had over the years were people I knew from a distance so that there would be no obligations, and I could stay in control. It is ironic that so much of my work in the past twenty years has centered on teaching about connections and community. Again the reminder — what you are most capable of developing in others is what you most need to develop in yourself. What I yearned for, but was not ready for until recent years, was community. I know now that this desire was a need to feel part of something larger than myself. Learning to show up for others, with all their warts and personalities and gifts; learning to love people, even when you don't like them; learning to subordinate feelings to higher principles; and learning to be in a community today as if you are going to stay there for the rest of your life have been an integral part of my journey. For in accepting the flaws of others, I accept my own. In investing in the lives of others beyond self-seeking motives, I come to know others and in the process, I come to know myself. In valuing others, I come to value myself. In caring about others, I learn to care about myself. Indeed, the words of my mother come to mind: "To know is to love." I need community to help me with this. The journey of authenticity, from time to time, is traveled alone, but we all reach a point where we need to invest ourselves in others to further the voyage.

* * * *

OPENING TO CONFIDANTS

Oh the comfort, the inexpressible comfort of feeling safe with a person; having neither to weigh thoughts nor measure words, but to pour them all out, just as they are, chaff and grain together, knowing that a faithful hand will take and sift them, keep what is worth keeping, and then, with the breath of kindness, blow the rest away.

— George Eliot

A confidant is someone who will stand beside you on the road of authenticity, someone who loves you and respects you for all you are. A confidant is someone to pour your heart out to about what is really happening, someone who will hold a confidence without violation and someone who is not afraid to tell you the truth. Confidants give you support and perspective and remind you, "I used to complain about having no shoes, until I met a man who had no feet." A confidant is someone who can put a name on your inner pain and deepest feelings, who will remind you of your worth, and who will support you with your aspirations.

Confidants are necessary in our darkest days when we are lost; surrounded by grief or besieged by inadequacy; in need of acceptance, support, reassurance, and confirmation; they are necessary to clean the lenses of our perception so we might see the world and ourselves more clearly. In moments of crisis we need to be reminded of that which we can so easily forget: our innate nobility, our worth. The language of a confidant may not even be words, but meanings and wisdom beyond the language of voice. A confidant is someone who will lift you up high enough to get a new perspective — someone who walks in when the rest of the world walks out. A confidant can be like a moon on a dark night, reflecting back to you a reminder of the constant presence of light even in the darkness. A confidant is not there to evaluate, judge, advise, or interpret your words, but simply to be present and help point you toward your own truth and meaning.

We also need confidants when we are ready to share our dreams, our values, and our deepest aspirations. At these times, we need to be reminded of our gifts and of our value, both to ourselves and to others. Confidants cherish our hopes and are kind to our dreams. A confidant is someone who can remind us why what we do is worth doing — someone who cares more about our soul than our ego.

Those who are committed to the authentic path need confidants to help us step back in the midst of action and to debrief at the end of the day by asking, "What just happened to you today? What didn't you foresee? What could you have done differently? How did you feel? What did you learn? What is the truth about this?" In a caring and respectful way, they will challenge you by saying firmly, "Let's take a look at what just happened." Or, "There you are; you just did the same thing you did last month." Confidants are there for the long haul. They help you see patterns of behavior and give you support to make necessary changes.

I am blessed with some wonderful confidants who have come into my life. In recent years I have been intentional about this because I recognize the need for daily connection with trusted friends I can open up with and who will offer me a listening ear and a fresh perspective. Val is not only my lifelong partner, she has also been my best friend for many years. It was certainly more challenging when the kids were younger to create undistracted time to sit with each other and open up and share our inner lives. But as the children are getting older and more independent, we are creating the space needed to do this. I love taking a longer lunch hour and spending time over a cup of tea just talking about our day. Whether I am frustrated with an issue at work, or feeling inadequate about an upcoming project, or simply in need of some fresh eyes on a problem, I feel blessed to have this gift of a listening ear, an intuitive mind, a compassionate heart, and an outside perspective in my life. Val also challenges me as much as she supports me. Although confrontation is not her strong suit, Val is known for her eyes — she looks at me and says, without words, "Do you really think that would be a wise choice?" She brings balance to my compulsive nature. She helps me slow down and consider a new viewpoint. It is not always easy to hear what a confidant will tell you, but I have to remind myself from time to time that if I opened up only to confidants who agreed with me, then I wouldn't need a confidant in the first place.

No one person can completely fulfill the role of a confidant. I have learned that I need a web of people to give me support in a variety of ways. As with any friendship, it takes time to develop a trusting relationship so that we feel safe enough to open our hearts. I have a wide range of confidants around the world. I have made it a habit in recent years to pick up the phone and talk with people about what goes on in my life. We share common ground in our shared spiritual practice, and these conversations give me tremendous strength. But these relationships don't develop overnight. It has taken years to build the trust. And the trust hasn't come so much from them as from me. The more I risk, the more I share, and the more the trust comes. I also travel to meet with these people face to face. The phone and emails are wonderful tools, but they will never replace face-to-face contact with another human being who cares enough about you to tell you the truth and hold you accountable for what matters most in your life. I need people outside my family with whom I can share my darkest side, my fears, my doubts, and my insecurities. Even though a marriage requires realness and honesty, if I bring too much to Val, it will contaminate the relationship. I need support from outside to enable me to bring strength and perspective *to* the marriage rather than always taking *from* the marriage.

Rather than giving answers, confidants help guide you to your own truth. Just last night I overheard Hayley talking to her dog about a problem she was having with a friend at school. Lucky couldn't offer much in the way of a new perspective, but it was fascinating to hear Hayley struggle through a lengthy monologue while her canine companion, through a compassionate presence, helped her to excavate her own hidden wisdom and reach clarity about the issue. Witnessing a child confide in her dog reminded me that confidants must "feel with" rather than "fix" and that we have the answers to our own problems if we have the support from another to trust the emergence of our own hidden expertise.

This is what confidants do. They affirm you and care about you without necessarily agreeing with you. They are not afraid to be honest and are able to do so without diminishing you. They help expose you to the truth that lies behind your blind spots and they offer hope, but they don't tell you how or whether to proceed. Confidants hold you accountable to live out what matters most in your life, helping you see the truth about yourself more clearly. The Sufis had it right when they said, "The eye can't see itself." We need others to help us find new ground to stand on and new eyes to see the view.

Reaching out and opening up does not come naturally to me. I am learning to reach out, to call on people, to build relationships *before* a crisis occurs. If I wait until a crisis to invest in a relationship with confidants, it's often too late. I need to foster these relationships along the way. I have also learned that risk precedes trust, not the other way around. If I wait for trust before risking vulnerability, the trust never comes. By being vulnerable, even when trust isn't completely there, the trust is strengthened. If it isn't, I move on and find different confidants.

One of the most beautiful qualities of true friendship is to understand and to be understood. Confidants are very precious. To think you can take the authentic journey without confidants is like thinking you can survive a Canadian winter without a coat.

* * * *

INVITING MENTORS

While playing the piano in the presence of my music teacher, I was becoming flustered and angry with myself for not playing the piece perfectly. Kristiana put her hand on my arm and said gently, "Stop." After a short pause, she continued, "Why did you decide to take piano lessons?"

"For relaxation and enjoyment," I responded.

"Well, for a person who wants relaxation and enjoyment, you don't seem very relaxed and you certainly don't look like you are enjoying yourself. You look like you are trying to perform rather than simply find pleasure in what you are doing."

At that moment I became aware of how difficult it was for me to be engaged in an activity for the pure joy of the experience. Instead, I took so many expressions of life and turned them into a competition, either with myself or with others. In the midst of this reflective moment, Kristiana then respectfully reminded me that I will probably never be a Mozart, a Beethoven, a concert pianist, or even the star at the annual student recital. "Why don't you let go of performing for me or anyone else, and do this for the simple and pure love of music?"

A sense of reprieve and freedom swept over me at this sudden and swift awareness of truth. I realized that this insight wasn't just about music. It was about my life. It was about my yearning for a new way of being in the world — letting go of pressure I put on myself and those around me, about the desire to be less hard on myself, and the freedom that comes from letting go of my addiction to perfection. Suddenly, I could enjoy playing the piano.

Kristiana challenged me and gave me perspective, compassion, and support — things that can only be gained through other human beings who have what you want, who have walked a path before you and have some experience and mastery in a place you want to travel, who have the ability to pass on their wisdom and skills, who care about you enough to invest in your life, and who are committed to supporting you — the attributes of a mentor. Mentors, like confidants, come in many forms. They can be parents, teachers, colleagues, or good friends you look up to.

There are three forms of mentors: "leg-up" people, teachers, and formal mentors. *Leg-up* is a term derived from working with horses. When small children can't reach a horse's mane to pull themselves up, they have someone alongside to push their leg up and give them a boost. Leg-up people are a kind of mentor, but are not necessarily sought after. They are people who appear when you need them most and they give you a "leg-up." They give you more support, affirmation, and encouragement than negative criticism. Teachers, parents, grandparents, aunts, uncles, neighbors, and even guardian angels are often leg-up mentors. The young need elders and mentors; they need healthy older adults who pass on their wisdom. And elders need to be needed. They need to be asked. We help feed and nurture each other through mentoring. We all need to support each other in knowing our value, our worth, and our contribution to the world. Authenticity calls us to awaken and acknowledge the leg-up people in our past and present life.

As an awkward, gangly, and undersized adolescent, I signed up for football in my first year of high school, not because I was talented, but because I wanted the challenge. All my friends played football and my self-esteem depended on being a starter. I was a kid with no skill and no size, but Coach Gustafson supported my passion and gave me the space to prove myself. He would often stay late after a practice to give me extra attention and help me learn how to block. He didn't spoil me or treat me more benevolently than other students, but he gave me a chance, he believed in me, and he gave me unfailing encouragement. I used to walk two miles to his house every morning in the autumn months for a ride into town to practice before school started.

My parents were both leg-up people for me. My father, Harlie Irvine, planted the first conscious seed of awakening in my deep core of authenticity on a frosty February morning in 1974 while we were out feeding the horses.

"As you prepare to leave home, David, the conventional thing to do as a father is to wish you success. If you define success by the world's standards (achievements, conformity, recognition, wealth, compliance, materialism, and pleasure), then success for you will be easy. I say this because I know how focused, ambitious, and determined you have always been. I see how you have overcome a myriad of obstacles and how you always seem to come through to the other side and achieve the goals you have set for yourself..."

"So," my father continued after a long pause, "my wish for you is not success, at least by these standards. My wish for you, instead, is that you discover, in your life, the difference between a successful life and a meaningful life. It is okay to live a life that is successful, but then go beyond success to meaning. That is what will bring you lasting fulfillment."

After another silence, I found myself fumbling for a response, wanting to ask him what he meant, and at the same time, not quite knowing how to reply. Then my father quietly took his hands out of his gloves and embraced me. Taking a step back, he put his hands on my shoulders and said, "I love you, David."

"I love you too, Dad," I mumbled. Then we walked silently back to the house and fixed breakfast.

This story demonstrates how difficult it is to be real with each other, to allow a connection to emerge between two people. An insecure seventeen-year-old, struggling for his autonomy and for space away from his parents, is not, at the best of times, open to the love and affection of a caring parent. I have often noticed how uncomfortable it is to stay in a moment of love and not back away from connection. This is one challenge of authenticity, to be real and courageous, to stand tall in the face of discomfort, and be willing to be touched by a simple source of strength that flows beneath outer appearances and facades.

This story is also about a father's love for his son and his willingness to be vulnerable in the face of rejection, loving in the face of fear, and compassionate in the face of bravado. It was as if Dad was a gardener throwing seeds on my soul, not knowing if or how they would take root, but trusting that although some seeds would fall on rocky ground, others would land in fertile soil and take root like tenacious grass that finds a home in the cracks of concrete. As a father of three daughters, I wonder now what my father thought on that winter morning. Did my aloof and rigid response make him wonder if his words had been a futile exercise of flinging seeds against stone? I suspect that Dad knew he was getting through somehow, some way. Regardless, he did what he felt he needed to do that day. His words were an act of pure love, an act of authenticity.

On that day in 1974, my father was calling me to be more than what the world expected — to be more than outer appearance, achievement, recognition, and compliance. He was calling me to an inner spiritual journey, to a path of authenticity. Some of the seeds he planted that day have taken many years to germinate. Over the past three decades, my comprehension of the significance of my father's wisdom on that day has been emerging. And I have a huge appreciation for the "leg up" he gave me. At times, the journey to meaning has been intentional and conscious. At other times a deeper, more powerful life force, quietly and painstakingly at work below the surface of my awareness, has been guiding and directing me.

Just as leg-up people have an impact that you don't often recognize until years later, teachers can influence you without knowing that they are doing so. If you have ever read a book that impacted you, the author could be a mentor to you without being aware of it. Whether you call them mentors or great teachers, authenticity calls to a grateful and generous heart by acknowledging these people in your life and by passing along what you have been given. Their writing, their art, their teachings and their poetry are left to you as their legacy. I have had many wonderful mentors in my life that I have never met or even talked with, yet they have changed me.

Formal mentors are people you seek out formally and identify by saying, "I want a relationship with these people. I want to study with them. I want to learn from them." Often when I read a book that impacts me, I will call the author, and if there is a meaningful connection, I will travel to see them. As a result, I have studied with some marvelous teachers, people who have had a lasting impact on my life and work. My mother, Joyce, also had an enormous impact on my work, particularly in my early days, and I view her as one of my most significant mentors. We could philosophize for hours about life and work and the future of our society. She honored and supported my passion for learning. I am filled with gratitude for the mentorship of my mother and the tremendous impact her teachings had on my authentic journey.

Formal mentoring begins when we reach out and ask to be mentored. When I first started to write on authenticity, I reached out to a man named Robert Terry whose books influenced me. Robert Terry wrote a book entitled *Authentic Leadership*. Robert was gracious, compassionate, and most insightful. Just six months after my first connection with Robert, after a lengthy struggle with ALS, he passed on to the next life. Although we never met, Robert and I corresponded via email and conversed over the phone, until his speech finally gave out. He was a master at frameworks and worked with me in the early stages of the framework of this book. His spirit, wisdom, and generosity made a tremendous difference to me.

When you are intentional and ready, mentors appear. In the last two years, Father Max Oliva, a Jesuit priest, has come into my life. His newfound calling of bringing spirituality into the business community has led us to many conversations. His love, compassion and wisdom have been evident on many occasions. The best mentoring relationships can evolve into friendships and such is the case in my relationship with Max. Our relationship began with me seeking his counsel and advice, but Max now appears when I am most in need of his support, friendship or a new perspective. Earlier this spring, in a moment of writer's block, Max arrived unexpectedly. That day, after a two-hour conversation, Max left me with renewed energy and my writing flowed for the rest of the day. When the student is ready, the teacher appears.

Don't let fear stop you from asking people to mentor you. Many elders in our society would love to be mentors, yet they are never asked. We all need to feel needed and to know that the world is a better place because of our contribution. Mentoring is a path to the joining of age and experience, to passing on a legacy of wisdom. Inviting mentors into our lives enriches us and also pays benefits to those providing the mentoring. We all reach a stage when we need protégés to acknowledge, appreciate, and seek our wisdom. This a necessary stage in one's life and work cycle. Without giving back what we have learned in life, we stagnate. In turn, protégés, too, must be respected and cared for by the mentor. Mutual affirmation is a critical component in the process of mentoring.

I derive great pleasure from receiving emails or letters from people who are impacted by something I have written or said, as well as from sending emails or letters to those who have influenced me. Authenticity asks us to acknowledge what others mean to us, make the process visible, and pass on what we have been given. Mentors are around us all the time. Community asks us to make this relationship explicit.

A mentoring relationship is a very special human connection. Mentors see what their protégés can be even when the protégés cannot see it for themselves. Mentors truly offer new eyes and bring new light to their protégés. Over my life, I have, at one time or another, had mentors in every area: I have had spiritual mentors and mentors that helped me with my health, my relationships at home, and with my business development.

A word of caution about mentoring is necessary. As in every-thing, the pursuit of community must be done in moderation. Mentors can pull us off the authentic path if we give up our own voice in a mentoring relationship. Mentors are here to help us find our own truth, not for us to rely on them for answers. It is ego enhancing to be a mentor, and the good ones will resist the seduc-tive power of being a guru. Mentors cannot take the authentic jour-ney for us. In this regard, all mentoring relationships need an accessible and safe exit, where the dignity and grace of both parties can be maintained. We walk the authentic journey alone, in the company of allies.

Parker Palmer, another generous mentor, once reminded me that the quest for community can be one more form of manic activ-ity if it is not rooted in a continual practice of silence and solitude. We need to balance time alone with the commitment to being in relationship. It is not healthy to be submerged in any relationship at the expense of your own identity. This is especially true in a rela-tionship with a mentor. Mentors are there to help us find our own voice, not to dictate what it should be.

*　＊　＊　＊*

THE OPPORTUNITIES OF FAMILY

A Poem for Papa
If you go out on a summer day
Go and see yourself at play
Call your dad
And you will see
Just how fun it will be.

— Hayley Irvine, age 9

As a child, my father was my scout leader. Through the scouting program he taught me some important, sustaining values, like doing your best, respecting and serving others, and caring for the land. I was blessed to have a father who was there for me as a teenager, hiking and camping with me while instilling some critical principles and values for a satisfying and meaningful life.

Before I had children, I carried on my father's legacy by becoming a scout leader myself. It was there that I had my first exposure to the critical role that parents — and particularly fathers — play in the lives of their children. Many of the youth who joined the group were dropped off and I saw little of most of the parents. I decided to create a joint activity where they needed to bring their fathers once a month. If they didn't have a father or access to their father, they were to round up an uncle, a neighbor, or an older male in their life to come with them. Our first project was a father-youth campout. As we were gathering our gear, a man in a black three-piece suit, whom I had never met, walked up and introduced himself as Jason's father.

"Jason is packed and ready to go. I just want to know what time I should pick him up tomorrow," he said.

Clearly the father did not intend to join us. Under his ball cap, Jason had tears welling in his dark eyes. I asked Jason's father where he was parked and what he was driving. He pointed out a brand-new Cadillac, parked a safe distance from any other vehicle. When we got to his car, I complimented him on it and leaned up against the front fender.

"Nice car," I said.

"Thank you," he replied, "but I would appreciate it if you wouldn't lean against it." I obliged.

"I respect the fact that you don't have time to take your son camping this weekend, and we'll be glad to take care of him for you.

I do need you to know, however, that as a requirement in this troop, you will be expected to join us for one activity a month."

"Oh, I won't have time for that," he replied abruptly. "I'm a lawyer and I'm either in the office or out of town most evenings and Saturdays."

I replied, "Well, if you can't join us, could I ask a favor of you?"

He nodded, hesitantly. "Sure, I guess."

"We are quite strapped for transportation to the camp, and I was wondering if we could borrow your car?"

A look of shock came over this man's face as he responded with, "I have never met you, why would I loan you my car?"

"With all due respect, sir, if you wouldn't loan me your car, could you give me one reason why you would loan me your son?"

Thus began the father's induction into the path of authenticity and his coming to know a wider, deeper truth about himself. While I took his son on this outing, he made time to join us in subsequent camping trips, and slowly learned to experience his humanness beyond his role of competence. Though neither parenting nor a love of camping are required for authenticity, what is necessary is an open heart.

For those who are parents, you know how families are doors to authenticity. Authenticity calls us, as parents, to recognize the value of community and extended family in the raising of our children. We also know of the brilliance and teaching opportunities that our children bring us and we recognize the value of our children and the legacy we are both leaving and living. Indeed, it takes an entire community to raise a child, and children can help us enormously to reach within ourselves.

Authentic parenting asks us to know, respect, and foster the unique nature that children bring into the world. My daughters all have very different natures. Mellissa is gentle and creative. She has needed a soft touch and a calm, supportive hand throughout her life. Hayley has a passionate spirit with a flair for performance. We are continually finding ways to channel her yearning to direct and to express herself. Chandra's gift is love, and we joyously nurture her compassionate heart. As we keep our eyes and hearts open to our children, they teach us so much about ourselves.

One mission of those who influence young people is to acknowledge and nurture the uniqueness of each child and recognize the exceptional contribution that is made through their presence in the world. This takes time and a conscious commitment. As parents or mentors in a young person's life, we also have a responsibility to bring our own authentic presence to the relationship. We help foster a sense of responsibility and authenticity with our children in the same way that we help cultivate their other desirable traits: first by our own daily practice and then by example. The greatest gift we can give is our own authenticity that will, in turn, begin to cultivate self-trust within the child.

While standing in a checkout line, Chandra asked if I would buy her a toy that was sitting on the counter. My first response was, "No, you don't want that toy." I then realized that I had diminished an authentic desire within her. The truth was that she did want that toy and I didn't want to buy it for her. By recognizing this and changing my response accordingly, I took a step toward fostering authenticity between us and within us.

Children have enormous wisdom within them. There are times when they need direction and answers from adults, but most importantly, they need adults to take time to listen and help them access their own inner wisdom. This is a skill that requires a lifetime of practice, beginning when children are born. As we intentionally support young people to think for themselves, to problem-solve using their inner resources, and to trust their wisdom, we are preparing them to live authentic, capable adult lives — long after we, as caregivers, are gone.

There are many parallels between parenting and gardening. No plants ever grew because I commanded that they do so or because I threatened them. Plants, like human beings, will only grow in the appropriate conditions, when they are given proper care, love, and nourishment. Finding the most desirable environment for the sustenance of plants — and people — is a matter of continual enquiry, awareness, and investment.

Extended family also plays a critical role in our authentic journey. I was visiting my dear Aunt Zona only a short time ago with two of my daughters. Visiting Zona, who lives over a thousand miles from me, is like visiting my spiritual roots. We told stories of my mother, of our heritage, and of our religious and Irish roots. After the visit, Zona sent me a card. Here, in part, is what she wrote: "So happy am I, David, for our time together. Yes, each time you visit it adds another dimension to our life's processes. It takes a lot of understanding to really know ourselves! And if we keep learning about who we are and about who the wonderful folks are that are close to us — it brings a ray of light for seeing ourselves. Like your mother so stressed in her life: 'knowing is loving.'"

Another aunt, Doreen, inspires me with her wisdom, her wit, and her passion for continual learning. During my last visit we stayed up late conversing about a stimulating discussion paper on Neurotechnology and Related Areas. I am blessed to experience a variety of richness in my extended family. We each bring the gifts of our crazy lives to the family stew. We have, as a family, had our share of breakdowns, both in marriages and in psyches. We each bring our challenges, our pain, our difficulties, and our gifts to life. Yet I believe that somehow, all of the collapses and brokenness and pains and joys are bringing us, like society itself, toward a higher level of spiritual integration and wholeness. As my father once said when we picked him up from the hospital after a severe and penetrating depression, "Dave, it wasn't a breakdown, as much as it was a breakthrough."

I was born into a dynasty of both courage and humanness. There was no pretense of perfection, just a willingness to face the suffering in an authentic human way. Nobody in my family has had it easy, just as no one in life has a trouble-free existence. Authenticity never guarantees it will be easier, just more meaningful and fulfilling. I have been taught and inspired to somehow embrace it all, appreciate it all, and use it all as fertilizer in my authentic garden.

I cannot leave this section on family without expressing my gratitude for the rich inheritance of love, values, character, pain, acceptance, wisdom, and the door to healing that I received from both of my parents. Soon after my mother's death, I found among her personal belongings a three-hundred-page handwritten history of her seventy-eight-year life, written over a forty-year span. The best way to honor my mother is to share some of the last three pages of this chronicle with you. These last pages were written just fourteen months before her death:

... Regrets eat at the soul — especially regrets over material things. I watched my father's pain because he had no inheritance to leave his children. What wasted energy!

I do know that I have a much greater legacy to leave my children than money or material things. That is the legacy of my writing about my own personal journey. In this sharing I hope I can help them to be open to living life more fully. The freedom to be — fully to be — who we are is the greatest gift any of us can give ourselves. And we must give it to ourselves. No one can do this for us.

My hope is that my journal writings will help my progenitors accomplish this task!

As I reflect upon my seventy-seven years I am enveloped in memories and love for this experience of "living life." What a gift it is. I am so grateful to the Creator of this miracle. My whole journey has been a mystery, a miracle, and a marvel. I feel strongly that an unseen hand had orchestrated it and has handed it to me as a gift! I know it has been a process, with peaks and valleys, with joy and deep pain, with laughter and tears, and with many wonderful experiences and the whole gamut of human emotions. Most of all it has been a privilege and I thank the Great Creator for such a wonderful gift.

— *Joyce E. Irvine*

Mother, as I read your story, I thank you for the rich heritage you left me that goes beyond your written story to a more complete life story. You have left your grandchildren and us the gift of your wisdom, your humanness, and the inspiration to carry on your legacy.

* * * *

PARTNERSHIPS AND COMPANIONS

My family of origin undoubtedly fostered the roots of my authentic journey, but now it is my family of procreation that contributes to the nurturing environment necessary for my progress along this path. I have been blessed with a mate and lifelong partner whose "partnership" stretches beyond the usual spousal roles. As partners, Val and I are doing a good job of working together in the raising of our children and building our business. We support each other tremendously and work most cooperatively as a "team." But I felt over time that, in the demands of children and work, we were missing time alone to share our inner, spiritual lives beyond our roles and responsibilities. There was love and caring and wonderful cooperation, but we were not making time for real vulnerability. I felt that our relationship needed some authentic presence. We talked about it and resolved to set aside time to practice opening up our authentic selves more fully. Now that the girls are in school, we try to make time over lunch to ask each other: "What's been happening for you today? How are you, really?" Sometimes we will walk or just sit together to create structured, uninterrupted time to open up with each other. I have a higher need to "push" for vulnerability and openness, and I have been able to talk with Val about this, own it, and then let go of some of my expectations.

Making a commitment to spend time together each day when I am home is taking us to a deeper level of intimacy. We are just beginning this habit. At first, like any new practice, it was awkward. We went through times when we didn't have a lot to say, or we would start by talking about the kids or the business or my writing. Little by little, however, we are opening up with each other and talking more about our inner, authentic worlds, our struggles, our upbringings, our feelings, our insecurities. We are becoming genuinely engaged in these communications, and in the process, the love that has always been between us is being rekindled in a new way. I am looking at and acknowledging some of my blind spots, some of the darker sides of my nature, my self-centeredness and inner fears, and how these surface as control and unrealistic demands on Val. In the process, the acceptance and deep respect between us is growing. We are seeing our differences and sharing how they can help us grow, both together and individually. We are both learning to act from a place of wisdom, rather than from a place of habit.

Working on our partnership is strengthening our marriage. We bring a deep respect to the process and a commitment to support each other. We are there to build, not to hurt, and either of us is free to back off and call it quits on any given day. I bring intensity to the partnership, while Val brings stability. We can both see the development of maturity as we support each other's growth. I treasure the love that I am blessed with. We have a very precious companionship that is growing each day. We look forward to growing old together — today.

The partnership that Val and I share goes beyond our marriage because we are also partners in our business. In addition to dealing with the "administrivia" of running a business, we have worked side by side in the writing of this book. And in the process, we have experienced a whole new realm in partnering. True partnerships bring different strengths to the table. My strength is my ideas, my experience, my heart, and my ability to tell stories in a way that awakens the human spirit. Val, on the other hand, keeps me grounded, helps my material stay relevant, and brings her healing, loving heart to this project. She has truly been a gift from God in my life, and I could not have completed this book without her endless energy. In one respect, she has been my faithful editor, but to call her an editor severely undermines the gifts that she has brought to the life of this book. There were days that I would write for eight hours and come home completely disheartened, wondering if I had written anything worthwhile. She would listen with her loving arms around me and then gently turn me around and point me back to the computer the next day. "Just keep at it. You are meant to do this."

Just as the completion of a project can be made more effortless by working as a team, partners and companions can enhance your efforts along your authentic journey. Like mentors and leg-up people, partners and companions can be invaluable assistants in the discovery of our authentic self. They are one of the many components of our community that will assist us along our way.

* * * *

LEARNING COMMUNITY IN NATURE

According to a Jewish folktale, one day a child, Honi, saw an old man digging a hole in the earth. Honi asked the man, "Must you do heavy work at your age? Have you no sons or daughters to help you?" The man kept digging.

"This work I must do myself."

Honi then asked, "How old are you?"

"I am seventy years and seven," answered the man.

"And what are you planting?"

"I am planting a bread fruit tree," was the answer, "and the fruit of this tree can be made into bread."

"And when will your tree bear fruit?" asked Honi.

"In seventeen years and seven."

"But you surely will not live that long," replied Honi.

"Yes," said the old man, "I will not live that long, but I must plant this tree. When I came into this world there were trees here for me. It is my duty to make sure that when I leave there will be trees here also."

At their very foundation, ecological awareness and the choices that emerge from that consciousness are spiritual. Land and nature are God's gift to us, the fabric that we are woven into. For those who honor aboriginal traditions, this innate reverence for the earth and the interdependence of all life is reflected in the notion of seven generations — making decisions based on outcomes for seven generations to come, knowing that we have a deeply seeded obligation to care for this land that has been entrusted to us.

Great spiritual teachers taught not in churches but went directly to nature, sitting under a Bodhi tree or on top of a mountain or in a cave. All the spiritual people I have met share a kinship with the land, a sense of connection with the divine in nature. Nature returns us to a source of inspiration and a connection to God. Nature gives a greater sense of ourselves, connecting us with something more sustaining, more powerful, more lasting. Our quest for authenticity is not only enriched by a reverence for the earth, it is incomplete without it.

The first step toward rediscovering this spiritual fountainhead is simple: go out and be in the natural world. Experience it, observe it, feel it, and be fed by it. The earth teaches us an eternal message that cannot be taught through a book. Spend time in the natural world. The sun and the air are good medicine, both for the body and for the soul. Sun and air are nature's great healing forces. The natural world is a good nurse for tired bodies and worn down spirits. Let nature have her way with you. Let her healing powers surround you.

The common view of land in today's economic world is that it is an investment. We separate ourselves from the earth in which we live by relegating it to an inert lump of rock, by buying and selling it as a commodity, often without even setting foot on it, much less stopping to appreciate its beauty or savoring its magnificence. We build on the earth, we take from it, we use it, and yet do we really experience it?

The economic model has its roots in Descartes' mechanistic model in which man began to consider himself "above" nature. This separation from the natural world has led to an alienation from the "laws of nature" and has instead given rise to a belief in a god-like superior "human nature." This in turn leads to a master (man)/servant (nature) relationship in which nature is to be tamed or governed.

While this approach has disastrous planetary consequences, the side effect is that we do not recognize our own natural rhythm. Instead, we create a myth-like perception of man's place in the universe, made in the image of a beneficent, paternal god. Out of this mythical hierarchy come our own organizational and family structures.

And herein lies the problem. The underlying premise of the mechanistic approach is that we don't trust the universe to act authentically in the affairs of human beings. We have to intervene and control to ensure the right outcome.

Authenticity asks us to go back to that place and time when we loved our land, when we were part of nature, not users of her, when we flowed with her energy and her rhythms, when we listened to her and sought to understand her instead of abusing her, when there was preservation of the natural balance between what we took and what we gave back. Instead, what if we could view the world as a giant living creature that sustains us in the way that a body sustains micro-organisms?

I grew up on lakefront property on the edge of a forest, rich with endless pathways for exploring. I look back now and see the quality of my relationship with the land in those formative years. I was a part of the ecosystem that surrounded and nourished me. As a youngster, I would spend time in "the wild" after school, grasping the magic of the caves that overlooked the lake, riding horses bareback through the trees, catching tadpoles and frogs in the river, witnessing our mares giving birth to new life, and watching the deer that came to feed in our backyard. These experiences held a quality that was very distinct from the nights when I came home, went into the living room, and turned on the television.

Our home today overlooks a small creek in the foothills of the Rocky Mountains in western Canada. When a ruffled grouse, killed by a hawk, was left to die in our backyard, my first reaction was to throw the grouse in the garbage to get rid of it. However, I recalled the experiences of my youth and, together with my family, we buried it in the field behind our home. It was a simple experience. We set it gently in the ground and each of the girls said a prayer for this bird and for life. It brought an unadorned reverence for life into our family at that moment. Recognizing that we are a part of the life cycle, with all its loss and its brutality, its healing and its joy, brings a quality of authentic expression to life. Since that day, my children have wanted to bury anything they find that resembles a lost life. Later in the spring, they found an abandoned sandpiper's egg and were determined, once again, to bury it. It was Chandra's job to carry the egg to the "cemetery." While her big sister was offering a prayer, and we were all attempting to be spiritual, our eager six-year-old squeezed the fragile shell just a little too hard. It exploded in her hands and covered us all with rotten, putrid egg. After regaining my sense of humor, I was reminded that being a part of the connection to the earth and what springs forth from it connects us all in community. As we remove ourselves from the land, we remove ourselves from the vital authentic connection that sustains life even in the face of death and decay.

Bringing an awareness and commitment to the land into discussions in our family has helped me to teach our children a reverence for all of life. It has made us all more conscious. Just this summer there was a large anthill behind the fence in our backyard. Angry at the "intrusion" on "my" property, my first impulse was to get out the ant poison, with no mindfulness as to the effect that might have on those around me or the ecosystem as a whole. However, I remembered that as a family, we are committed to make decisions that are economically, socially, and ecologically sound. So before I took any action, we observed the ants and talked about why they are there. What purpose to our environment do they serve? Nobody had an answer to these questions, so we got on the Internet and studied ants and became educated about their role in the ecosystem.

We discovered that the inconvenience they were causing us did not come close to the environmental cost of getting rid of them with harmful pesticides.

Making these small, seemingly insignificant decisions about my part in the ecosystem supports my connection to authenticity. This awareness and commitment bestows a reverence for life that extends to my interior life and to those around me. Separation from the environment indicates separateness in all areas in my life.

Unlike the boredom that eventually results from today's fast-changing fads, television shows, video games, computer programs, or any of the myriad of recent technological advances, I never tire of witnessing a sunset, a waterfall, or a blooming flower. I am always closer to God in the natural world than in a world created for the purpose of materialism. My soul will always prefer plants to plastic, terrain to technology, and trees to television. Authenticity asks me to join with that which is genuine, with that which has substance, and with that which will sustain me — long after my computer and microwave oven have been discarded.

The daily habit of getting out of the house and off the concrete has taught me to observe, listen to and smell what nature offers me. As I walk among the plants and flowers, I learn about selfless giving, of the manifesting of beauty with no expectation in return. From nature I learn about gestation, and that brings patience. In a world whose velocity continues to increase through more advanced means of communication, faster computers, credit cards that give us instant gratification, fast food, powerful cars, and drugs that "fix us" faster, accompanied by more demands, we, as a culture, are growing increasingly impatient. Gestation reminds me that a healthy birth is one that goes full term and is not rushed. Gestation also reminds me that anything worth doing is worth doing s-l-o-w-l-y. It teaches me to wait, to allow for the needed time to pass for maturity. Nature doesn't force or control, but rather seems to unfold. I cannot push the tomatoes to blossom in our backyard, any more than I can push the love in a relationship. I cannot command the roses in my garden, "Bloom!" I cannot demand the cut on my hand, "Heal!" Nature teaches me to pay the price of patience and reap the reward of healing and growing in its own time. Nature teaches me that often I just need to get out of the way, trust, and "let it be."

From nature I learn to stop the busyness and notice what is really going on, both inside and around me. I learn to discern and listen to the soul's promptings as I sit by the river. Nature teaches me to go within.

From the natural world I learn the law of the harvest — that if I want to reap in the fall, I must plant in the spring. Nature does not allow me to cheat, to try to cram the planting into early fall, hoping that I can squeeze out a late harvest. Nature teaches me natural consequences for my choices and thus quietly lectures about the lessons of responsibility.

I learn about the value of the seasons — that for everything there is a season, a time to plant and a time to reap, a time to work and a time to rest, a time to build and a time to reflect, a time to do and a time to be. I have learned that every winter is followed by a spring, and every spring precedes summer, and after every summer, there is a fall, and then again winter. As with the seasons, so, too, come consistency and flow and the trust that every night is proceeded by day, and every day is followed by night. Winters and darkness are part of life, and I know that the sun will return along with the promise of a new day.

Nature can also teach us the value of rhythms. Most generations who lived in pre-industrial societies adapted themselves to organic rhythms, setting internal clocks to dawn and dusk. We have constructed an artificial time line that has little or nothing to do with the animal and biological world in which we live.

I have learned some things about parenting and helping from nature — that the plants that stand firm are those that develop their own roots; that excessive watering produces weakness, not strength; that in spite of your best efforts as a steward of the land you till and care for, sometimes plants don't turn out as you hoped.

Nature teaches me humility and a reverence for life which is essential for the authentic journey. Spirituality was born within me on those early days on the farm. I planted tiny seeds and watched them grow and I witnessed the miracle of the birth of many foals and calves and piglets. No one, as yet, has been able to invent a seed or an egg capable of reproducing itself in any living form. I have reverence for the mystery of life. Nature teaches that a greater force is at work in my life.

> *To see a world in a grain of sand*
> *And heaven in a wild flower*
> *Hold infinity in the palm of your hand*
> *And eternity in an hour.*

> **— William Blake**

Nature, from the brutality of her hurricanes to her blossoming spring flowers, from her underground springs that nourish us to droughts and floods, is authentic. Nature is real, and as we connect with the reality she offers, we are nurtured and strengthened on our own authentic path. Spending time in nature is good for authenticity.

* * * *

ABUNDANCE

Someone else having more doesn't mean I have less.

— Don Campbell

Five hundred years ago in England, one of the Oxford colleges built a "great hall" using huge oak timbers for beams. The dining hall is still in use, but recently the beams needed to be replaced because of rot. The current college administrator, deliberating and researching a solution to the problem, found in the records of his counterpart five hundred years ago that an oak grove had been planted near the college at the time of the erection of the dining hall — specifically so that large timbers would be available when needed. The great old trees were harvested and used for a purpose foreseen five hundred years before. The foresight of the original builders reflected an abundance attitude — that we must provide for others and for the future by replenishing and replacing what we use up now. An investment in the present ensures an abundance of resources when we need them.

This abundance mentality can be viewed as "the law of the pot." My friend, Don Gray, passed this theory along to me and I have taken the liberty to elaborate on it so as to make it my own. I have come to view the world as a great big pot. Every time we need something, we dip in and take something out of the pot. Everything we need is here. Sometimes we have to ask. Sometimes we need to take a step and reach into the pot. At times, the miracles just overflow into our lives. Sometimes I have been receptive to what comes to me, and at other times I am just too busy or too unconscious to even notice the spillover. At times, the blessings come in many different forms. Yet, as I look back over my life, I realize that every time I have needed something, there has always been someone there to help me, or something appears that I needed to take me along to the next stage on the journey.

When we don't need something from the pot, we need to put a little in it every time we can: support, comfort, kindness, love. If we all throw a little in every day, then when we need it, the pot will have just what we need.

The promise of community is the awareness that we are not alone on this journey, but rather a part of a network of interconnected relationships. In community we realize that normal discontent is not a symptom of unsatisfied needs, but is a challenge from which none of us is immune. The discontent may mean we simply need a listening ear, a compassionate heart, and a wise perspective from those who care about us. Community reminds us that the authentic journey is not a quick and easy road to salvation, but is both a painful and joyous journey. When we open up to and surround ourselves with those who matter most to us, we find support for both our dreams and our disappointments.

The triumph of the industrial economy is a challenge to community. Let us be committed to not let community fall and to see how necessary and precious it is. Authentic communities welcome and respect the authentic contribution of every member and consider the implications of decisions for generations to come. They ensure that the children are loved by the entire neighborhood, not just the parents; that both the young and the old are needed, that their unique gifts have fertile ground in which to grow, that every person has something to contribute. Authentic, compassionate communities do not isolate the old or warehouse the young in impersonal, under-resourced care centers. Authentic communities do not place education at the bottom of their budgetary priorities, realizing that we all shoulder a stewardship for the education of our children. Authentic communities do not frighten the elderly by jeopardizing their financial support systems. Being a part of authentic communities means not abdicating personal accountability to government services alone because each person shares the responsibility for community. Community holds us to the commitment to support each other through all stages of the life cycle. There is an old saying that if we treated every person we meet as if they were the Messiah, then it wouldn't make any difference if they weren't.

* * * *

CHAPTER 3

&

Building Character

When I do good I feel good.
When I don't do good, I don't feel good.
— *Abraham Lincoln*

* * * *

AS I REFLECT ON MY ADOLESCENCE and early adulthood, even into my thirties, I realize that I spent a great deal of my life trying to fit in. I spent much time during those early years giving the world what it wanted, being who others wanted me to be. I spent a good part of my life seeking approval by meeting the expectations of others — my friends, my teachers, my church leaders, my university instructors, my bosses, my parents, my clients, my colleagues, my communities. I was also fortunate to meet and associate with very successful people during this time, and I ended up seeking their approval by trying to achieve what they achieved and to own what they owned. Because I lacked the ability to see myself on the inside, I failed to see inside others. Void of self-assurance, the driving force behind my ambition in those early adult years stemmed from unacknowledged insecurity, fear, and uncertainty. I had a hard time with close relationships with other men because I was always jostling for position, either comparing or competing with their external accomplishments. Somehow I was trying to imitate in order to integrate, and yet the opposite was manifesting itself.

To escape the burden of conformity and responsibility, I would, from time to time, rebel. I went through periods when I abandoned my conscience and sought only comfort. For years my unarticulated values were subordinated to my feelings. At that time, I had no sense of an inner compass, no awareness of any accountability, even to myself. "Oh, what a tangled web we weave," wrote Shakespeare, "when first we practice to deceive." Running from yourself by either compliance or defiance leaves a trail of deception where no sense of inner peace can be found. I was too driven and too afraid to be with myself. The ambition for more never filled the gap of less.

My life was, for the most part, an extreme of either compliance or defiance, opposite ends of the spectrum of inauthenticity. I was also living a life that was outer-directed, following the dictates of what society and those around me expected. On the one hand, there was incongruity between my espoused values and my choices, and on the other, I did not even have enough clarity about my own values to know that there was incongruity.

I know now that this was a necessary stage in the evolution of my authentic self, but at that time I really had no foundation of who I was. This showed up in the incongruity between my personal life and my work life. My life was divided, instead of integrated. I preached simple, balanced living and yet I traveled over two hundred days a year. I lectured about accountability, but had difficulty keeping promises to myself. I taught people how to have meaningful relationships and yet I had difficulty being in one. I preached the value of community, but lived much of my life alone. I used to go back to an empty hotel room after a lecture and truly have difficulty looking at myself in the mirror. I felt like a fraud. I kept myself busy because, as I know now, it was just too painful to stop and face the truth about myself.

The emphasis in my life at that time was almost exclusively economic. My life was about materialism and success, and even more about appearing respectable and decent to the world. It was about looking wise and successful while my inner life was out of sync with myself. I was not integrated. I was making a good living, but I was not building a very good life.

After a series of painful events, I began to stop and feel the incongruity between what my inner life was yearning for and what the world was furnishing. I began to look inward and realize that what really mattered was getting buried under the cloak of compliance and defiance. In those days I would awaken in the middle of the night in a cold sweat. With no crowds to affirm me, alone in a hotel room, my reserves were depleted. There was nothing to draw from, nothing to sustain me. My character was smothered under the accouterments of comfort, popularity, and materialism.

In researching the origin of character, within its roots one will find the word "chisel," a tool used for stripping away waste material from an object. In the context of character, chiseling is stripping away trappings that might get in the way in order to get down to the essential things, to what really matters. When I first read about this concept of "stripping away waste material to get down to the essential essence," in the context of character, I thought again of Michelangelo creating magnificence and beauty within a slab of marble.

Chiseling out your character from the raw material of yourself is akin to the work of a great sculptor. The raw material is there, but you must carve away the exterior — the parts that are restrictive — to enable your true character to manifest itself. Everything that happens to you — good and bad — is an opportunity to chisel toward your true character. Character is the person you are after you have chiseled away the unnecessary material to what, underneath, is most vital.

Building character calls us to stop and take notice of the sense of incongruity within ourselves, to become honest with ourselves, and begin to realize that below the trappings of what we have — whether in the form of possessions, achievement, roles or financial success — lies the deeper essence of who we are.

Character isn't how you act when life is going the way you want it to. Character is what people close to you — your kids, spouse, staff, or colleagues — see when you are under stress, when your life seems to be falling apart, when you are angry, tired, scared, or in the midst of enormous change and uncertainty.

Character is the set of virtues or traits that make up who or what we are as persons; it goes beyond personality or charisma or even skills and encompasses, instead, the foundation, the very core of a person's essence. Character calls us to be trustworthy before we expect trust. Character asks us to make certain essential choices: ownership over renting your life, citizenship over consumerism, integrity over dishonesty, accountability over entitlement, abundance over scarcity, service over self-interest, and courage over comfort and superficial security. Character blazes the trail of authenticity.

By consciously cultivating the inner qualities of character — maturity, integrity, courage, humility, gratitude, service, and, clarity — we are tilling the soil of our own mind and ensuring that it can serve as a source of strength and correct action in our lives. These inner qualities support the foundation of authentic living and cannot be imposed, legislated, or decreed. They can only be cultivated by our own conscious choice to behave ethically — a deeply misunderstood concept in our world today.

I once heard someone define ethics as "obedience to the unenforceable." This comes close to my perspective. You make choices, not because someone is watching or keeping score or because you might be punished if you break the rules and get caught. You are following your own inner gyroscope and listening to an inner voice that leads you to a commitment to ethical choices. This eventually turns into ethical habits and reaps the promise of strong character.

Aligning your daily choices with your core virtues — your attributes of ethical goodness — forms the basis of strong character. Character is independent of economics. Character costs nothing and thus is perhaps worth more than anything we own. After all, true financial independence comes not from having wealth, but from your ability to create wealth. Everything you buy can be replaced. Character has lasting value because you can't buy it. It costs no money to be a person of character. You can lose it all — your material possessions, relationships, income, job, even your health — but no one can take away your character without your consent. Remember, when your wealth is lost, something is lost; when your health is lost, a great deal is lost; when your character is lost, everything is lost. Character is the quality that determines the value of your life. In order to ascertain this value, we must establish a standard. If we establish that a life of worth is one that demonstrates such virtues as honesty, purity, unselfishness, and compassion, then, by these standards, many people revered by our culture have little value. What shall we profit if we gain the whole world, yet lose our soul?

The decision to build your inner self won't just happen. It is a series of conscious decisions to do the next right thing rather than to take the path of comfort and least resistance. As you slowly carve away the parts of yourself that allow your true character to emerge, keep in mind the words of Thomas Paine, "That which we obtain too easily, we esteem too lightly. It is dearness only which gives everything its value."

* * * *

CO-CREATION: TAKING OWNERSHIP OF YOUR LIFE

One of life's greatest paradoxes is that nearly everyone wants to improve their circumstances, but hardly anyone wants to improve themselves.

— *Milton Sills*

One evening I called a friend about something important and his boarder answered the phone. When I asked if my friend was home, his reply was a faint, "No." When asked if he knew when he would be in, his reply was a pale, "I don't know."

"Could I leave a message for him?" I asked, trying to be courteous and patient.

"Yeah, but I don't have anything to write it down with," he replied.

"Is anyone else home?" I inquired.

"I don't know," he said.

"Do you think you could find out?" I answered.

"No, I'm just a renter," he said and hung up.

I don't intend to be critical of this poor lad and I want to give him the benefit of the doubt. Who knows what kind of a day he had or what his intellectual status was at my moment of calling. I am also not critical of the often very sensible decision to rent your living space.

What I am saying is that many people go through their lives as "renters." They don't own their work or their lives. They are waiting — for retirement or for the kids to move out or for a job or for the next lottery. You'll know renters when you meet them at work. "That's not my job," will be the first words out of their mouth. In relationships, they are the ones who lay all the blame and responsibility for change on the other person. Renters wait for something or somebody to make them happy. They do not take accountability or responsibility, in other words, ownership, for their lives, and until they do, their authenticity will fall short.

Kids are not born accountable. They are dependent and need to learn to take ownership. When my six-year-old spilled her juice at the supper table, she exclaimed, "Dad, it got spilled!" and not "Dad, I spilled it." What she is saying in her fearful world surrounded by adults is, "I didn't do it. Something did it to the glass. Somebody or something made me do it!" The most common response from a child when they make a blunder is to respond with, "It was an accident" or to blame something or someone else. These are appropriate reactions from six-year-olds who are on a learning curve to take ownership for their lives, but this sort of immaturity commonly continues into adulthood.

Sydney Harris, a journalist, said, "We have not passed that subtle line between childhood and adulthood until we move from the passive voice to the active voice — that is, until we have stopped saying, 'It got lost,' and say, 'I lost it.'" Making a decision to be an owner is ultimately making the decision to grow up.

Nearly everyone has an excuse when things go wrong. A lack of ownership and accountability is always easier to see outside ourselves, in every level of our workplace and communities. We seem to be in a hurry in everything we do today except to take ownership when mistakes are made. While there is no rush to take responsibility for things gone wrong, there seems to be no shortage of persons ready to claim the credit for an endeavor that goes well.

In the end, we are answerable for the kind of character we have made for ourselves. "That's just the way I am!" is not an excuse for thoughtless or contemptible behavior. Nor is it even an accurate description, for we are never just what we are. Aristotle was among the first to proclaim that we become what we are as people by the choices that we ourselves make. Owners of their lives accept responsibility for being what they have made themselves and refuse to make excuses.

Responsible persons are those who take charge of themselves and their decisions without blame. It's only when we have at last grown up that the two messages: "I'm totally dependent on you" (the outlook of a young child) and "I'm totally independent of you" (the outlook of an adolescent), finally turn into: "You can depend on me" which is the truly mature, authentic outlook.

At the time of my mother's death in 1999, I inherited her quote book, a list of ideas and thoughts she had collected for nearly eighty years. It was a great treasure and captured much of her wisdom. Within that book, I found a definition of maturity written by my favorite author, "anonymous":

> **Maturity is:**
> *The ability to do a job without being supervised.*
> *To finish a job once it is started.*
> *To carry money without spending it.*
> *And to be able to bear an injustice without wanting to get even.*

Maturity is not a passive process, where we sit submissively as injustice tramples us. Maturity, instead, is a courageous decision to stand tall in our fight against injustice without a motive of revenge. Character begins with a decision to be an owner, not a renter, of your life, to decide to claim full responsibility for your life, your happiness, and your development, rather than waiting for someone else to do it for you. Authenticity will not grow in the barren sand of blame and immaturity. I so clearly remember those adolescent urges I had for unconditional approval, absolute security, and ideal romance, urges that were understandably appropriate for a teenager, but yet if continued as an adult would prove to be an impossible way to live. Only by growing up do we shed the attitude that the world is devoted to our happiness and recognize that we must accept responsibility for our actions.

By taking ownership for how you respond to every disturbance that comes your way, you become the co-creator of your life rather than being the result of circumstances. Taking ownership begins with a decision to no longer be a victim, a spectator or a bystander in one's life, but to be a participant. There is no one or nothing to blame. There is no "they" doing it "to you." Owners take accountability to respond in the face of whatever happens to them. You must accept responsibility for a problem before you can solve it. Ownership means trying to be part of the cure of every situation. If you are not part of the solution, then you are part of the problem.

Before you can move the world, you must first move yourself. The great teachers of the world have all said the same thing: If you want to make a change in your life, don't look to others. Look within yourself. You can have the government lower taxes. You can have this person do that and that person do this. But there is a good chance that all the external changes won't mean much nor will they sustain authenticity until you change what is within you. I am a firm believer that you can place me in the best or the worst circumstances and sooner or later I will create outside whatever is inside of me.

In practicing as a family therapist and consultant over the years, I witnessed many people who leave relationships — jobs, marriages, or communities — because there was something wrong "out there" — in something or someone else. In fact, family therapy has a concept that is useful here. We call it the "identified problem." Every family who has come to see me as a therapist had one member among them who was seen as the problem — if we could "just shape this person up" or "get her to behave differently" or "get him to pull his weight," then it was assumed that all obstructions for the rest of the family would miraculously be eliminated. The same concept, not surprisingly, emerges in consulting with organizations. There is always a team member who, if we could just "fix" him, would alleviate all the problems of the team.

The assumption is that they are the problem. The problem is "out there." It is interesting that when someone exits a relationship or fires the "identified problem" or transfers the "bad boss" to another department, without first looking within — either within the system or within themselves — after the six-month honeymoon, the problem returns. Then someone else takes on the role of the "identified problem" and you either come up against the same wall or find a new problem that is the opposite to the old one. Sometimes, for example, if the last boss was too controlling, then this one is too passive. If you end a marriage without taking ownership or looking at your part of the problem, you will meet the same problem again in your next relationship. Again, the problem may take an opposite form. For example, if your last partner had a hard time showing feelings, then the new one may be too unstable.

Individuals who appear to be the problem — in an organization or in a family — are not the problem. They are a symptom. "Identified problems" merely carry and express a problem that is not faced from within. What we don't own, what we don't face, we project onto another. Centering the attention on another helps us avoid the accountability that comes with ownership. As co-creator of their current reality, owners realize that they carry the responsibility for how others treat them. Ownership does not mean that you own the blame, but simply that you own the responsibility. Owning responsibility means that you look at your part of the problem, you change the things you can, and you stop trying to control others by forcing them to be different than they are. This acceptance of life on life's terms, instead of on your terms, allows you to get on with authentic living rather than living life as a victim.

Nearly everyone wants to improve their circumstances or change their partners or bosses or children, but hardly anyone wants to take an honest look at themselves and say, "What is my part of the problem?" "How could I be contributing to the current situation?" Ownership calls us to courageously look within and clean up our own side of the street. If you don't, you will inevitably bring the perceptions and the problems with you. Unless the vessel is cleaned on the inside, whatever you pour into it turns sour. Choosing to be an owner means having the courage to look within and decide to let it begin with you, no matter where you are.

The quest for the authentic self, for one's true being, is what Joseph Campbell calls "the hero's journey." Such an expedition almost always begins with an awareness of a disturbance, of a sense of incompleteness, tension, or incongruity in one's relationships, either in love relationships, work relationships, or community relationships. To set out on the journey, the hero must first recognize that the cause of the disturbance lies not out there, but within. Owning responsibility for the cause of the disorder enables the hero to be the co-creator of his or her own life.

"Owning" the disturbance in your life may sound like self-blame, as if you brought this trouble upon yourself or others, but it really is the antithesis of this. Seeing yourself as a co-creator is a way to support you and free you by looking at your current troubles with a new set of lenses. It is a way that invites you not only to be in charge of your responses to life's situations, but also to be a student of your life rather than a victim. It helps in building character. Disturbances will always surface in your life when you have something to learn. Someone who needs to learn the lesson of trust, for example, will experience distrust of others. He or she will mistakenly interpret the words and the actions of others as distrust, which will lead to tensions and unpleasant outcomes. Victims will blame the other person and thus will rob themselves of an opportunity to learn. When you take ownership of the situation, however, you can begin to see your part in it. This does not abdicate the responsibility of the other. There are still evil people in the world, as there always will be, but this perception and subsequent action will give you the freedom to look at yourself and refuse to be owned by others. If you simply get mad and either leave or stay in the relationship without taking the time to learn what you need to learn, be assured you will continue to meet distrust in your life.

Years ago I was in business with someone I considered very controlling. I perceived him as making all the financial as well as short and long-term business decisions in the partnership and I grew increasingly resentful. I was ready to split up the partnership, when I realized that I was there to learn something. I was in this relationship for a reason. Being an "owner" of the disturbance that was going on within me did not, in any way, mean that I was responsible for his personality, but simply that I was contributing to the problem by my lack of awareness and skill. I realized I was there to learn to be more assertive, to trust myself more, to speak my truth in a way that was both respectful to myself and to others. When I learned to do this, he stopped being so controlling. After all, he could no longer be controlling because I no longer allowed myself to be controlled. This was a difficult and risky process. It was a six-month period of trial and error, getting perspective and coaching from others (not to "fix" my colleague, but to learn about myself) and practicing new ways of relating in a more self-trusting, self-assured way. To this day I am grateful for this person and what he taught me. He gave me the impetus to grow up. Had I stayed in the relationship and remained a "whiner and complainer" without the lesson, he would have continued to control me. Had I left the relationship before the lesson was learned, I would have continued to meet "controlling" people. We did eventually end the partnership, and have become good friends. And I meet far fewer "controlling" people these days. You have no power over anyone else, but when you change, the world changes, because you have on a new pair of glasses. Ownership asks of us, "If it is to be, let it start with me."

Carl Jung wrote that disobedience is the first step toward consciousness. Character calls us to distinguish between defiance and authentic disobedience. Defiance is about disobedience for its own sake. It is about running away from the truth by lashing out and hurting people. It comes as a result of previous compliance. Conscious disobedience, on the other hand, says that we are not here to fear or please those in authority. Authenticity recognizes that there is worth and meaning in our acts of disobedience as a more complete expression of our distinct destiny. Disappointing authority may be a sign that we have begun to live our own lives. We do not know that our lives belong to us until we have stood tall in the face of fear. This is not against anything or anyone, but for our soul. The promise of freedom is realized when we hold our own viewpoint, our own ground, in the face of rejection and disapproval. I call this the authentic moment of truth, when we choose courage over comfort. When I am angry with someone for controlling or manipulating or abusing me, it is usually an indicator that I have betrayed myself by not standing tall on my convictions. The answer, as usual, lies within, calling me to character. Even today, I sometimes put people in a position of being my parents, needing their endorsement, approval, and sanction. When I own my part of this problem by saying no to anyone I put in a position of authority over me — a boss, a client, even a friend that I respect — not out of defiance, but from my own truth, I recover my freedom.

Know that others might not see this authentic courage as a gift to their relationship with you. Don't count on them having a favorable opinion about your no longer needing their approval. However, any courageous, respectful act of authenticity invites others to see the truth about themselves so they can initiate their own transformation. Character calls on us to not wait for others before we accept the invitation to change. Whether or not they accept the invitation, we will have done our part to bring balance to the relationship and sovereignty to our own spirit. When done respectfully we can bring connection through our own strength rather than alienation through fear. Herein lies the seed of trust in any relationship — self-trust through self-respect. For only when we trust ourselves by being true to ourselves can we begin to trust another human being.

* * * *

THE CONSCIOUS CITIZEN

The true value of a human being is determined primarily by the measure and sense in which he has attained freedom from the self.

— *Albert Einstein,* The World As I See It

Citizenship is a term we seem to be less familiar with today. It is almost outdated and not well understood anymore. Citizenship goes beyond the pride of carrying the flag or singing the national anthem. In a democratic country it means the right to vote and the freedom to mark a ballot as you wish. However, we vote in this country with more than our ballot. We also vote through our commitment to our community and our country. Citizenship renews our social contract for action. Whether we pump gas or run a multi-national corporation, we all have a vital and valid role to play. Citizenship is about choosing full service over lip service. We may be called members of a society, but only we can choose to define ourselves as citizens. It is a personal decision.

A requirement of authenticity is a desire to be a contributing citizen. The call to authenticity goes beyond self-centeredness and narcissism to a commitment to the community. We are co-creators, not sole creators, of our lives and of our collective society and planet. Being a person of strong character means a decision to be a citizen rather than a consumer. Consumers bring an "entitlement" mindset to their lives and their work. They feel entitled to be served and entitled to be happy. They consume more than they give. They complain more than they create. They wait to be told what to do. Consumers are still waiting to grow up. They have needs to be satisfied rather than a commitment to serve. A culture of consumers results in hatred across borders because people don't take responsibility to know each other. We hold onto the past rather than the present and the future. We blame others instead of accepting personal accountability.

The "entitlement" mindset that comes with our consumer society can be seen at all levels of the culture. In the workplace we feel entitled to job security as if it were a right with no responsibility. In the marketplace we demand good customer service as if it were an entitlement with no obligation on our part. We do needs assessments in organizations, communities, and even families, forgetting that the work of leadership is not to meet people's needs so much as it is to foster an environment where people can make a meaningful contribution through the expression of their gifts, allowing authenticity to emerge.

Citizens, on the other hand, realize that every right is accompanied by an obligation and that with every entitlement comes a responsibility. They choose service over self-interest. Citizens have a strength of character so they work for the betterment of the whole rather than for "what's in it for me?"

When discussing the virtues and necessity of citizenship with a group of farmers in western Canada, I lamented that we are a culture with a charter of rights and freedoms void of an accompanying charter of responsibilities. I remarked that rights can be legislated, while obligations must be chosen. A woman came up to me after my presentation. As a recent immigrant she excitedly reminded me that in Canada, there is a charter of both rights and freedoms as well as an accompanying charter of responsibilities. All new immigrants are presented with this on the day they take on the right — and responsibility — of citizenship. She emailed me the document and I have since contemplated that those birthed in Canada could benefit from renewing their citizenship.

Under the *Canadian Charter of Rights and Freedoms*, Canadian citizens are guaranteed the right to: be a candidate in elections, be educated in either official language, apply for a Canadian passport, vote, and enter and leave Canada freely. As a Canadian citizen, we each share the responsibility to: vote in elections, help others in the community, care for and protect our heritage and environment, obey Canada's laws, express opinions freely while respecting the rights of others, and eliminate discrimination and injustice.

Since embarking consciously on the journey of authenticity, I am more aware of my place, and of the responsibility involved in being a citizen. By choosing citizenship I realize I am not just in it for my own comfort and pleasure. I am a part of a larger whole, a citizen of my community and of the world.

There are opportunities to express citizenship every day, if you are open to them. I was jogging through my neighborhood on an early morning run when I came to a red light, but there were no cars crossing my path. Consumerism would mean darting across the street, not wanting to waste time waiting for the light to turn with no thought as to the effect of this choice on others. Citizenship demands looking around and noticing a car full of children waiting for the same light. I now acknowledge that I am not in this world alone, that I have a responsibility to be an example to those children, to show them the importance of respecting the law. Authenticity calls us to abandon self-centeredness.

Citizenship calls us to kindness, respect, and decency when dealing with those who serve the public, whether it's the clerk at the bank, the cashier at the grocery store, the civil servant at the post office, or the nurse at the emergency room. Citizenship calls us to carry our portion of the tax responsibility with gratitude. Citizenship calls us to take accountability to bring our children to school learning-ready, to be a partner in the education process and to stop expecting schools to compensate for a failure in the home or a broken community. Citizenship calls us to do our share for the child down the street who has no father in his life and to stop abdicating responsibility for anything outside our backyard fence. Citizenship asks us to remember that the land we walk on belongs to all of us and that the air we breathe will soon flow through all of our lungs. Citizenship calls us to turn the lights off before closing the door of our hotel room. Citizenship asks us to bring a servant heart wherever we go so that, through our presence and actions, one burden can be lifted today. Citizenship asks us to be committed to a social cause. Citizenship asks us to cease defining a good day by one in which everything goes our way, but instead as one where, through some act of ours, we were able to make the day better for someone else. Citizenship reminds us that we are not alone, that we are a part of a web of life that exists beyond our borders.

When I do my job as a consumer, my goal is to be rewarded. When I do my job as a citizen, my goal is to serve. Citizenship means a decision to make the world a better place, starting with ourselves. Citizenship begins with the person in the mirror.

* * * *

THE BEDROCK OF INTEGRITY

There is no real excellence in this world that can be separated from right living.

— David Starr Jordan

Integrity comes from the word *integer*, which means wholeness, integration, and completeness. It includes a sense of cohesion and congruence. This can sound esoteric and abstract until we discuss integrating the fragmented pieces of ourselves in a very practical and simple approach to authentic living. In relation to strong character, what does it really mean to operate with integrity?

Stop for a moment and think about a time someone agreed to do something for you and then failed to fulfill their promise. Ask yourself, "What was it like to be a recipient of a dishonored promise?" Now consider a time when you said yes to a request and then, upon a few moments of reflection, realized that you didn't have the time or the resources or the capacity or even the will to keep your word. We have all had the experience of saying *yes* on the outside when we really feel *no* on the inside and thus we all struggle with personal integrity. An integral part of the foundation of strong character, integrity, means promising only what you intend to fulfill and honoring the promises you make, both to yourself and to others.

When you let someone down, when you don't show up for a meeting at the time you agreed to, or when you miss a child's concert you promised to attend, it is important to stop and notice your level of consciousness about your promise. "No one but you cares about the reason you let someone down," my friend Gerald Weinberg has said on more than one occasion. Failure to honor the promises you make affects the accomplishment of the task and the level of trust in the relationship involved. But most importantly, failing to keep promises erodes your personal integrity at the level of who you are and how you live your life. When you make a promise and then tell yourself that your promises are not worth much and it doesn't really commit you because you just say things that you don't mean, you breech your integrity and erode the fabric of your personal character.

The first part of integrity — only promising what you intend to fulfill — encompasses three elements: sincere desire (you genuinely want to honor your promise), ability (you have the capability to fulfill your promise), and means (you have the resources to keep your commitment). If you make a promise that you do not intend to keep, or if you promise to do something that you know you don't know how to do or don't have the resources to fulfill, it constitutes a breech of integrity.

The second part of integrity is the honoring of your promises. By honoring, I do not necessarily mean fulfilling, even though that would be a worthy ideal. There is a difference between lying and committing an error. Mistakes are not a lack of integrity. We are all entitled to mistakenly commit to something and find out later it was different than we thought. This is a mistake, and even if we sincerely intended to keep the promise, our understanding changed, still leaving our integrity intact.

How do you keep your integrity intact when you are unable to fulfill a promise that you sincerely wanted to and had the capability to fulfill? Integrity does not demand perfection. Circumstances arise. With a change of circumstances it is possible that it may not make sense to fulfill a promise as originally stated. As soon as you realize your promise is at risk, call your creditor (when you make a promise, you are like a debtor, and you have a creditor, someone who owns the promise). Call your creditor and explain that your promise is at risk (or a concern that you will not be able to deliver). Explain the circumstances. Do this as soon as you learn about the change of circumstances. Apologize, and give an acknowledgment of regret, that you have made a promise that you are now unable to fulfill. Then inquire and negotiate with your creditor about how you can minimize or reduce the damage caused by not fulfilling your promise. Then recommit to a new promise, a new course of action. The final step is to reflect on and learn from the experience.

What was it that prevented you from fulfilling this promise? What could you take from this experience so it doesn't occur again?

Now, what about the integrity that emerges from keeping promises to yourself? Just this morning, I had a conversation with Hayley, my nine-year-old, about the rewards of keeping promises to herself. She reflected upon one of her responsibilities — to walk her dog twice a day without having to be reminded. She has made this promise to Lucky, to us, but more importantly, she has made this promise to herself. Hayley replied, "I know that Lucky likes it when I take her out. And I know that you like it when I take her out because she doesn't get antsy and poop on the carpet. But I would say that the greatest reward for taking her out would be that I feel better about myself when I do something that, at first, I don't like much but know it is the right thing to do."

Perhaps all promises we make to others really come down to promises we make to ourselves. When I have promised to take my kids to the park after supper, but once the kitchen is cleaned and fatigue emerges, I really want to say to the kids, "Not tonight, I've changed my mind. I just need some rest," then a stronger part of myself — the person who desires to live life with a strong character — must step forward and say, "You made a promise. Follow through, David, whether it is comfortable or not, whether you feel like it or not, because you are learning to be a person of integrity."

Many of us have had the experience of letting ourselves down after a lofty New Year's resolution. Self-respect comes to those who think carefully about any promises you make to yourself — whether it be to develop good health habits, spiritual disciplines, regular study habits, or time for the important people in your life. For example, when you promise yourself to exercise each morning, the reward of self-respect will come to those who, when the alarm goes off and comfort comes on, choose mind over mattress, put their feet on the floor and start moving with a smile on their face. Strong character, it has been said, is the ability to carry out a worthy decision, after the emotion of making that decision has passed.

When a CEO makes a promise to shareholders, perhaps she is making a promise, first and foremost, to herself. As the CEO of your own life, whenever you make a promise, you are, in essence, mixing the concrete for the foundation of your own personal integrity, upon which the company stands, and where you will build strong character. How strong is the foundation you are setting down? Is your work trustworthy? Have you skimped on the cement? Are you a person of strong integrity by keeping your promises?

Before you make any promise, either to yourself or others, take a deep breath and center yourself. Become conscious of your intention. Be careful that the promise in front of you is yours, not someone else's. Ask yourself, "Is it right for me, for my authentic self, to make this promise or am I doing it just to please someone or out of obligation and/or fear?" Then take a second breath and ask yourself, "Do I sincerely desire to keep this promise?" Honesty with others begins with honesty with yourself. Take a third breath while you ask yourself, "Do I have the skills, the capability, to keep this promise? If not, do I have the capacity to learn?" On the fourth breath, ask yourself, "Do I have the adequate resources to fulfill this promise?" If others are involved, that is, if you are making a promise on behalf of someone else, you will need at least a fifth breath to ask whether the person you are speaking for can and will answer yes to these questions. If the answers to any of these questions are, "I'm not sure," then to keep your integrity intact, wait before you promise.

Being a person of strong character means that we pay attention, that we are conscious before we commit. You may need more time than four or five deep breaths before deciding to make a promise. Take the time you need so you can decide from a centered place. When I am conscious and centered, I like to give myself a minimum of twenty-four hours before making any major decision in my life that requires any action in the future. I need time to stop and go inside. Sometimes I need time to talk it through with confidants. Sometimes I just need to sleep on a decision before I make a promise. Living a life of integrity enables us to seek, discern and move toward the truth about ourselves and to have the courage to act on that truth. To keep the trust in your relationships strong, it is better to under-promise and over-deliver, than to over-promise and under-deliver. To keep your character intact, your authentic self asks the same from you.

I've learned in my lifetime that you are only as good as your word. When you decide it is time to say yes, then decide it is time to be a person others can count on. No matter how difficult or uncomfortable a task is, you know within yourself that you are a person who will follow through. The people in your life count on you, but most importantly, your authentic self counts on you. There are no excuses once you have stepped up to the plate of strong character. Maintain your personal integrity by being a reliable person, and enjoy the promise of wholeness, integration, completeness, and self-respect.

* * * *

CLEARING

As you prepare the way for a deeper, more authentic self to come forward in your life, you will need to create the space for something new to materialize. And creating space for something new first requires a willingness to let go. To initiate the process, take some time to reflect on what you want to take with you on the authentic journey and what you want to let go of. I invite you to pause and take an inventory of what, in your life, is supporting your authentic journey and what is holding you back. Consider three categories: objects, past wounds and relationships.

In terms of objects, we all have clutter that builds up around us collecting dust. But objects don't just collect dust; they collect energy. Authentic living and growing requires you to keep energy moving within and around you. One way to do this is to clear out objects in your life that block energy. One of the places that energy collects for me is in my bookcase. New teachers, new awareness, and wisdom begin arriving the day I clean out my bookshelf and filing cabinet of material I have outgrown. Discerning which books I have outgrown, and which ones remain important to me, is vital to my ongoing growth. I have one drawer of files. Once that drawer is full, it is time for another clean up. Cleaning my garage is another clearing activity. I love to have a garage sale or take stuff to the recycle depot that no longer serves me. Another place that old energy can collect is in your wardrobe closet. Try going through your clothes and taking the stuff that is no longer "you" to your local consignment store. Letting go makes room for something new to emerge in your life.

My mother claimed that she spent the first half of her life collecting stuff and the second half getting rid of it. She grew up in the Depression, and her experience with deprivation led to collecting "stuff." I learned from my mother, who was accustomed to accumulating, the importance of keeping my life simple by simply keeping less stuff in my life. It is never too late to clean up the stuff in your life. Scheduling three or four "clean out" days a year has been an important discipline in the recovery of my authentic self. These are days specifically devoted to noticing where stuff is collecting and energy is blocked in your life, and clearing away those things that were once useful. One of my purposes for writing a book is to clean up the pile of thoughts and quotes and stories that have been growing on the top of my filing cabinet over the past few years!

Keep in mind that energy collects in different places for different people, so be respectful of yourself. For some, keeping books serves your authentic self. We are all unique here. The key is to be conscious of what objects are blocking your energy and your subsequent authentic growth. As well as being therapeutic, one of the by-products of clearing away clutter is a simpler life.

Besides clearing away tangible objects, it is critical to have a way to free yourself from past wounds. We have all been hurt or shamed in some way. The nature of living is the path of some pain. Denying or holding onto past resentment and old hurts inevitably insulates you from the sunlight of your authentic self. Just as it can be useful to clear away the clutter blocking you, so, too, is there value in creating a structure and space to clear the wreckage of your past. By releasing and healing the past, we open the door to new possibilities for the future, we transform our wounds into our gifts, and we find inner peace.

An old story tells of two monks walking in the woods at sunrise. Both had taken a vow of celibacy, a commitment to avoid touching a person of the opposite sex. Early in their walk, the two came across a woman drowning in the river. The older and wiser monk reached into the raging water, took her by the arm, picked up her chilled and weakened body and carried her to the nearby village where she found refuge. For the remainder of the day, the younger monk remained troubled by this, continually asking his mentor if performing this act of service was, in fact, a breach of his vow of celibacy. For many hours, the older monk was silent, patiently listening to his protégé's tedious inquiry. Finally, by late evening, he turned to his young companion and explained, "It is true that I carried this woman from the river to the village. Yet, you, my young friend, have carried her all day!"

My own experience of clearing away past wounds has been a personal and powerful process. In past years I found strength and perspective from psychotherapy. In recent years I have found healing power in taking an honest inventory of my past and pouring it all out — wheat and chaff together — with a trusted and respected spiritual advisor. She helps me see my past, and thus myself, with new eyes, and because she operates from a spiritual center, I find freedom to not just talk about my past, but access the tools and the power to have my past "released." When my history blocks me and I go back to familiar patterns, I now have the structure for changing the old habits and outdated reactions. Through daily awareness and practice, spirituality becomes practical.

Regardless of the structure you choose, it will take some intentional effort, some perseverance, and a sincere willingness to face the truth about your past and let it go. The structure itself is as unique as the authentic path. Find one that works for you. Stick with it and follow it through, whether your process includes a structure within a therapist's office, a twelve-step program, or your religious practice.

To take inventory in the third category, relationships, take an honest look at the people in your life. Start by clarifying which are fostering your authentic growth and which are currently blocking you. I recently made a list of the twenty or so most important people in my life, people I admired and respected, people who have made a significant positive impact on my life, people I care deeply about, and people who are currently supporting me on my authentic journey. I called or wrote to them (some of them were deceased) and acknowledged what they have done and been in my life and what they meant to me. This is a good affirmation for them, but you will find it even more therapeutic for yourself. Others are a mirror for us, so when you acknowledge the magnificence in others, you take a step toward recognizing it in yourself. Take time, in your own unique and meaningful way, to acknowledge the people in your life who support you on your path of authenticity.

Now, make a list of those people in your life who do not support you right now. These may be institutions or groups, such as your current workplace, or they may be friends, relatives, or even significant relationships. Look closely, in the spirit of ownership and personal responsibility, at why these relationships are unhealthy for you at the present time. Are you compromising yourself? Are you seeking their approval and conforming to their wishes and in the process giving up a part of yourself? Not everyone needs to be nurturing. Some relationships in our life give us an opportunity to serve and to extinguish self-centeredness. But life is just too short to be spending much time with people who are damaging and unsupportive to our spirit.

I remember some time ago, a longtime friend went through a bitter divorce and would call me a couple of times a month for support. For a while, I was glad to be a sounding board and offer what support I could, but soon his grieving turned to bitter complaining and criticizing. He was not interested in building his life or taking responsibility to change. He was not at all interested in healing or searching for new perspectives. His bitterness was becoming toxic and was contaminating my spirit. I felt worse about myself being in his presence, especially because he became so bitter that he was often critical of me. I did the best I could to reach for the pain below the negativity, hoping that my compassion would help lighten his load. But it eventually became evident that instead of a mutually beneficial friendship, I was being used. I finally ended the relationship.

When ending destructive relationships use caution: be sure you take a close look at yourself before discarding a relationship or you will face this part of yourself in the future. Don't give up too soon. There is an expectation that surrounds us that life should be free of pain and should be filled with continual ease. This is not about seeking short-term happiness at the expense of long-term integrity. I know that there is a part of me that gives up far too easily and abandons relationships when the going is tough. So many of us expect the "happily ever after," rather than being open to the possibility of the prince and the princess being occasionally depressed. At the same time, the authentic journey requires you to let go of those people in your life who are blocking you, who are genuinely holding you back from being who you are meant to be. Some people are just plain destructive to your soul.

Preparing the way for authenticity means creating a structure for examining those relationships in which you experience pain and resentment, where you look at your part of the separation and where you can practice forgiveness and letting go. As you clear away the damage and pain of your past relationships, clarity will come about the current relationships that you will need to let go of.

The process of clearing — whether of "stuff," past wounds, or relationships — requires ongoing consciousness and effort. It is necessary, from time to time, as you travel along the authenticity path, to stop, take stock, and determine where you need to create space for new elements to enter your life and how you can do this in a way that is meaningful and unique to you.

Ron McMillan was Val's uncle and a train engineer with the Canadian Pacific Railway for thirty-eight years. Last year Ron succumbed to cancer, and although he had a tough exterior after engineering trains for almost four decades, underneath was a poet. Not long before his death, he wrote to me about trains, and clearing, and life.

Life Is Like a Mountain Railroad

Life is like a mountain railroad, from the cradle to the grave.
Over the canyons, round the mountain, and across the grade.
If you find that you are running at a speed that is hard to maintain,
and there are pressures all around,
Pull over, take the side track, the branch line, the "lollypop,"
let the flyers, the express train, go by;
then you can open the switch when you have cleared all the fast trains,
and proceed at your own speed,
and work by your own special orders and time table.
Otherwise, a wreck is inevitable.

— **Ron McMillan**

* * * *

MAKE ROOM FOR THE SHADOW

We all have a darker nature that lives below the surface of what we show to the world. There is a piece of us that we are unaware of, or blind to, that if we do not bring to the surface and face will bring pain to ourselves and/or others. "Shadow" is Carl Jung's term for this hidden part of ourselves. The shadow is that dark, unlit, and repressed side of ourselves that we do not currently know. The long-repressed shadow of Dr. Jekyll arises in the shape of Mr. Hyde, a deformed, ape-like figure glimpsed against an alley wall.

My own understanding of the concept of "shadow" deepened when I started to do work in institutions as an organizational development consultant. Anyone who has worked inside bureaucracies knows that every organization consists of at least two organizations: the visible system and the shadow system. All employees are part of both. The visible system consists of formal hierarchy, recognized lines of authority, rules, and communication patterns. The shadow organization, on the other hand, lies below the surface of the obvious. It consists of hallway and coffee conversations, the grapevine, the rumor mill, and the informal procedures for getting things done.

Within the shadow system lies immense creativity, wisdom, and interconnection. It is, after all, where a good deal of the real work — the work that means something — happens. While the visible system is often focused on procedures, policies, job descriptions, and routines, the shadow system has few rules or constraints. Any good leader knows that to have lasting impact on the organization, you have to listen to the shadow. You have to make time to get down to the cafeteria or the places where people take their breaks and talk about what matters most. You have to listen to the hidden network. If you try to battle against the shadow by attempting to "overcome resistance" without respecting the shadow, it will go underground and sabotage any opportunity for new growth.

Wise and authentic leaders will not try to fight the shadow, but rather recognize it for what it is: a natural part of the larger system. It is simply more interconnections among agents, often stronger interconnections than those in the visible system. These leaders will be confident and courageous enough to not dishonor, agonize over, or do combat with the shadow in their organization. Rather, they will recognize the value of these "hidden" and powerful networks, using the interconnection to enhance information flow, respect, creativity, and wisdom, while diminishing anxiety.

The shadow side of ourselves is like organizational shadow. Just as facing and listening to this hidden energy in organizations leads to a more meaningful, authentic workplace, so, too, facing and listening to the hidden sides of our own nature will lead to a more meaningful, authentic life. My own immense interest in the concept of the human shadow stems from facing depression, addiction, rage, anxiety, worry, and mood swings, and from dealing with desolate periods in my life. From within these dark sides of myself came both the misery and the gifts. By listening to and respecting these hidden, darker parts of myself, I have come to appreciate their contribution to my authentic path. Everyone struggles at times. While pain, suffering, and darkness remain a part of life, there are constructive and necessary strategies to face these darker sides of our nature in the authentic journey.

It was not long ago that we adopted Lucky, a wonderful little eight-year-old Bichon Frise, from our local humane society for Hayley. This dog has a lovely temperament. She is smart, cuddly and loving, and she blended into our family beautifully — until we left her alone. Her separation anxiety was so great that she would scratch the door and run wildly around the house in extreme fear if we left her alone for just one minute. There wasn't anything wrong with her. It was simply how her character was manifesting itself at this stage in her life. She didn't need punishing or ignoring. But we all had to face this "darker" side of her nature. Learning to create a structured, nurturing way to help her feel more secure in our absence has made her a better pet and has helped each of us bond with her, and her with us.

I can identify with Lucky. I, too, have an insecure side. Granted, it doesn't show up with frantic scratching at the door. Instead, on the surface it looks like procrastination, anger, obsession, over-ambition, workaholism, or jealousy, but the root cause is self-doubt, fear, and insecurity. Unless I have the courage to move toward this uncomfortable, hidden side of my nature, to name it and let myself experience what I want to avoid, to acknowledge and face it, and to have a structure to let it go, this darker side of myself will take over my life through the symptoms listed above.

A pattern for me is to be loving and supportive and compassionate to the world, but what is often unacknowledged is my fear and insecurity. I appear caring when I am really afraid, yet my amiability and pleasing nature can actually be covering up fear. Resentment, if left unacknowledged, can build and be released on the people I care most about. They see my fury when the world sees only my kindness. In reality, both kindness and fury, both compassion and insecurity, and both courage and fear are real parts of me, and authenticity calls me to look honestly at all of these. In the process of being open to all sides of ourselves, and making more conscious choices, we are freed from the shadow, that hidden darker part of our nature, so it doesn't unconsciously become a tyrannical master. By working with my anger in this way, I make socially responsible decisions before it turns to rage — which is abuse. I become more whole, more human, and thus more authentic.

Today I know that I am more than these darker sides. I recognize the enlightened, optimistic, and beneficial forces operating in me. I also know that there are forces in my shadowy, darker side that are destructive in their expression. The shadow contains those aspects of ourselves that we do not want to own or recognize and that we continually sweep under the carpet of consciousness. Turning away from the shadowy side keeps us from understanding who we are. It keeps us from the full expression of our authentic self and will eventually destroy us. Turning toward this dark side is fearful and risky; we may lose control or do something destructive. We may see something of ourselves that we dislike, even hate. Yet I am quite certain that a step toward finding your authentic self is to extract the negative projections we make on people (projections that serve mainly to mask the fears we have about ourselves) and acknowledge and embrace our limitations. For example, if you find yourself angry or hurt with the world or even with those around you, it is a good opportunity to look inside, to courageously excavate the source. I often find myself overly stressed by certain circumstances. Looking at the shadow means I stop and acknowledge that much of the stress in my life stems from an old belief, an old pattern, of taking too much responsibility *for* others and not giving enough responsibility back *to* others. Denial and projection block the doorway to authenticity, while being open to see all opens the door.

The promise of approaching and facing the shadow is that we will learn more about ourselves so we can bring more of who we are meant to be to the world. The willingness to face our whole self will open the door to authenticity. You express your full potential when you are willing to face your shadow, openly acknowledge the reality of its presence within you, and then take steps to deal with it. Facing your darker sides enables you to access your inner resources and remove the clouds that cover your inner beacon and, in the process, live within the knowledge that genuine power exists within and beyond you.

* * * *

YOUR QUALITY OF LIFE

A rich industrialist from the North was horrified to find a Southern fisherman lying lazily beside his boat, smoking a pipe.

"Why aren't you fishing?" asked the industrialist.

"Because I have already caught enough fish for the day," replied the fisherman.

"Why don't you catch some more?"

"What would I do then?"

"You could earn more money," responded the industrialist. "With that you could have a motor added to your boat to go into deeper waters and catch more fish. Then you would make more money to buy more nylon nets. These would bring you more fish and more money. Soon you would have enough money to own two boats... maybe even a fleet of boats. Then you would be rich like me."

"And what would I do then?" asked the fisherman.

"Then you could really enjoy life."

"What do you think I am doing right now?"

This Southern fisherman expresses two final and vital qualities of character — clarity and congruence. Clarity is about knowing what matters most in your life, in spite of the influence of the culture. Congruence is about aligning your life's choices with what is most important. Much of this book is designed to help you go inside and excavate an awareness of yourself so you can find this clarity and have the courage to live life with more congruence. In the building of a strong character, the "Quality of Life Statement" is a useful tool for clarifying your goals in life and it provides a framework for decision making so you can live life with increasing congruence.

St. Augustine gave useful advice seventeen hundred years ago, which is applicable for us today, when he said, "Start with the end in mind." In reality, few of us ever take the time to ask the question, "To what end?" If we look around our culture, most goals driving human choices are aspirations such as a new car, an achievement, a bigger house, a more productive business, or further education. Yet when these goals are met, it is often at the expense of other factors we failed to consider. I have learned the importance of writing down my goals, but I have also learned the importance of ensuring that these goals address both short and long-term needs, human values, economics, and the environment. Unless the clarity of our "end" takes into consideration each of these areas, we run the risk of focusing on what is immediately pressing at the expense of what is most important in the support of our authentic self.

Allan Savory, author of *Holistic Management: A New Framework for Decision Making*, has had a great impact on my belief that personal leadership is built on a foundation of clarity about one's desired quality of life. Allan, a former wildlife biologist and farmer, developed a simple approach to personal and organizational leadership more than three decades ago. His original work with land management and stewardship has evolved into a valuable guide for all who seek to make better decisions within their business, community or any other aspect of their lives.

Allan proposes clarifying and writing down a three-part holistic goal for yourself and, if applicable, for your business. This goal encompasses three components — quality of life, production, and environment — which will guide every significant decision you make. The *quality of life* portion of your holistic goal expresses the reasons you are doing what you are doing, what you are about, what kind of person (or organization) you are, and what you want to become. It is a reflection of what matters most to you and why. It speaks to what needs you want to satisfy now as well as the vision you seek to accomplish in the long run. The *production* portion of your holistic goal expresses the level of production, achievement, financial success, or amount of work that is required to sustain the quality of life you desire. The *environmental* portion of your holistic goal reminds you that all households and businesses — even those that are solely service-oriented — affect ecological health. A goal relating to the environment needs to be included because, in the long run, the well-being of every family, business and community depends on the stability and productivity of the land that surrounds them.

This concept of managing holistically has widespread application for an industrialized society that rarely stops to examine the questions: "What kind of quality of life are we personally and collectively committed to sustain?" and "What level of production will support the quality of life we most desire?" and "How do our business and life decisions affect ecological health, which we all depend on for our future?" At a personal level, having a strong character means facing these questions within ourselves and with those who matter most in our life. We then must ask these questions of the organizations we lead and the communities we live in. Clarifying your most desired quality of life first, and then aligning your level of production and decisions that are ecologically sound with your quality of life, compels you to ask, "How much is enough?" This critical question forces us to examine honestly within ourselves the difference between *needs* and *wants*. Remember that your holistic goal is not meant to serve as a marketing tool the way a mission statement would. It is meant to be personal and meaningful only to you and to those closest to you. It is the deep, abiding, and sustaining mission that lies beneath a mission statement.

No one can specify what is or is not appropriate for inclusion in your quality of life statement. What needs to be included is unique to you. However, there are seven areas you might want to consider in thinking about your quality of life.

The first is your *purpose and contribution*. Think of the contribution you are making to your family, your workplace, your community and the world as it relates to your quality of life. What is your current expression of service to the world? Authenticity calls us to a level of success and self-expression that has little to do with the world's measurements of achievement. Are you at peace with what you are giving back?

The second area encompasses your *core virtues and values*. What qualities do you bring to your life? This aspect of a quality of life statement defines what kind of a person you most want to be. It is a list and a description of virtues such as humility, integrity, maturity, prudence or compassion that represent what you stand for as a person — the kind of character that you most want to express to the world. Virtues answer the question, "What kinds of actions do I want to bring to the world?" while values answer the question, "What matters most in my life?" and includes ideals such as spirituality, health, family, and community. You can work on virtues to improve your character, while values are something you set. As you clarify and make choices that are aligned with these core inner qualities, you begin to live an integrated life, rather than a fragmented life based on pleasing others, popularity, pleasure or power.

The third aspect of your quality of life statement is *relationships*. Who are the most important people in your life and how are your relationships with them? Who is supporting you? What is your community? After listing the important people in your life, reflect honestly about the quality of these relationships. What is it like when you are together? How much deep compassion and respect is there between you? What are your needs in the relationship? How much can you share about these questions between you? How much time will you set aside for these people? What actions need to be taken to create the quality of relationships you most want in your life?

Challenge and growth is a fourth area to include in your quality of life statement. We all need to grow and expand beyond our comfort zone and be challenged. Examine your commitment to your ongoing growth. What areas are most important to you for your own renewal? What are you curious about? How are you fostering your curiosity? There are many different areas for personal growth and development such as musical abilities, new skills, creativity, wisdom, time spent with mentors, professional skills associated with your work, interpersonal skills, or personal development courses. What kind of development and growth is important to you? How much time, realistically, would you like to spend developing yourself in the course of a week or a year? Are you learning something new every day? What areas have you neglected? What are you doing to stay fresh? I keep a picture on my desk of my children picking up shells on the eastern coast of Canada to remind me how important curiosity and endless learning are to me. My dad used to sit on my bed each night and ask, "What did you learn today?" He would hold me accountable to learn something new every day and to teach him what I had learned. He started a tradition of sharpening my mind with a continual influx of new and stimulating information and established the habit of lifelong learning that I have carried on with my own daughters. "In times of change," writes Eric Hoffer, "learners inherit the earth, while the learned find themselves beautifully equipped to deal with a world that no longer exists."

The fifth area is in the realm of *physical health*. Our quest for authenticity, for wholeness, may include a new relationship with our body. Think about your health and current choices around your health. Even though genetics are a given, we can influence our health, and subsequently the quality of our lives, by the choices we make. Good health is a source of wealth. Without health, happiness is not impossible, but it is difficult. We tend not to appreciate our health until it's not there. What is your vision of health?

Grace is the sixth component of your quality of life statement. Grace is a quality of character that creates a space for wonderment and awe in your life. A calm mind is like the surface of a still lake; it reflects the beauty that surrounds it. But like the windswept surface of a lake, a troubled mind reflects a distorted image of all that falls upon it. Grace not only allows us to see an exact reflection of the universe, but also a connection with the source from which the beauty originates. Grace unifies and brings reverence to life, connecting us to the divine force of the universe. How much room do you make in your life to notice the grace within you and around you?

Community is the seventh component to consider in your quality of life. Where do you want to live? What kind of surroundings support you, give you the sense of being at home with yourself? Personally, we chose to raise our children in a small community in the foothills of the Canadian Rockies, where we can care for and enjoy the outdoors, surrounded by neighbors and friends who provide mutual support in the raising of our family.

After your quality of life statement comes the production portion of your three-part holistic goal. This deals with the kind and amount of production that is necessary to sustain your defined quality of life. This is where you set achievement goals and create parameters around the amount of financial success you will strive to sustain, without compromising your defined quality of life. This portion of your holistic goal deals with the forms of production: "What form of work can you engage in that will support the quality of life that is important to you?" "Will you have the courage to say 'no' to types of work that lack meaning or do not support your quality of life?" "How much do you want to work?" "How much free time will you take?" "What financial goals do you need to support the kind of quality of life you desire?" "How much is enough?" "How will you produce more than you need, in order to contribute through your production?"

No matter what life stage you are in, another aspect of production is to begin to define for yourself what retirement means to you. Under the quality of life portion of your three-part goal, you will want to begin to clarify how you envision spending your time in your later years. Production challenges you to ask yourself how much money you will need to invest now to create the kind of quality of life you desire as you age.

The third and final portion of your three-part holistic goal concerns the environment. What is your commitment to sustain the environment for the generations that follow? With no ecosystem, there is no life, let alone quality of life. What landscape do you want to surround you that will support your soul? Even though you may not be involved specifically in managing land, we all play a part in creating an ecosystem — both internally and externally — that will sustain us. As citizens, we all have a responsibility to be caretakers of this planet. Within your holistic goals, you will undoubtedly find value in bringing your commitment to the environment to your conscious awareness. Not only is it good for the land and for our future generations, it is good for the soul.

*   *   *   *

THE COURAGE TO STAND ALONE

Great spirits have always encountered violent opposition from mediocre minds.

— Albert Einstein

Those who pursue the authentic life, who seek to live by inner *principles* rather than what the society says is *popular*, and who seek the higher life of wisdom must be prepared to stand alone. Taking the courageous path of authenticity requires that you let go of the need to be liked or to be popular or to be secure. Authenticity is not a journey to win social acceptance or find life's comforts. When you start being real, at least in the early stages, you can expect to be alone. Your relationships will change. Your job, whether you decide to leave or stay in your current position, will change. Your friends, if they decide to stay in your life, will change. You may feel both lonely *and* peaceful — lonely because no one can take these initial steps into authenticity with you; peaceful because you are following your heart's desire.

On a hot Saturday afternoon my six-year-old daughter, Chandra, decided to take on an entrepreneurial venture. I helped her make up drinks while she did the poster: "Kool-Aid for Sale — 25 cents for large, 20 cents for medium, 15 cents for small." When she realized that our street didn't have enough traffic to make a decent profit, she convinced me to move her stand to a busier intersection. Then she wanted me to stay with her. "I don't need your help," she exclaimed emphatically. "Just stay and keep me company. I want someone to talk to!" But she didn't have time to talk to me. She was too busy drumming up business by calling out to everyone who drove by.

Have you ever sat at a Kool-Aid stand with a six-year-old while she waves cars down? I wanted to put a paper bag over my head, pretending that I didn't know this stray kid. It was at that moment, in my fear of what the neighbors would think of me, that I had two important insights. First, Chandra, standing on that street corner, was expressing a vital quality of authenticity. She didn't give two hoots what people thought of her. She was there to sell Kool-Aid. The second realization was that Chandra, with her passion and lack of fear of rejection, will make a great entrepreneur someday if she can keep this spirit alive. After all, she was thrilled with the $1.80 total profit she put into her piggy bank on that Saturday afternoon, which incidentally, was more than I earned sitting there being self-conscious.

Children continue to teach me. The principle is that authentic people are not afraid to stand alone. Chandra did not care about the approval or the affirmation of others — she had a purpose and she fulfilled it.

It is the mark of the saint, and probably of every authentic person, to stand alone. Mother Teresa was an example of authenticity. She did not depend on the approval or the affirmation of others to do her work. In Calcutta there were some Hindus who, inclined to regard poverty as an unalterable part of the divine scheme, looked askance at her efforts to relieve it and concluded that she must be a CIA agent. To the Western liberal conscience, it appeared as a particular reproach that her works of charity stemmed from an unyielding conservative religious stance. In 1990, the feminist Germaine Greer launched an attack on Mother Teresa as a religious imperialist who used her charity as a method of foisting Catholicism on vulnerable people. But her courage to continue in the face of criticism can teach us all to be more courageous in doing what needs to be done in our lives, regardless of the risk.

* * * *

CONCLUSION

Character defines the very soul of an authentic person through ownership, conscious citizenship, integrity, clearing, making room for the shadow, and creating and sustaining a quality of life. We are the architects and artisans of our own character. We come into this world as a seed of unique possibilities, but we are not born accountable. Sadly, destructive habits such as laziness, dishonesty, selfishness and irresponsibility are easy to pick up. Choosing the good ones — courage, honesty, compassion, maturity — requires conscious discipline and is necessary work if we are committed to being people of strong character.

The nineteenth-century British writer William Makepeace Thackeray captured much about the nature of the process of character building in four lines:

> *Sow a thought and you reap an act;*
> *Sow an act and you reap a habit;*
> *Sow a habit and you reap a character;*
> *Sow a character and you reap a destiny.*

Indeed, it is not the fierceness of the storm that determines whether we break, but rather the strength of the roots that lie below the surface. The promise of strong character is that you will have deep roots that will hold you steady during the storms of life. Clarity and courage are the inner citadel and character is the bedrock upon which this quiet place sits. People with a strongly developed character possess a fervent and passionate willingness to put forth good in the world. They care less about what others think of them and more about the respect they have for themselves. Their world is no longer built on emotions but on a core deep within that is essentially changeless.

Character is what Abraham Lincoln was talking about when he said, "I desire to conduct the affairs of this administration such that if at the end... I have lost every friend on earth, I shall at least have one friend left, and that friend shall be down inside of me." Character is the realization that greatness stands on the foundation of goodness. Character consists not so much of the outward things we do for the sake of appearance, but of the inward condition of the mind and spirit that represents who we are. The noblest contribution anyone can make to the human race — and to the foundation of an authentic life — is that of an unshakable character.

* * * *

CHAPTER 4

———— ❦ ————

Seeking Calling

Life is no brief candle to me. It is sort of a splendid torch which I have got hold of for the moment, and I want to make it burn as brightly as possible before handing it on to future generations...
I want to be thoroughly used up before I die.

This is the true joy of life... Being used for a purpose recognized by yourself as a mighty one, being a force of nature... instead of a feverish, selfish little clod of ailments and grievances, complaining that the world will not devote itself to making you happy.
— George Bernard Shaw

* * * *

Stop for a moment and reflect on the following questions:

- Have you ever found yourself at work only to discover that there is some vital, valuable part of yourself that didn't travel there with you?

- What happens to your soul when your special gifts cannot seem to find their place in what you are doing?

- How often have you worked in an organization where there is far more talent, brainpower, wisdom, and resourcefulness than the job required or even allowed?
- What is the result of living without a sense of purpose?

These questions get to the heart of your calling. Living a purposeful life, while discovering and expressing your passion and unique gifts in the service of others, contributes to the development and expression of your authentic self. Calling is where the world's needs meet the soul's desires. In the decades that I have been involved in the field of personal and organizational development, this is the area that people inquire about more than anything else. People who hear my presentations and hire me to mentor and coach them most often ask, *"How do I find my purpose in life?"* and *"How do I know when I have found my purpose?"*

What is your calling? Why do you get out of bed in the morning? What are you supposed to do with your life? How would you articulate the meaning and purpose of your life? Is what you are now doing really the whole story? What are your unique gifts?

Those who face the immense undertaking of seeking answers to these questions — of living their calling — while simultaneously living in a society that tells you how you "should" live, are the real heroes of the modern-day world.

Calling taps into a deep source of energy from which life springs forth. When you make a decision to seek and heed your calling, hidden hands will be there to help you live the life you are meant to live. When you search for a life of purpose with a firm resolve to live in a way that matters, you will find yourself on a path that has been there all the while, waiting for you. Doors will open to places that you didn't know were there. Following your calling — or in the words of the mythologist, Joseph Campbell, following your "bliss" — means being willing to set aside the life you have planned in order to live the life intended for you.

It is not my intention to provide a complete treatise for finding and fulfilling the central purpose — or purposes — of your life. What I offer is my experience of seeking my own calling, along with some clues for listening to and heeding yours. For it is in your calling that the core of authentic living lies. Far bigger than your jobs, goals, strategies, and planning, more eminent than your current perception of self-fulfillment, and more meaningful than the rhetoric of a hastily written mission statement, calling speaks to the very essence of your existence.

Recently, after leading a session with a group of senior managers on Authentic Leadership, I was debriefing with the company's CEO over dinner. During the retreat, the group had shared some very personal material about the meaning of leadership, legacy, and calling. The CEO was reflective afterwards and wanted to continue the conversation.

"As I look back over my prosperous career, I am fortunate to have had the success I have," he said, "but, frankly, I am at the stage in my life when I am questioning my sense of purpose and inner contentment. For most of my career, I have sought success in the form of recognition and power. Although this was important at the time, what I want now is to make a contribution that goes beyond achievement. What I desire most at this stage in my life is to leave a legacy." The intensity of his resolve was expressed in his entire body.

"I would give anything right now to discover what it is that I am meant to be doing with the next stage of my life. I have been driven, but now I sense the emergence of a calling."

This CEO was beginning to listen to and seek his calling — a voice within him that was summoning him to respond to his authentic self. Like so many of us, out of necessity, he had spent a large share of his life attempting to meet the needs of the world: his parents, teachers, friends, church leaders, and, for the past two decades, his customers, shareholders, employees, community, board of directors, and family. Yet, during the past several months, he found himself lying awake at night, knowing that something in his life was missing, that something was out of balance. He talked of feeling incongruent between what the world was offering and what his authentic self was looking for. Unknown to him until we spoke that day, he had begun to seek his calling, embarking on the hero's journey.

In this chapter, I offer a list of statements I hold to be true about finding your calling in life. Then I give examples of people in my own life who are seeking and living their calling. Finally, I leave you with some clues and potential strategies for discovering what you are called to be and do in this life.

Here are some of my beliefs about calling. I invite you to take some time to reflect on how they connect with your convictions.

- You can be unemployed, but you can't be uncalled. Every person enters the world as a seed of possibilities with a destiny to fulfill. We each bear a uniqueness that asks to be lived and that is already present, waiting to be expressed. The calling does not go away, even if one's awareness of it does. Every individual has a central and unique guiding force. This force compels us, knowingly or unknowingly, to a destiny and essence of life we are meant to have. Whether we live one day or one hundred years, we are called to make a unique contribution in the world. If you don't yet know what your calling is, then your calling is to discover it and live it as best you can.

- It is more important to *live* your calling than it is to *articulate* it. Many people are living the lives they are meant to live without a formal personal mission statement or even the ability to communicate what that calling is. Although crafting a statement of what your calling is can help you find it and stay connected to it, the best test of how aligned you are with that destiny is the degree of inner contentment you experience in your life. In *Seat of the Soul*, Gary Zukav writes, "When the deepest part of you becomes engaged in what you are doing, when what you do serves both yourself and others, when you do not tire on the inside… but seek the satisfaction of your life and your work, what then? Then you know you are doing what you are meant to be doing."

- There is a difference between a "vocation" and a "job." A "vocation" is work that you get paid for that is aligned with your calling and provides an opportunity to live your purpose and express your unique talents and passions in the service of others. A "job," on the other hand, is a place of employment that gives you a role, an opportunity, and the financial means to live your calling away from your paid work. It is authentically legitimate to have a job where you go to work and a calling that you come home to. I once met a lawyer who described his vocation as being a musician. "Music is my heart and my passion. It is what gives me fulfillment. Music feeds my spirit. I practice law during the week so I can play on the weekends."

- Everyone is unique. This matter of calling is highly individualized. What you are called to do or be may have nothing in common with what I am called to be or do. It is how you use your passions, gifts, compelling desires, firm resolve, and highest aspirations — in the service of others — that expresses your calling.

- An awareness of your calling evolves over time as your consciousness evolves. While a rare number of people find and live their calling in their youth, most don't find and express it until later in life, as the authentic self emerges. Early experiences and roles prepare you for your calling later in life, while a hidden force moves you toward growth. You will become more in tune with your calling as you connect with your authentic self through: finding center, building character, and nourishing community. It will be common to sense incongruity when you are out of step with your life's work. It is critical to be flexible and courageously respond, without judgment, to the authentic voice from within, and move into new frontiers as you are called.

- Calling outlasts a career. You will likely be seeking calling your entire life: honing and developing it, learning to say "no" to the wrong opportunities, and paying attention to your authentic place in the world. You may retire from your job, but there is no retiring from your calling. As Henri Nouwen wrote, "Those who think that they have finished are finished. Those who think they have arrived have lost their way."

- The antidote to exhaustion — times when you experience "bad" tired rather than "good" tired, a life that is out of balance — is not rest. The antidote to exhaustion is alignment and wholeheartedness. If you want less stress and more balance and authenticity in your life, you don't necessarily have to work less or quit your job. Maybe you just need to be more authentic in your work. Start by looking for what you can say "no" to that will make room for you to find and express what your heart most desires.

- It is important that you pay attention at the commencement of the call — when you begin noticing yourself living an inauthentic life. Awareness of calling will come to you from within and in many forms. It can come in sudden bursting flashes of insight or in subtle, gradual awakenings. It may come in the form of insomnia, depression, difficult feedback, or the loss of a loved one — or it may just come as a vague sense that something is missing in your life. Regardless of how the call comes, if you start to feel a sense of incongruity, know that you are making progress. There's nothing wrong with you. Just be sure you do not suppress it, run away from it or keep yourself distracted from it, or you'll end up paying a price. Regardless of how it comes to you, calling is relentless. Be aware: if you don't pay attention to the voice within, you'll either get sick or bitter.

• Having a sense of calling in life does not necessarily bring complete clarity or relief, void of any further struggle. You don't simply "arrive" once you have a well-articulated purpose. Calling goes beyond sitting down for a few hours and writing a personal mission statement. In all likelihood, you will spend your lifetime coming to know what you are called to do and to be.

Here are some examples of people in my own life who are seeking and living their calling:

Val, my lifelong partner, came to this life with a call to be a healer. Healing is her life's work, her innate gift, her calling, and her vocation. Every living thing that comes in contact with her spirit and with her hands becomes more alive as a result of being in her presence. The plants in my office blossom when she nurtures them. Our children's spirits flourish when they are in her presence. I know that I am a better person because Val is in my life, and all who come into contact with her will attest to this.

Val has had many jobs. She has taught school, she has been both a college and high school administrator, and now she is a household executive and the administrator for our business, as well as editor of my writing, all of which are a means for her to express her authentic self — her innate capacity to heal. These roles are all tools for expressing this calling. Val brings her healing presence to everything she does. She has never written a personal mission statement. She has never been on a vision quest or read a book on the subject or taken a course for finding her life's purpose. She intuitively lives her calling. If you meet Val, you will feel better about yourself just by being in her presence. She is the kind of person who can't *not* heal through her gentle spirit, open heart, and authenticity. Healing and brightening the world she touches is simply a natural part of who she is. It is a light she brings to any darkness she enters. Indeed, I would not be here today in the way I am without the gift of this woman in my life.

My oldest daughter, now in her twenties, is an artist. Her calling is to create. If she's not creating she gets depressed. She is a potter, and clay is her medium, her means to express her calling. For years she spent hours a week at the pottery studio, developing her craft on the wheel. She also does graphic design work on the computer, another way to express her creativity. Now, as a young mother, she has learned that there is more to parenting than creating. However, to sustain her well-being, she must make room to get to the pottery studio at least once a week.

I have a young niece who is a professional human-rights advocate, with expertise in the Muslim world. She has been working as an activist on women's rights and peacebuilding since she was 15 years old. Lauryn holds a B.A. Honours in International Development Studies, an M.A. in Human Security and Peacebuilding, and is working on her doctorate. She is the recipient of numerous awards and distinctions, including the 2000 Chatelaine Women of the Year. Lauryn was born to be a "disturber." Her call in life is to create social change by disturbing the status quo. Ask her parents and you will know that she was a disturber in her family at a very early age. In a recent interview in *Canadian Living* magazine, she was quoted as saying, "It's my goal to make activism cool." Lauryn is also a "connector." "It's important," she said once, "to see a violation to a woman anywhere as a violation to yourself." She is eloquent, articulate, and determined. She is not just surviving. She is *living* — because she is listening to her call. When asked, "What advice do you have for young women?" she replied: "Never set limits. Never close your mind to what your talents are and to where they can take you. Growing up, I don't think anyone thought that being a human-rights activist was something to pursue. I did because no one told me that there was a certain path I had to take. I remember announcing to my parents one day at dinner that someday I was going to run the UN. No one blinked an eye. That made me think, okay, I guess I can do it."

Some years ago, during a very unsettling personal time, I made a conscious decision to go out and "look for" my calling, thinking that if I knew what my calling was, it would give me the inner peace I yearned for at that stage. I saw some of the personal mission statements of respected colleagues hanging on the walls in their offices. I, too, wanted what seemed to be a definitive answer to the question of who I am once and for all. For more than two years, I read every book and took every course I could find on the subject of finding purpose in life. I flew to Arizona, where I went on a three-day fast and vision quest in the desert. I studied with a Shaman. I sat in sweat lodges and spent time talking to aboriginal elders, priests and other religious leaders. With each of these experiences came a residue of growth. Without ever finding a way to articulate it at the time, I know today that I am called to be a seeker and a teacher in my life. This is my life's work. I just didn't see it at the time.

During all these learning experiences I repeatedly tried to formulate a personal mission statement about what I was called to do in this lifetime — without any success. In the process of searching for my calling out *there*, I discovered it was actually right *here* all along. I also realized that I had to add what I wanted to be into the equation. Instead of the old description, "I am what I do," I had to flip the emphasis to "I do what I am." After my last intensive "personal calling" retreat in the Mendocino Forest in California, I decided that instead of trying to "pursue my calling" I would look for daily opportunities to respond to the simple needs of others, and find a way to use my gifts in service. I would simply try to be myself and see what emerged.

On the way home from my vision quest, I read an article in an airport magazine that I would not ordinarily pick up. It was written by Oprah Winfrey about Dr. Martin Luther King's purpose in life and about his influence on her life. His prayer, every morning, was simply, "*Use me, God. Show me how to take who I am, who I want to be, and what I can be, and use it for a purpose greater than myself.*"

Finding your authentic self has often been equated with discovering the perfect job. What I have come to realize is that the goal of calling is to find satisfying work — either paid or unpaid — that fills your destiny and brings you satisfaction. If you can't find that, then you need to find a way to be satisfied with what you are currently doing and do it in a way that is satisfactory to you. Remember that *all* acts of service contribute to the good of the whole and that there is no single act of greatness, just a series of small acts done with great passion or great love. Your authentic self and accompanying calling will come to you as you bring the very best of yourself to whatever is in front of you each day. T. S. Eliot expresses it well: "We must not cease from exploration. And the end of all our exploring will be to arrive where we began and to know the place for the first time."

Ironically, since I let go of the compulsive need for clarity about my life purpose, clarity has come to me. Shortly after my decision to let go of trying to figure out my calling, I came across a book called *The Path: Creating Your Mission Statement for Work and for Life*, by Laurie Beth Jones. Just for the fun of it, and wanting to learn more about myself, I spent the good part of a summer working through the exercises in the book. The drive for clarity had left me and there was a lightness in the exploration.

At the end of the summer, after some soul searching and conversations with people who know me well, I finally did come up with a personal mission statement. Since I began writing my personal mission statement years ago, it has evolved and grown with me. Although the words have been important tools to inspire me in the low days and guide me on the good days, what matters most is not that I have a mission statement, but that I have a *mission*.

Here's my personal mission, as it stands today:
I work to change the world by changing myself first.
Through the experience and strength of my authentic presence...

I inspire and guide leaders — in all capacities — to authentically connect with themselves and those they serve, so that they may amplify their impact in the world, and in the process, find meaning and significance in their lives.

I hold up both a beacon and mirror to everyone I come in contact with, that they may know, more fully, their intrinsic worth.

My purpose is to teach and to learn, and in the process, to evolve my soul. Clarity about your authentic call in life is more emergent than it is deliberate. It is not a goal to be achieved, but a gift to be received. A poem, written by the seventeenth-century poet, George Herbert, describes the force of having a "call" in life:

The Call

Come, my Way, my Truth, my Life
Such a Way, as gives us breath
Such a Truth, as ends all strife
And such a Life, as killeth death.

Come, my Light, my Feast, my Strength
Such a Light, as shows a feast
Such a Feast, as mends in length
Such a Strength, as makes his guest.

Come, my Joy, my Love, my Heart
Such a Joy, as none can move
Such a Love, as none can part
Such a Heart, as joyes in love.

* * * *

There is no formula for finding your calling, and for me to offer one would be inauthentic, so what I present is a list of clues and potential strategies for discovering what you are called to be and do in this life.

START SMALL

One of the barriers to detecting, listening for, and sensing your calling in life is to think of calling as one specific laudable vocation. Calling often brings us up against such widespread legendary images in Western culture as Martin Luther, Mother Teresa, Jean Vanier, and the Dalai Lama. It is important to understand that images of heroic expressions such as these are undoubtedly inspirational to those who seek their calling. Each of these heroes are certainly "called." However, they represent only a very small spectrum of ways to be called.

The ordinary life, fueled by the consciousness of a deep and abiding call, is extraordinary. The little things in life are often the big things. Just because you may be called to simple expressions does not make them unimportant. You might feel called to look closely at yourself every time you get angry, to see where the anger is coming from and ask whether it is an appropriate response — and make socially responsible choices accordingly. Calling can be as simple, and as important, as working with this emotion of anger and turning from an explosive, abusive, self-centered response to energy that creates.

I sometimes hear excuses for not hearing a call or having a call. "I was not well mentored in my childhood, and therefore cannot be expected to make a contribution to the world" is a familiar one. If any illusion holds our modern society in a relentless grip, it is that we are our parents' children and that the primary instrument of our fate is how our mothers and fathers raised us. Know that no matter who you are, no matter where you have come from, you have an important story and you have a choice. No matter what your upbringing, it was exactly what you needed to prepare yourself for your unique call in life. Your past is what you need because your past is what has been given to you.

When I am alert and receptive, I continue to look around and find all sorts of calls that beckon me, for example, to be more gentle when I want to lash out, to be more attentive to a loved one when I would rather withdraw, or simply to be more loving and kind to a stranger when I would rather be indifferent. By giving credit to these little calls, I prepare the soil for a bigger call to character.

We live in a society that values and adores those of celebrity status, while often undermining the worth of small and vital contributions. Collectively, we applaud and revere the gold medalists, the Oscar nominees, the successful entrepreneurs, the Everest climbers, the billionaires, the platinum CD artists, and, to a lesser extent, the Nobel Prize winners. We are in awe of anyone who has attained fame, notoriety, and celebrity status, especially if they have overcome a devastating misfortune to reach the pinnacle of their dreams and their vocation. I have great respect and admiration for successful people who follow their passion and perhaps even their calling and manifest their destiny by pushing the boundaries of possibilities to their outermost limits. There is, without doubt, a time and a place for great achievements. I certainly appreciate my achievements in this lifetime.

While I acknowledge the inspiration in stories of greatness, I am now reaching a point in my life where I am drawn to Mother Teresa's adage, "We can do no great things; only small things with great love."

I am increasingly finding value in simply being and doing good work, with or without fame. I am respectful of the hundreds of people I meet each year who will never achieve fame or recognition by the world's standards, but quietly and steadily go about their daily lives volunteering in their community, standing tall on their convictions, painting an unsigned masterpiece, recovering from an addiction, lying beside a parent while they die, or compassionately standing by a loved one with a terminal illness.

At my daughters' "last day of school" celebration, when Chandra graduated from kindergarten and Hayley completed grade three, I sat and watched the children say good-bye to their wonderful teachers. The children had tears streaming down their cheeks. Hayley would cry herself to sleep that night, knowing that after two years of being with Josee-Lyne Seguin she would be moving on to a new teacher the following year. Then I went by Denise Breault's kindergarten class to thank her for the wonderful gift of her presence to Chandra during the year and found another little girl weeping in Denise's arms. She, too, just wouldn't let go — of her kindergarten teacher or of her experience of being a part of this community of gifts.

Neither of these two magnificently talented public education teachers will ever get a gold medal or a platinum CD or an Oscar nominee for the lives they have touched and changed. They, like so many who quietly serve their communities with their presence and their gifts, won't get into any "hall of fame" or receive a Nobel Prize for the passion and energy they bring to the classroom every day, in spite of their weariness and the demands placed upon them. Neither of them will get recognition in the press for their dedicated day-in and day-out contribution to the lives of children. They won't get paid what they are worth, nor will they receive public acknowledgment for their unique gift to powerfully influence our next generation through their devoted presence and through the expression of their gifts. Nonetheless, they are following their authentic calling.

Everyone is called to bring a unique contribution to life. The challenge is to slow down, listen, and *respond* to your call. The key is to be open to what is right in front of you. You don't have to look for it like you would a lost piece of jewelry. It will come to you like the sun in a darkened room when you open the drapes. You are a complete package as you are. The call to greatness is the call to be yourself.

* * * *

WHAT DO YOU DO WELL THAT YOU DON'T REMEMBER LEARNING?

The real voyage of discovery lies not in seeking new landscapes, but in having new eyes.

— *Marcel Proust*

Near Eleusis, in Attica, there once lurked a bandit called Procrustes or "The Stretcher." He had an iron bed on which travelers who fell into his hands were compelled to spend the night. His "humor" was to stretch the ones who were too short until they died or, if they were too tall, to cut off as much of their limbs as necessary to make them short enough. None could resist him, and the surrounding countryside became a desert.

There is nothing more important in this life than becoming yourself. Yet, too many of us are so compelled to sleep in the Procrustean bed of a culture that wants everyone to be the same size that we insulate the calling present in us all. We are told, for example, that we must have a certain level of intelligence in order to be capable of offering something of value to society. In reality, there are many forms of intelligence including mechanical genius and spatial intelligence. There is emotional intelligence, which links emotional stability and aptitude with relationships, an increasingly recognized capability in the business world. When I was a teenager, I remember my dad hiring people who were intellectually challenged to work on our acreage. These were people who probably had an IQ of less than eighty, but if there were a way to measure their compassion — their *LQ* — their *love quotient* — they would score over two hundred. These people with disabilities had astonishing freedom; they did not seem imprisoned in prejudice or bound by the shackles of the need for prestige and societal approval. They were magnificent people, hard workers, and wonderful role models for me. To this day, I am grateful for the gifts their presence brought into our home and into my life.

One very powerful way to rediscover your true gifts in life is through a question asked by John Scherer: *What do you do well that you don't remember learning?* Take a few moments to reflect upon your early experiences, how your life has evolved and where you are today. The answer to this question will help you step back from the Procrustean bed of the culture and renew your ability to find your gifts that have been there all along. Taking time to reflect on this question will give you a start in clarifying your gifts and help lead you to your calling. When you start asking this question, your gifts — and your calling — will begin to emerge.

When I stop and reflect on the answer to this question, three words come to mind: heart, teaching, and music. Heart and the innate ability to feel with others have been with me since birth.

They are both a part of me and developed in me as I was raised in a family where pain, conflict, and tension were a part of life. Several early memories include nurturing dolls, comforting a hurt friend in elementary school, stepping into the middle of my parents' anger as they fought, and, more recently, weeping when I inadvertently ran over a family of ducks crossing the highway. The pain of this event stayed with me for days. This gift of heart led me to the profession of social work, where I practiced as a psychotherapist for nearly a decade.

Next is my gift to teach. I recall standing in front of an entire church congregation at the age of six, speaking to three hundred people, presenting a three-minute talk. During the entire time, I was completely at ease and even had to be asked to sit down because I used up both my own and the next person's allotted time. For many years, I have continued to practice, develop, and strengthen the skill of teaching and speaking, but it does seem to come naturally and easily to me.

My third answer was the gift of music, which has always been with me, but took a different path to root within my spirit. As a child, I took Royal Conservatory on the piano and quit, discouraged and bored, after three years. My mother was disappointed by this and always said, "But David, you have so much music in you!" I didn't recognize it then, but know now that I was discouraged not with the music, but with the mechanics of the music. I naturally play by ear, something I didn't learn, but was born with. After forty years I have found a marvelous teacher and returned to music. After a day of writing or speaking, I find unspeakable joy when sitting at the piano playing Beethoven or Pachelbel or Enya. I have done so little in my life for pure joy, and this is it.

What I am learning is that we don't really find our gifts, but rather our gifts find us. Teachers, like gifts, will show up when we are ready. Gifts are an expression of the marvelous creative life force with which we are blessed. When we reach for an understanding of our gifts, we can be drawn closer to others as we express ourselves. It might be a gift for music or for painting or for writing or story-telling. A talent is a call, for it draws us to a vocation that uplifts our own spirit and helps us find fulfillment as we share it with others. Relating to children, crafting a workshop, carpentry, gardening, or working with persons who are mentally or physically challenged are all examples of gifts that awaken us to a special relationship and cause the world to be better off through our presence.

As I come to know and trust my gifts, I use this awareness as a filter for the decisions I make. More and more often now I find myself telling potential clients that I want to choose work that is aligned with my gifts. That way we all win. They get the best part of me and I get to give the best part of me. It doesn't always happen so cleanly, but my work is evolving in this direction. I am blessed to have a vocation in which I can express the gifts that have been afforded to me. And if I don't do it in my work, I need to be doing it elsewhere in my life — otherwise my soul will suffer. Until I returned to the keyboard, I didn't know just how much I had missed playing the piano for the past four decades!

Depression has also been a gift to me. She has helped me slow down and create a kind of garden in which inspiration, compassion, and wisdom could take root and grow. Depression has been a voice from my soul that says, in essence, "Respect the winter in your life. Remember to let yourself hibernate for a season when you are called in that direction. Listen to your spirit."

Depression always comes to me as a teacher, if I will pay atten-tion to her. Often in her visits, she reminds me that my life is out of balance, that I was spending too much time alone in my office doing work that is misaligned with my gifts and my passions. When I lis-ten to this voice and begin reaching out and connecting with friends and colleagues who nourish, stimulate, and challenge me in meaningful ways, she usually goes on her way.

Our gifts, and then our calling, often spring forth from our wounds. If you track your wounds, the places where you have been hurt, you may well find your gifts. The pain we have felt in life is often the driving force behind the contribution we make to the world. My gift to work from the heart and to teach with compassion has arisen, to a great extent, from the pain in my life. As a youth, I frequently found myself in the middle of other people's confrontations, attempting to be the peacemaker and taking on their pain. Tuning in to their pain helped me learn about and express compassion. My response to the conflicts around me was the catalyst for developing one of my gifts. I realize now that what happened to me in the past was exactly what was needed to bring me to my gifts today.

We draw closer to freedom when we can look for the wisdom that comes from unexpected and difficult events: the death of a loved one, an illness, an accident that creates a disability, or an apparent misfortune that breaks the pattern of our life and obliges us to reflect and reevaluate ourselves with renewed values and perspective.

Such experiences come as surprises that open us up to new possibilities. They appear to be tragic and come with enormous grieving and loss because they move us from the secure world of the predictable to the chaotic world of the unknown. But later we may discover that they are blessed events. Many parents of children with disabilities have told me the horror and disbelief they felt at the birth of their child. But over time they unearthed the awareness that their child had transformed them, opened their hearts, and awakened them to unknown gentleness, compassion, and wisdom. Crises and unexpected changes can lead us to denial, anguish, anger, and revolt, but these emotions can gradually help us to accept reality as it is and discover in the new situation renewed energy, perspective, freedom, and meaning in life. Indeed, every curse can become a blessing, just as every blessing can become a curse.

Our family had the privilege of having Kano, a Norwegian Elkhound, spend his life in our home. I am going to tell you about Kano's nature, his gifts, and his contribution to our family, but before I do that, I want to tell you what his gift wasn't. Kano was not the brightest dog in our neighborhood. He failed agility training and we worked far too hard to give him an advanced understanding of obedience. We tried for three winters to teach him how to pull a sled. He was born for the cold northern climate, but he was not born to pull a sled.

Kano's greatest gift was love. When he first came into our family, Val and I lived alone, and Kano was the center of our family life, until children arrived and the focus on Kano shifted. It was no longer the dog that jumped up on my lap; it was the kids. Walking Kano was no longer a priority because the children needed our attention, and his gift of love began to be lost in a house where he was no longer needed. Ever so slowly and subtly, Kano began to withdraw. He began spending more and more time asleep in the garage. Soon it was difficult to get him excited about going for walks; even when I had the time to take him to his favorite trail by the river, he was no longer interested. He lost his spirit, that sparkle in his eye.

Shortly before my mother's death, she took me aside and in her wisdom said, "David, promise me that you will get Kano out of the garage. He is depressed and needs resurrection, and in the process, he will teach you something."

Having struggled with my own depression in life, I have come to know that depression is exacerbated when our life is not aligned with the nature and spirit of who we are, when we allow those gifts to go to sleep in the garages of our lives. Depression is a voice from the soul, an indication of a lack of congruence between our choices and our gifts. Given that our society emphasizes what we own and what we do, rather than the celebration of who we are, is it any wonder that sixty billion U.S. dollars is spent annually by businesses in North America to pay for depression claims by employees? Where are our untapped gifts and contributions to the world? Where do we find our sense of meaning? Four times as many North Americans were being treated for depression at the end of the 1990s than ten years earlier, despite a decade of unparalleled prosperity.

So, for a year, we created a family project to get Kano out of the garage, to awaken his gift of love which, for years, had been dormant in the garage. In the evenings we shut off the television and took Kano for walks. At noon I would come home and take an extended lunch break and get him back in those woods that I, too, had neglected. And in those walks and those times together, as Kano came back to life, something in turn was awakened in me. Kano helped me to rediscover long-neglected gifts.

For years, I had facilitated various forms of strategic planning retreats and accountability agreements with executives. This work was very lucrative, but Kano helped me realize, in the stillness of a morning walk, that my work was no longer feeding my soul. My gift, like Kano's, was to work from the heart, and by not honoring that gift, a part of me had gone to sleep with Kano in the garage.

My next strategic planning retreat was scheduled for the following week. At the end of the first day of a two-day retreat, I turned to the group and said, "I have to be honest; I am not having a great deal of fun today. I made a mistake by taking on this contract. Although I feel competent doing this facilitative work, it is no longer fulfilling. I take accountability for the contract, so I will give you three options: 1) I will bring in one of my colleagues to complete the process; 2) we can cancel the retreat now and I will not charge you; 3) I'll offer you a storytelling day, where each of us can tell stories about what our heart's desire is in this organization. What is our unique contribution? What is our vision and our dream for creating a more fully human workplace? You have talked in your strategic planning about your commitment to create a more fully human organization. Why don't we start by doing it with this group?" (By the way, they told me they weren't having much fun either.)

Unanimously, they chose the storytelling, and day two turned out to be a rich, fulfilling experience for us all and the beginning of a significant cultural shift for the organization, as well as the beginning of a personal shift for me — a renewed commitment to follow my heart rather than my ego and my paycheck.

So thank you, Kano, for spending the last year of your life living your gifts and helping me to find mine. Months later, Kano faced a painful battle with arthritis. He was put down in our back yard surrounded by those who loved him and were loved by him. His gift lives on in our family.

* * * *

BE INFORMED BY PASSION

The history of mankind is the story of people selling themselves short.

— Abraham Maslow

You are more than you believe and passion is a key that unlocks the door to new possibilities. One of my favorite stories, a tale from the late Mort Utley, illustrates what is gained by following your passion:

A little boy trying to sell a dog sat by the sidewalk with a sign that read: "DOG FOR SALE: 25 cents." On his way to and from work, a man walked by the boy for five days. Finally he said, "Are you having trouble selling that dog?"

"Sure am!" The boy replied.

"Would you like a suggestion?" the man offered.

"Sure would!" the boy said.

"You are not thinking big enough! There is no passion in your work. Who wants a 25-cent dog? Take that dog home, give him a bath, brush his hair, and put a ribbon around his neck. Then raise your price, and you'll sell him!"

The next day the man was amazed when he saw the boy and the dog. The dog was all washed and brushed with a big yellow ribbon around his neck. A huge sign said: "DOG FOR SALE: $10,000!"

The man said, "Son, I told you to be passionate and think big, but this is ridiculous. Who is going to pay ten thousand dollars for a dog?"

The boy replied, "Mister, you told me to think big, and that is the biggest number I could think of."

Not wanting to discourage him, the man went on his way. The next morning, the boy was gone, but the sign was still there, with "For Sale" crossed out and "SOLD" written over it.

Curiosity got the best of him and he knocked on the boy's door. When the lad answered, the man congratulated him. "Son, I see you sold your dog."

The boy exclaimed, "Yes sir, and I want to thank you for helping me find passion and think big."

The man then asked the boy, "How much did you get for him?"

"Ten thousand dollars," was the boy's reply.

After a moment of silence, the man responded, "I know he's sold, because he's gone, but I know that you didn't get ten thousand dollars for him. How much did you really get for him?"

"Mister, I told you. I got ten thousand dollars."

"How in the world did you get ten thousand dollars for that dog?"

"I sold him for two five-thousand-dollar cats!"

This story illustrates the power of the passion we all had at some point in our lives and how, in the course of "fitting in" to the culture of what is "appropriate," "proper," and "sensible," we lost touch with this wonderful indicator of our heart's desires — our passion. Passion is pure enthusiasm, but it is more than that. Passion is the deep, abiding voice within us that informs us of the blueprint of our lives. Many of the people I meet in our Intensive Authentic Leadership programs draw a blank when we invite participants to "go inside" and listen to their passion. We have shut off so much of our heart in our culture that we are out of touch with what our passion is. Passion is a torch that can guide you through the dark tunnels of your inner life. Passion is the energy that can sustain you in discouragement; it can nourish a depleted spirit and be a friend that gives confidence in the face of insecurity. Passion will move you to divine presence because when you are passionate, you are completely present.

Passion is used to describe the love in our life, but it extends far beyond the love of a significant person. Stop and ask yourself two questions: "Where in my life do I experience passion?" and "What activities do I do, that when I do them, I lose all track of time?" Passion is power. Passion is what we are most deeply curious about, most hungry for, and will most hate to lose in life. My experience as a psychotherapist is that the repression of passion or the life force is the most common reason people come for therapy. By discounting our passions, we block our energy and insulate ourselves from the call. Underneath all passion lie the needs of the spirit. Suppress passion and despair will follow.

It is often difficult to admit honestly what our passion is because we feel we can't do anything about it. We may not be able to afford to travel or parachute or buy a motorcycle or an RV or even have time to read the books we want to read. In response, we stop listening, shutting the door on any new possibilities, afraid of seeing truth and shutting down the source of energy that sustains us from within.

Authenticity calls us to listen to these passions, whether we can "afford" to do them or not. Use the energy around the passion as a torch to look inward. For example, if you stop and notice that you have a passion for motorcycles, but can't yet afford to buy one, you have two options. First, you can set a goal to buy a motorcycle and put money aside each month. The passion will then fuel the flame of perseverance and give you some energy to go to work because now you are working for a higher purpose. But the second option is even more powerful. If you have a passion for motorcycles, even if you cannot afford one right now, take some time to use this energy to go inside. It may be that the passion is not for the motorcycle, but for what the motorcycle will offer you. The authentic way is to ask, "What desire does the motorcycle fill?" Is it a yearning for freedom? power? escape? fun? As you reflect on these questions, you will unearth the source of a river that flows through you — a river called passion. In the meantime, while you save for your motorcycle, maybe there is another, less expensive way of following your heart's desire.

Passion is the voice of the inner spirit that is always alive, but sometimes sleeping. I have a passion for learning, for conversation, for helping others. I have a passion for connection, for engaging in meaningful dialogue that leads to new insights and new directions for living. I have a passion for certain kinds of music. When I lie on the floor with the speakers turned up, listening to Beethoven's *Ninth Symphony*, my heart sings. I also have a passion for connecting with my body and with nature. When I go for an early morning run through the hills and along the river as the sun is rising, painting the sky deep red, every cell in my body reverberates with exhilaration. Connecting with my body through the practice of yoga has been a recent discovery for expression of this passion. Taking time to listen to your passions will provide a powerful inner navigator leading you to endeavors and activities that nourish your authentic spirit.

It is far too easy to let ourselves be involved in work, in tasks and roles for which we have no real passion, or in jobs that give us rewards in the world's eyes — success, financial rewards, even fame — but do not fill our soul. Our passion does not necessarily have to be fed by our work, but if we do not nurture our passion somewhere in our lives, our spirit will begin deteriorating. It is crucial to find outlets to express our passion, for passion is woven deeply into the fabric of our authentic self, and when we suppress it through conformity, we put our spirit to sleep. Awakening our passion arouses our soul. When making choices that are aligned with our passion, we will not tire on the inside. Too many go through life without expressing their passion and thus resign themselves to exhausted desperation.

Passion also has a dark side when it crosses the line from being a hunger to being an obsession. Passion for more, for greater heights, for bigger achievements, for more wealth, can be consuming when it diminishes our sensibility for balanced living. I speak from my own experience because I have had periods in my life when I was so consumed by passion that it put my family, those closest to me, my health, and my spiritual life at risk. Certainly there are times in our lives when being focused and driven by our dreams is an important expression of the authentic self. But when our egos consume us, when our passions flood our entire existence for too long, we can lose contact with our authenticity, and our soul begins to erode. The key is to stay centered, to allow our passions to inform us, fulfill us, and express us, without defining us.

Remember: keep an open mind and listen to the clues. A friend of mine, an adventurer, world-class athlete, and highly successful entrepreneur, was confronted with cancer at midlife. The cancer was his greatest teacher because he took time to stop being consumed by his passion for external achievements. His authentic journey turned inward and he was inducted into a new level of spirituality as he was forced to stop being driven by his passions.

Oprah Winfrey speaks a great deal about passion when you listen to the voice of her authentic life. "If you don't know what your passion is," she says, "then realize that one reason for your existence is to find it." Your life's work is to find your life's work and then to fulfill it. Ignoring your passion is like dying a slow death. Your life is speaking to you every day, all the time, and your task is to slow down and listen to it.

* * * *

LISTEN TO LOSS

Remember the bell, whose beauty is released by a sudden, ferocious blow.

— *Crispinano*

A voice on the other end of the phone told Don his father had died of a sudden and massive heart attack. Don spoke on the phone as his wife and five children silently and expectantly continued to eat their supper. Calmly Don put the receiver down and returned to the table and articulately explained to his family that he would be catching the first plane out in the morning to make the necessary funeral arrangements.

"I'll need to call Nancy [his administrative assistant]. She'll take care of my cases until I return on Monday." Nothing more was said as a family until Don left on the plane the next morning and the kids started asking questions of their mother. Don flew three thousand miles to his old family town. He and his only sibling, a younger brother, buried their father. Don returned to his law practice in less than six days.

Three months later, Don was playing catch with his golden retriever in the front yard of his home. The ball that he threw bounced off the nose of his dog, and she eagerly bounded onto the road to retrieve it. Suddenly, brakes screamed and tires skidded on dry pavement. Don's young daughter found her father fifteen minutes later, sitting on the curb with his dead companion in his arms, still weeping uncontrollably. Less than a week later, Don came to see me, seeking some executive coaching toward the discovery of his authentic self, open to begin making changes in his life.

Calling comes from deep within us, from beyond the demands of our culture. Facing loss can open a door that leads to a depth where we can find our calling, loss thereby being our teacher. Loss and suffering through facing death, illness, or catastrophic events has deeper meaning when we understand that it can lead us to a new awareness of ourselves. Pain, in fact, presents opportunities for wisdom, compassion, and the emergence of the authentic self. Instead of averting our eyes from the painful events of life, look at them squarely and contemplate them often. By facing the realities of death, infirmity, loss, and disappointment, we free ourselves of illusions and false hopes and avoid the misery of denial. Helen Keller, who lived through enormous suffering and loss, wrote: *Character cannot be developed in ease and quiet. Only through experience of trial and suffering can the soul be strengthened, vision cleared, ambition inspired, and success achieved.*

To accept life as impermanent and death as inevitable does not mean that our attention must focus only on loss and endings. The life energy in living things is powerful and doesn't easily surrender to the forces that threaten it. Look at the way a blade of grass, seeking light and life, will manage to grow through even the smallest crack in a sidewalk. But by accepting that everything will eventually be taken from us, we can allow loss to be a teacher.

Loss is part of the natural rhythm of life. It is not only normal to grieve, it is necessary to the authentic journey. To deny or run away from loss is to shut the door to authenticity. Embrace it and the door to authenticity opens. We suffer because we are human. No one is immune from loss and subsequent grief. Death is the great equalizer and our common human destiny. If there were one word that captures the essence of passing through the losses in life, it would be "humility" — the awareness that all of life is temporary and that a stronger, more lasting force beyond ourselves is at work in our lives. Humility teaches us that the only constant in the universe is that all things are in the midst of change. Everything is impermanent. Humility invites a reverence for life, an appreciation and a desire to fully be here now. Humility helps me find the simpler, more lasting joys in life. For a person who has taken my share of pleasure in the material world, I am learning from loss and an accompanying connection to an enduring force to find freedom in letting go of my attachment to possessions, to recognize the difference between preferring nice things and needing them. It is precisely this perspective of anguish that gives birth to new consciousness. When we are no longer able to change a situation — whether an incurable disease or the loss of a loved one — we are challenged to look within and, over time, change ourselves. It is within the dark times that we begin to see.

Where were you on September 11, 2001? Like the day that John F. Kennedy was shot, the memory of September 11 is branded into the collective and individual memory. The events of that day marked one of the darkest times ever experienced by Western culture. The murderous scenes, replayed countless times, smothered our innocence and crushed the core of our humanity. Collapsing towers evoked intense feelings, from rage to unfathomable grief, catapulting us into a descent that I had never known to that point in my life. After sitting in front of the television with Val, shocked and dismayed for more than an hour, the crisis soon inspired concern and compassion. The desire to seek others was overpowering. My first impulse, when the waves of shock began to recede, was to call my sister in San Francisco, my daughter in Utah, and my friends in the Boston area. We wept helplessly together. Even the most tragic experiences can bring gifts. On that September day, amidst the tragedy of lives lost and the horror of evil's effects, something greater emerged — the indomitability of the human spirit — courage, kindness, steely determination, and wisdom. Of course we saw it in the fire fighters and emergency workers, but I also saw the effect of the disaster as my twenty-two-year-old spoke with new wisdom and insight. I saw newfound compassion in my family and friends. A yearning to touch others, to express feelings, and to experience deep community surged around me and around the world. What should not and could not be carried alone was shouldered collectively.

Coretta Scott King, the widow of one of history's greatest peacemakers, Martin Luther King, Jr., was asked once if she had any advice for how to get through life's tough times. She replied, "If you look deep enough, you'll find the strength."

During the times following the deaths of both of my parents as well as family and friends whom I have lost, the authentic journey calls me to make room to grieve, to take time away from my busy routine, to slow down, and to share with my community. Indeed, death magnifies our awareness. After a funeral the tendency is to run, to stay busy, to return quickly to the routines of life. In part, during these times it was necessary for me to move forward, but the call was to resist the temptation to escape and to allow the losses to push through like that blade of grass in the hardened sidewalk. I am grateful that I have learned how to feel grief. It has become a friend to my authentic self and allowed me some serenity. When experiencing the excruciating pain and mystery in the midst of loss, I find comfort in the words of the German poet, Rainer Maria Rilke:

> *Be patient toward all that is unsolved in your heart*
> *and try to love the questions themselves like locked rooms*
> *and like books that are written in a very foreign tongue.*
> *Do not now seek the answers, which cannot be given you*
> *because you would not be able to live them.*
> *And the point is, to live everything.*
> *Live the questions now.*
> *Perhaps you will then gradually, without knowing it,*
> *live along some distant day into the answer.*

Authenticity asks us to hold the tension of opposites, grief and gratitude, to embrace living fully while knowing that death and loss are unavoidable. As we open our awareness to both life and death, to both suffering and delight, we step into authenticity — the fullness and joy of life — honoring our complete self, while acting on our priorities with greater clarity and wisdom. We come closer to knowing who we really are and who we are meant to be. There is enlightenment in the old New England adage, "Farm like you'll live forever, and live like you'll die tomorrow." It is only in accepting loss and death that we may truly learn to live. Authenticity invites us, as we accept and face loss, to live life with more richness.

> *I walked a mile with pleasure, She chatted all the way,*
> *But left me none the wiser for all she had to say.*
> *I walked a mile with sorrow, And ne'er a word said she;*
> *But, oh, the things I learned from her when sorrow walked with me.*
> **— Robert Browning Hamilton**

Pain has been the compelling force for many of the great artistic contributions to the world. Beethoven's music was inspired by his pain and introduced a new emotional, dramatic, passionate era of composition. On one occasion, Beethoven was grieving his rejected marriage proposal to Countess Giulietta. He sat at his piano as moonlight beams trickled through the windows of his flat, unable to express his anguish. As happened so often, his music spoke the language of his heart, and he composed "Moonlight Sonata" for his love of the countess.

The recognition that suffering and loss are part of the great impermanence of the universe can cause us, as a wise person once told me, to either become "bitter or better." We have a choice to either remain angry or to open our hearts to the wide spectrum of life. I conclude this section on loss and its role in authentic development with a short parable:

Hasidic Jews have a story about the sorrow tree: on Judgment Day, each person will be invited to hang all of his own miseries on the Tree of Sorrows. Each person will then be permitted to walk about the tree and take a good look at everyone else's miseries in order to select a set he likes better than his own. According to Hasidic legend, each person then freely selects his own personal set of sorrows once again.

* * * *

PRACTICE AUTHENTIC SERVICE

We have no more right to consume happiness without producing it, than to consume wealth without producing it.

— **George Bernard Shaw**

Something I have learned over the years is that if you want success, don't make success your goal. Make service your goal and success will follow. Don't go after money, go after helping others to get what they want, and you will always get what you need. Make it a point to make your contribution bigger than your paycheck.

Getting out of yourself to be of service to others is not an easy campaign. The tentacles of selfishness are insidious and they permeate our Western culture. One evening, a few years ago while I was becoming conscious of my self-centeredness, I was walking down the street and spotted a colleague about a block away. When we met, we spoke to each other for about five minutes and went on our separate ways. About a block further down the street, I was struck by a significant insight. I realized that for the entire ten-minute period from when I had first seen my acquaintance until that very moment, I had been totally preoccupied with myself. For the two to three minutes before we met, all I was thinking about was the knowledgeable things I might say that would make an impact on him. During our five minutes together I was listening to what he had to say only so that I might turn it into an intelligent response. I watched him only so that I might see what effect my remarks were having upon him. And for the two or three minutes after we separated my thoughts were of those things I could have said that might have impressed him even more.

When the light of self-awareness first shines on an old familiar pattern, it can be painful. If I were really honest with myself, I cared more about myself than I did about this person. I was not concerned with what his joys or troubles might be or what I could have said that might have made his life a little less arduous. I cared about him only as a reflection of my own capability and a mirror of my brilliance. I was able to see my self-centeredness as I began reflecting on how it stemmed from fear, emptiness, and loneliness so many times in my life. I once read: "It is the nature of plucked flowers to wither." Living life mired in self-centeredness and without service is living life as a plucked flower, for it is in giving that we receive.

As I reflect upon this story I am aware of how I have matured over the years and how learning to serve has been an integral part of my authentic journey. In contrast to the previous occurrence of self-centeredness is a recent experience I had helping Val with her annual commitment to canvass for the Canadian Diabetes Association. Hayley and I did a stint of door-to-door canvassing together. I discovered, in the process, that our neighbors are very generous. Many spontaneously donated money in significant amounts, stating that they had a personal experience with and thus a special loyalty to the Diabetes Association. As Hayley and I walked home together after our route was completed, we reflected on how good it feels to be a part of the spirit of generosity. We discussed the difference between taking versus doing our share in the world to make our community and our world a better place — the difference between consuming and contributing. I then asked this little nine-year-old philosopher what the difference was between expecting a present at Christmas and performing service like the canvassing. "You never get enough at Christmas," she replied, "but what we did tonight fills your heart — right to the top."

There are many ways that service helps direct me to my calling and thus uncover my authentic self. My predisposition to depression and mood swings requires that I maintain daily structured disciplines to stay centered. For example, I watch carefully what I eat because I know that certain foods fuel depression and instability. I take daily quiet time. I reach out to confidants, I try to get out in nature, and I make time for enjoyable, moderate exercise. Service is one more aspect of my day that is crucial to my mental health and vital to the sustenance of my authentic self. When I get too self-absorbed, I become like a sponge that sits stagnating in the dark cupboard of my mind, like the Dead Sea that only consumes without giving back, thus lacking balance in the sustenance of a healthy ecosystem. Service can lift me out of the darkness of my soul, drain the sponge of self-absorption, and take me into the sunlight of the spirit. No matter how small — a smile, a kind word, an anonymous coin in an expired parking meter, some encouragement to the cashier at the grocery store, or a thank-you card to a colleague —

any service that adds to the quality of another person's life will add to the quality of your authentic self.

In serving others with a sincere desire to offer what you can, your gifts will emerge freely and effortlessly. For in giving to others, your soul is required to bring forth what is needed, and what is needed in the response to help another is inevitably needed for your own soul. I can't tell you how many times I have offered suggestions to a friend in need and am strengthened by hearing my own suggestions and realizing they can help solve one of my own problems. Service helps you access inner wisdom.

Once again, a word of caution is necessary when practicing authentic service. Like all spiritual practices, service has its dark side. From my own experience with burnout, I know that service must come *from* a sustaining center, rather than *to* a sustaining center. Be careful that you do not define yourself by the service you render. Service with no expectations will not tire you on the inside. You will serve from overflow rather than emptiness. In my early years as a therapist, my burnout stemmed partly from my identification with my role of helping. With no sustaining center from which to serve, I took on the problems of my clients. Unknowingly, I *needed* my clients to get better in order to feel worthwhile as a therapist. I was giving, but underneath my giving was a hidden agenda for the affirmation of my worth. This kind of service becomes exhausting because it does not come from love. It comes from unacknowledged neediness. It is filled with unconscious resentment and guilt. When giving is done out of neediness, conditions are attached, disappointments set in, and resentments are fueled.

When service comes from a sustaining center, it is energizing because you are detached from the outcome of the service. You will receive fulfillment by the act alone. You will find that giving and receiving are integrated, not separate. Service from a spiritual perspective always awakens you because you are using your gifts and take no responsibility for others changing or being different as a result. You let go of outcomes and simply "show up" as best you can, no matter how large or small your contribution. You give to live, rather than give to gain.

* * * *

BEWARE THE PITFALLS:
DISCERNING AND RESPONDING

Our lives begin to end the day we become silent about things that matter.
— *Martin Luther King, Jr.*

Callings can be spawned by a life-changing event or by a quiet knowing from within. They come in many forms and range from the subtle, when you sense within you that something in your life needs changing, to the dramatic, when the death of a loved one, an encounter with a life-threatening illness, or hitting the bottom of an addiction spurs you to action. Callings can be sudden or can evolve over a period of years. I know many people who attribute their fulfilling life today to being laid off years before. I also know a person who, while attending university, awoke in the middle of the night and knew he was meant to change the direction of his education. You can be conscious of the call and know a clear message has come to you, or you may be unaware for a while that your life is being gently pulled in a new direction. And there are many responses to choose from to answer the call. You can surrender completely, let go, and see where the current will take you, or you can fight it all the way, kicking and screaming.

I have increasing respect for the variety of calls that come to people, and I acknowledge how difficult it is to listen, discern, and act on the call, especially because our society seems set on dictating to us how we should be. "Is this a call or is it an obsession?" "Is this the voice of God or is it merely an emotional response?" "Is this my will or is it truly a voice from beyond me?" These are all questions I have wrestled with and usually can't answer at the moment they occur. But when I trust myself and give myself the freedom not to be in a hurry, clarity inevitably comes.

We have discussed thus far some of the clues for listening for and seeking your calling — slowing down, making room for quietness on a daily basis in order to turn off the voices of the culture and tune in to the voice within, starting small, reflecting upon your gifts, being informed by your passion, listening to loss, and practicing authentic service. Now let's turn our attention to responding to the call. Are there universal guidelines that will help you discern whether the call you receive is genuine or merely fabricated in your own mind, and just what do you do when you become conscious of being called?

Often a strong emotional impulse can leave you wondering if it is an authentic call or just another obsession. Although paying attention to feelings is important, emotions are generally not a reliable barometer with which to make life decisions. Often, during a crisis, our emotions want to take us to new places, but this is not necessarily a call. Distinguishing a call from an obsession or deciphering a call from an escape mechanism in a crisis is not always easy. Although there is no foolproof formula, there are a few guidelines for discerning the authenticity of a call. In order for a call to be authentic, it must meet at least three criteria.

First, if you are truly being called, your calling will take you further into responsibility, not away from it. If you wake up one night and feel "called" to leave your wife and five children and move in with a woman twenty years younger, this would likely be an escape from reality, not a call. Just because you desire something doesn't make it a calling.

Second, a calling will always require service. If you feel "called" to climb a mountain or train for a challenging athletic event, it may be a passion or a dream, but it is not an authentic calling until you can somehow use your experience to serve, support, or inspire others.

Finally, a calling must stand the test of time. If you feel you are called, ask yourself if it would still be right a week from now, a year from now, a decade from now. If you feel called to do something, give it a little time. Let it gel. You don't have to jump right in to a calling. The adage that "anything worth doing is worth doing slowly" is an important one here. Take your time. If it is a calling, it will persist. If it fades in a few days, it was not a calling but a whim.

It is important to realize that callings change and evolve over time. Be open for callings that ask for a change of direction. What is termed a midlife crisis is often a time of vocational change, when we are called to revitalization and resurrection. This is a call to a new level of authenticity and it may require a radical shift in activities and focus. Most people experience some kind of change at midlife, usually starting with pain or discomfort or fear. These changes can come when a relationship we are in puts new demands on us, when we lose a job, when our children gain more independence and need us less, when an illness or death strikes, or when a relationship ends. These painful experiences are very often wake-up calls, beckoning us to new opportunities for growth. Midlife is a time for letting go of the once useful but old patterns of who we think we are and making room for the authentic persons we are now meant to be. Challenge lies in front of us and we can either go back to sleep in the comfortable warmth of a familiar bed or put our feet on the floor in anticipation of a new adventure.

Here are four actual examples of some of the ways people respond to a call at midlife:

- A colleague I worked with many years ago received a call to leave her profession and become a nun when she was in her forties. She sold everything, became a Catholic, and entered a convent.

- A client, a successful entrepreneur, sold his business at the age of forty-two and began coaching other CEOs to find a quality of life they were missing.

- A friend, at the age of fifty-five, let go of the ranch he had owned and developed for more than thirty years and started a consulting business mentoring other ranchers, passing on what he had learned during the course of his lifetime. While he still lived and worked on the ranch, he turned over ownership and leadership to his adult children, using the family business as a tool for building what mattered most in his life rather than as a rigid definition of himself.

- A participant in one of our programs decided that it was authentic *not* to leave his job, but instead, commit to doing his job in a more authentic way. He took a careful inventory of the kind of work he would love doing, and had a courageous conversation with his boss about how he could move toward creating his "ideal job" in his current position.

These moves came from authentic awakenings. Each individual grew beyond their attachment to the material world — their need for external approval or security. Each one was wise enough to know it was time to heed the call to express another aspect of themselves. During the first half of life we tend to be consumed with the physical aspect of our existence, the need to be a part of the culture, to fit in, to make a living. The second half awakens us to the spiritual aspect of ourselves. The more we resist the call, the more the sometimes painful crisis of midlife is prolonged. When a call is refused, the crisis cannot be resolved and the human soul progressively deteriorates.

So just what do you do when you get a "call?" There is not much you can do, except trust and resist the temptation to either ignore the call for too long, escape, or take too much immediate action. Go slowly. "Direction is more important than velocity" is an important axiom, especially in the early stages of sensing a call. A good friend of mine has discovered in recent years that she is a gifted writer. She has listened to her still, small voice and enrolled in a creative writing class. She doesn't need to quit her job or attempt to publish her work yet. She just needs to write, whether it is thirty minutes a day or every Sunday morning. Then she needs to start sharing her writing with the world. To ignore this inner call would suffocate her authentic self, deaden her spirit, and put her health at risk.

When called, expect to feel at least one or more of these responses: fear, grandiosity, or emptiness.

Fear will accompany most callings. After all, the very nature of being called to something seems to involve simultaneously being called away from the mainstream. If, for example, you feel called to enter a path different from the one you or others have come to expect, a path that takes you in a different direction from what you or others have anticipated, you may face some rejection or resistance from both yourself and others. If you are called to follow your creative urges, you will feel some aloneness. All kinds of fears will naturally accompany a calling, for your calling implies stepping into the unknown without a road map. Calling does not necessarily entail following a well-marked trail, but instead making your own tracks and leaving a path behind you. When it comes to facing fear, the truly brave are not people without fear, but rather are those able to find a way to face and let go of their fears. Even though it helps tremendously to find at least one person who believes in you, don't expect the support of the world. Remember, in the end, the most important person to believe in you has to be yourself.

The second response, grandiosity, can occur when you receive a call and have a sense of being special — that you are being called to something unique because of the distinctive gifts you possess. You might even come up with a long list of impressive visions to tell the world how grand you are. But the truth is that when you are called, it is not because you are great or extraordinary, but simply because you can give of yourself to the world in some way or perhaps simply live a life of greater depth and meaning. A calling never fully defines you. It simply identifies an opportunity to offer something to society. Authenticity asks you to resist the seductive tendency to allow your call to define the entire meaning of your life. The result of my calling to authentic, spiritual work has been to move me toward a more reflective, gentle, and intentional life. I spend more time with my kids. I am more grounded and balanced. I play a little more. I am more alive and at peace with myself. Grace finds me more often. And I know that I am just one person on this planet of more than six billion, but I am one, and my unique contribution makes a difference. I am not any more special than anyone else, for we are all called, in our own authentic way, to our own unique contribution. Just as I am learning to resist the human tendency to escape from the fear, so, too, am I learning to resist the same inclination to grandiosity.

Also, a sense of emptiness can occur if we feel we are not called. However, we are always called, in one way or another. We might go through winters, periods of drought or of emptiness, when the force of our calling seems to weaken or even evaporate altogether. These periods may last for days or even years. I have learned to trust myself, to flow with these periods, and know that even when my calling is dormant, it remains alive. It just needs time to germinate from the inside. It seems that every five to seven years, my business takes a downturn, the bookings for teaching and speaking engagements diminish, and I have extra space for more reflection, study and writing. I have learned to trust during these periods and to resist the temptation to get anxious. They are vital resting periods in my growth.

Finally, we must resist the temptation to compare ourselves to others. Everyone receives a calling in his or her own way and at his or her own time in life. I have had calls that were direct and sudden, but mostly my calls have been subtle, gradual sensings, rather than clear voices. The ebb and flow of a calling is part of the journey. Sometimes I will feel in the flow. I will feel guided and carried. And then, suddenly, it will be gone. I am learning to trust both the emptiness and the aliveness and realize that all of it is necessary. As I become more trusting, I don't judge it so much. It is great to feel the flow, to feel called, and it is equally important to have times of silence, when we are invited to simply enjoy life for a while without the intensity of having to *do* anything. Sometimes we are called simply to be patient and enjoy the journey.

* * * *

SEEKING THE CALLER

Calling implies a relationship. If one is called, something or someone must be doing the calling. This expression of "the caller" comes in many forms. Some describe "the caller" as a deeper part of their being, their soul, or their "inner voice." Many begin merely by noticing that there is incongruity between what the world is supplying and what their soul is yearning for. The uneasiness within them is, in itself, a call from a more substantive part of themselves beneath their usual awareness. This relationship between the called and the caller is a very personal one, one which I cannot prescribe or judge.

I have come to a perception of "the caller" as my Creator, or God, for whom I am prepared to search and with whom I seek to develop a personal relationship. I find sustaining peace in having

God at the center of my life, and in this work of calling, I find both strength and solace in reaching for God to give me direction. I have wrestled much of my life with "calling." "What am I meant to do? Why am I here? What is my purpose?" These questions created never-ending anxiety until I came to believe that there was a power, a creative life force, a personal and compassionate source greater than myself which could direct me, guide me, and bring me "home." Seeking a higher power in my life through spiritual practice frees me to trust more and let go of my obsessive need for clarity.

Many people are living their calling without knowing that they are responding to it. If asked, they might describe themselves as simply being "on track." I know a stay-at-home mother, for example, who is completely assured and at peace with herself. This is where she is meant to be at this time in her life, and yet she was not consciously aware of any "calling" until I posed it as a possibility. "Yes," she exclaimed rather matter-of-factly, "I guess you could say that I have been 'called' to be a mother. This is where I am needed and what my passion is at the moment. I am not doing this 'for God' or even for my soul. I just can't possibly fathom doing anything else right now." This woman is a fine mother, fulfilled in her task of raising children. On sabbatical from her career as a health care administrator until her children are in school, she unknowingly listened and responded to her call at this stage in her life.

Opening, seeking, and staying conscious of a connection to the caller keeps me centered. It keeps me engaged with and detached from the other calls I get in life at the same time, by keeping me from identifying too closely with the call. I have been excavating my calling all my life but without a caller to relate to, my calling was too narrow. My search was limited because I was looking solely to my work and my roles for fulfillment. I am learning that my calling is entwined into a mosaic of a life that is much bigger than a career. How I live is just as vital as how I define myself by the contribution

I make through my work. A calling goes beyond any career or role we assign ourselves.

The promise of a calling is that it gives us a deep strength and solid foundation below the surface of this frantic and fragmented world. It provides a sense of continuity and consistency and helps us stay focused in the midst of the chaos. It brings clarity to what needs renouncing in the midst of the pace and the pressures. Clarity about my calling enables me to sit quietly in the face of the urgent pressures and make decisions in line with my calling to be a better father or husband. Knowing that I am called to show up in the daily responsibilities of life helps me turn away from distractions when I need to be focused on my loved ones. Calling is our compass in life, a constant motif running through the fabric of our existence. A calling helps us to finish well. A calling is a *yes* to our authentic self, to something important, and a *no* to the frenzied demands of the world.

* * * *

CHAPTER 5

—— ⚭ ——

The Challenge

Our doubts are traitors,
and make us lose the good we oft might win,
by fearing to attempt.
— Shakespeare

* * * *

I WANT TO LEAVE YOU with three challenges one faces when embarking on the journey of authenticity: the challenge to sustain a quietness of heart amidst the chaos of life, the challenge to separate your worth from your successes and your failures, and the challenge to stay on track amidst the distractions that pull you away from what matters most. Along with these challenges to remain authentic in the face of the world's demands, I offer some practical strategies to respond to these challenges by developing and sustaining a spiritual practice.

* * * *

SUSTAINING QUIETNESS OF HEART

It is better to light a candle than to curse the darkness.

— The Christophers

We live in unsettled times. As I pick up the morning newspaper, I wonder, "What will be in the headlines today? Another terrorist attack? Another shooting in a school? A new epidemic of a virus without a known cause? Which war will be featured on the front page?" I look around and see so many people struggling with meaning and questioning what is holding us together. Fragmented lives seem to be so common.

At times, I begin to believe that we have entered into another dark age. I can easily pick up despair over the seemingly inevitable devastation of our planet through rapid climate change, the fear of the release of weapons of mass destruction, or the violence and alienation in modern-day human relationships. On some days, we may be inclined to anesthetize ourselves to life's experience, allowing the deadness to further our separation and inner anguish.

The disciples of a Hasidic rabbi approached their spiritual leader with a complaint about the prevalence of evil in the world. Intent upon driving out the forces of iniquity and darkness, they requested that the rabbi counsel them. The rabbi's response was one that can help us all to come to grips with the malevolent forces of darkness that, at times, seem to surround our world. The rabbi suggested to his students that they take brooms, go down to the basement, and attempt to sweep the darkness from the cellar. The bewildered disciples applied themselves to sweeping out the darkness, but to no avail. The rabbi then advised them to take sticks and beat vigorously at the darkness to drive out the evil. When this likewise failed, he counseled them to go down to the cellar once again and to protest against the evil. When this failed as well, he said, "My students, let each of you meet the challenge of darkness by lighting a lamp." The disciples descended to the cellar and kindled their lights. They looked, and behold! The darkness had been driven out.

There are times in our lives when the world seems filled with darkness. No one is immune from tragedy, loss, failure, rejection or fear. Being human means we are sometimes touched by pain and uncertainty. No defense is strong enough to give us immunity to the unpredictability of life.

As we attempt to sweep out the shadows and beat at the darkness that besets us, it is easy to forget that the most powerful way of combating darkness is through the principle of light. We meet the challenge of darkness when we bring light to the world by bringing our unique presence to whatever we do — by being fully and authentically ourselves. Serenity begins when we put our energy into that which is changeable and when we accept and let go of that which is not. Our inner peace allows us to act in the world in a good way. Today I am more afraid of spirit-unrest, soul disturbance, and *internal* wars than I am of terrorism or sickness or wars on the planet. When I am calm in spirit, my inner light can guide me gently through the darkness. Without inner strength, I am lost.

When my inner flame is burning brightly and my spirit is centered, I can pick up a newspaper and know that what I read on the front page is a very tiny piece of all that is happening in the world, a tiny drop in the ocean of the human experience. There are so many possibilities and the challenge is to not become limited by my way of thinking. As you find your own truth, the universe will open a door for you that is so wide you cannot help but step through it into new life.

* * * *

SEPARATING YOUR WORTH
FROM YOUR SUCCESSES AND FAILURES

All success and failure are imposters.

— Rudyard Kipling

The postmodern era is the age of "more." We thrive on more wealth, more material goods, more speed, more technology, and more intense experiences. In our passion to possess and to achieve, we have accelerated the pace of contemporary culture to a point where we have become splintered and disjointed. We feel stressed, rushed, and out of breath. When I reflect on the rat race we seem to be in these days, the words of Lily Tomlin come to mind, "Remember, even if you win the rat race, at the end, you are still a rat."

Deep authentic satisfaction and contentment do not come from your ability to accumulate possessions or to achieve. The authentic journey is not about becoming more successful, if you define success by the world's standards. Rather it is about becoming a whole, integrated and more fully developed person who can encounter the entire spectrum of the human experience and possess peace of mind and then brighten the world more fully by your presence. It's about showing up for the journey. It is about letting go of defining life by externals. Achievements and failures are merely tools for becoming more fully human, for moving closer to authenticity. Success and failure are means to an end, not the end in and of themselves. It is much better to live a humble life unimpeded by grief and fear than to live affluently plagued with worry, anxiety, doubt and unbridled desire. The good life is a life of inner serenity, whether you are successful or unsuccessful, rich or poor. The good life comes when you tune in to the clues that will guide you to the person you are meant to be and you have the courage to be more of who you are destined to be.

STAYING ON TRACK

In the midst of all the darkness, there has been a surge of spiritual awakening. Walk into any bookstore or go online and you will find a proliferation of spiritual literature. Never has there been a greater explosion of information about spirituality. Now, as never before, we have access to all major religions in every major city. Buddhist monasteries, Christian churches, synagogues and mosques are opening their doors to those seeking solace and reflection in our fast-paced, stressful and uncertain society. Never have the teachings or the paths to awakening been so abundant. Never have the century-old teachings of the East and West — from Christianity, Judaism, Buddhism, and Sufism, to Chassid, Hinduism, Muslim and Native American — been so accessible and so sought after.

Despite the rise in spiritual interest, many in the postmodern population view traditional religion as having let them down. We now have millions of people who have reached adulthood without a faith-based practice, while at the same time they yearn for something to sustain them. In their search for alternatives, many today are asking, "What do I do?" "Where do I go?" "How do I do this?" And thus, their quest for spiritual awakening begins.

FOCUS ON ACTIONS

It is good to read about authenticity, to reflect upon your life, to shift your consciousness through new awareness. But to actually live authentically you must ultimately move beyond analysis into action.

After a large dinner at one of England's stately mansions, a famous actor entertained the guests with stunning Shakespearean recitations. Then, as an encore, he offered to accept a request.

A shy, gray-haired priest asked if the actor knew the twenty-third psalm.

The actor replied, "Yes, I do, and I will give it on one condition: that when I am finished, you recite the very same psalm."

The priest was a little embarrassed, but consented.

The actor did a magnificent rendition and the guests applauded loudly when he was done. The priest got up and recited the same words; this time there was no applause, just a hushed silence and the beginning of tears in some eyes.

The actor savored the silence for a few moments; then he stood up and said, "Ladies and gentlemen, I hope you realize what happened here tonight. I knew the psalm, but this man knows the Shepherd."

Just as you cannot know the Shepherd by a rendition of the Psalms, so you cannot know authenticity through reading a book about it. Knowing takes a daily practice.

BE A SEEKER, NOT A DRIFTER

Seekers look both without and within. Seekers understand that everything they learn they already know. Seekers trust their own inner guide and exercise careful discernment when conversing and learning. Seekers have a passion for continuous learning, yet, paradoxically, know that all wisdom and happiness come from within.

Drifters, on the other hand, manifest themselves in two forms. A drifter can be a person who floats aimlessly through life like a cork on the open sea, swept along helplessly by the currents of life. A drifter can also be a person who keeps looking for the next solution, the next quick fix, or the next fast-acting insight to rescue him from the discomfort of uncertainty. On this human journey there is a natural tendency to look outside of ourselves for understanding and happiness. We may find ourselves longing for an ideal future or seeking easy comfort to protect ourselves. It is hard to accept that there is no cure for living. Searching endlessly for quick fixes and easy answers gives us temporary relief from our pain and offers fleeting distraction, but it doesn't provide sustaining strength and results in perpetual restlessness and unsettledness. As we drift from teacher to teacher, from book to book, or from philosophy to philosophy, undoubtedly a residue of growth will be left behind, but be careful on your road that you are not seduced by temporary, self-serving, "fast food" solutions promising an easy road to salvation.

FIND A PATH THAT WILL GUIDE YOU TO YOUR OWN TRUTH

A rabbi taught his followers always to seek the answers from within themselves. But his followers always came back expecting more answers from him.

Finally, the rabbi set up a booth with this sign: "Any Two Questions Answered for $100."

After some deliberation, one of his richest followers approached the booth with two important questions. He paid the money and asked, "Isn't $100 rather costly for just two questions?"

"Yes," said the rabbi, "and what is your second question?"

The fundamental message of every great spiritual teacher is that we must eventually stop modeling ourselves after another person, or even emulating our spiritual teachers no matter how much we admire them, and begin to see through our own eyes. Trust your deep inner knowing and follow a path that is right for *you*.

It is vital, regardless of the path you choose, that it be one that helps you find your own way, helps you listen to your own inner guide, brings you back to your authentic self, and strengthens your sense of self, rather than one that demands obedience or conformity to a human structure. Great spiritual teachers do not introduce new moralities, but rather remind you of what you already know. People need to be *reminded* more often than they need to be *instructed*.

FIND A PRACTICE THAT WILL HELP YOU OVERCOME SELF-CENTEREDNESS

We do not find authenticity by simply going out and meditating on a mountain or reading a book or sitting in church. We find it in everything we do in the world: reaching out to a child, putting our needs aside momentarily for an aging parent, or courageously bringing our highest aspirations in the service of others. Each of these is an action of the spirit. In my view, unless your spiritual practice contributes to the betterment of the world, it cannot be called authentic.

An act of service can be a mere smile, writing a thank-you letter, offering kindness, listening when inclined to leave, or respecting when inclined to judge — these are the little things that are the big things in living a full life. Sanctity grows in an environment of compassion. An authentic, spiritual practice must hold us accountable to look beyond ourselves, to do what we can when we can. Authenticity, like spirituality, is defined by one's actions.

ONCE YOU FIND A PATH AND A PRACTICE THAT IS RIGHT FOR YOU, STICK TO IT

There is no standard map to authenticity. While we might initially explore several traditions and practices, in the end we must choose an honorable practice, a sturdy vessel to carry us on this journey, and stay on it with our whole heart. By "sticking with it," I do not mean to imply that your needs will not change or that you should rigidly adhere to one form of dogma for the remainder of your days. What I do mean is that it takes years of study and practice to root ourselves firmly in any one of the many traditions offered that our hearts are led to. What matters is the authenticity that we bring to the way we have chosen, a determination and a willingness to stay with it and see what opens within us.

There is an art to acting from a place of wisdom rather than from a place of habit, to creating a life of broader design rather than default, to discovering light amid the darkness, healing amid the pain, and calmness amid the chaos. Like any other art, this path of authenticity requires a daily practice of discipline. If you want your new insights to become sustained change, you eventually have to alter your course and make the journey a daily practice. Flitting from one religion to another or continually changing philosophies and approaches does not give you an opportunity to secure yourself firmly with the roots necessary to weather the storms of modern-day life. It is like pulling up the roots of a young sapling every time it breaks ground and reaches upward.

BE GENTLE WITH YOURSELF

Living life authentically, with strong character and a desire to center our lives on correct principles, listening carefully to our call, and creating a sustaining community, isn't easy. It isn't a quick fix. But it is possible. It begins with a decision, today, to take one thing we have learned from this book and respond to it with some action. By taking the journey of authenticity, we become a gardener of our soul. Gardening the soul, like gardening a flowerbed, is much less about controlling and manipulating and much more about tilling and trusting. Authentic living is meant to be a gentle process of learning and letting go of our mistakes from yesterday, forgiving ourselves and others for being human, starting anew each day, and trusting that a power greater than ourselves is carrying us.

It requires being both patient and persistent. Consider the miracle of the Chinese bamboo tree. When the seed of this amazing tree is planted, you see nothing, absolutely nothing, for four years, other than a tiny shoot coming out of the bulb. During those four years, all the growth is underground in the massive, fibrous root structure that spreads deep and wide in the earth. But then in the fifth year the Chinese bamboo tree shoots up to eighty feet! An authentic journey is like that. So much of the work, particularly in the early stages, is done beneath the world's, and even your own, awareness. Trust the process. Practice patience.

If you have truly committed to follow your heart, there exists beyond you and beyond your own will a powerful force that helps guide you along the way, that cultivates your growth. Unseen hands guide your journey with infinitely greater accuracy and power than is conceivably possible through your unaided will, enabling you to relax as you take your foot off the gas and begin to let life happen rather than working so hard to make it happen. Our Creator is the source of all of the principles I have passed along in this book and the source of our conscience.

The key to unlocking the freedom that allows this to happen is to "let go and let God," or as Antonio Machado poetically states:

> *Last night, as I was sleeping,*
> *I dreamt...*
> *that I had a beehive*
> *here inside my heart.*
> *And the golden bees*
> *were making white combs*
> *and sweet honey*
> *from my old failures.*

As we persist on the authentic path, the new consciousness gradually becomes the new familiar. Perhaps Emerson said it best, "That which we persist in doing becomes easier — not that the nature of the task has changed, but our ability to do it has increased." To the degree that you live by a renewed and inspired conscience, you will grow to fulfill your truest nature.

With newfound awareness and new choices comes assurance. There are no guarantees for an easier life or a life with less pain or uncertainty or fewer challenges or even a more successful life (at least by the world's standards). Authenticity is not a panacea for all that troubles you or a snake oil for all your grievances or ailments. The promise of authenticity is that you will have a commitment to stop the denial, to be available to go beyond the blindness to what is really going on within and around you. You will be a more whole, unified, and fulfilled person. This commitment to be open and to learn brings you more fully to the life you were meant to live and has its own reward — the inner calm in the storm, the inner strength that surpasses all understanding or human challenge, and the self-respect and peace that comes from living your life in alignment with your deepest, truest nature, regardless of the external environment or outcomes. We begin to understand that the presence of light is not the result of darkness ending, but of bringing light to the darkness. Peace is found not in the absence of difficulties, but in our ability to embrace the challenge of living fully without judgment or resistance and with new perceptions and resources. We discover the healing power beyond ourselves as we stand courageously and compassionately in this moment, knowing that we are not alone.

On the voyage, you will inevitably encounter one or more extreme ordeals. These are tests of your commitment to the direction you have taken. They provide opportunities for spiritual growth and breaking through personal limitations. Once these tests are completed, you will be a more authentic person with greater substance, character, and inner trust.

When we are in contact with our spiritual nature, our emptiness, and our humility, we exert an enormous attraction to other human beings. There is a compelling magnetism in that state of being that I call an "authentic presence." It is beautiful. And when others are in that same space or entering it, they resonate or connect with us and immediately doors open to us. This is not strange or mystical. It is part of the natural order.

This state is available to all of us. It is waiting for each of us. It is the greatest of human treasures. Achieving unity — oneness — first with ourselves and then with others in our lives is the highest and most delightful fruit of authenticity. Most of us have tasted this fruit of true unity from time to time, just as we have tasted the bitter, lonely fruit of inauthentic living. We know how fragile unity is. But after a time, we will realize that we are standing firm on a brand-new foundation. We have searched thoroughly down the dark crevasse of self-deception. We have looked at our lives painstakingly with both prudence and compassion and are content.

My friend Walter described spending the last days with his dying brother as both "unbearable *and* beautiful." The journey to authenticity is the same — a delicate balance between light and dark encompasses the whole spectrum of the mystery of life. It begins with the "barren desert," the awareness of an inauthentic life. Old ways of being, emotional patterns, and choices no longer fit. A time for passing into a new beginning is at hand. The call to adventure comes in many ways both subtle and explicit. It is the call to service, to giving your life over to something larger than yourself, the call to become what you are meant to become — the call to achieve your essential blueprint.

Some who are called to the adventure choose to run away from it. Others may grapple for years with fear and denial until they can face, and move through, the anxiety with courage. I once denied my own destiny out of insecurity and the dread of rejection. But I now know that cooperating with fate brings personal power, freedom, and responsibility. By engaging in our destiny, we surrender to the design of the universe, which speaks through our inner personal code. Refusing the call means continued restlessness.

And then, as if from nowhere, a guide appears: an event, a voice from within, or someone to help us over the threshold. When we say yes to the call, we begin the adventure. At this moment of decision, Buber says, "And even this is not what we 'ought to' do: rather... we cannot do otherwise. There is a point where our freedom and destiny merge. Here I stand. I can do no other."

So, I end this book, which is really just another chapter in my own authentic journey, with the Law of the Echo: it came to me from my friend, Ian West, an authentic leader and CEO of a long-term care facility. The Law of the Echo states that whatever you give to the universe, you will get back. Mahatma Gandhi inspired this law when he said, "Be the change you expect in the world." In other words, if you want more love in a relationship, be more loving. If you want more respect from someone, be more respectful. If you want more value from your life or your work, then bring more value to those you serve. If you want more peace in the world, then bring peace to the world. If you bring light to the world, the world will return light to you.

As idyllic as the Law of the Echo sounds, I must remind you that it doesn't guarantee the results you might expect. One day, as I left a stimulating and uplifting conversation with a friend, peace and tranquility surrounded me. I was radiating good energy and wanted to experiment to see if I could transfer this inner goodness I was feeling on to the rest of the world. I wanted to see if I could create a peaceful society wherever I went, just for one day. I thought I was doing pretty well, waving at drivers as I slowed down to let them into my lane. They waved back. The Law of the Echo was manifesting itself before my very eyes! That is, until one driver pulled up beside me and angrily made a rude gesture before squealing his tires and spewing rocks as he drove off.

This was a good lesson for me on two fronts. First, living authentically requires that we let go of expectations. Authentic living is not about manipulating people into responding in a way that will meet your needs, but instead it is about having the courage to live your life and let others live theirs. Second, sometimes we just have to resume our course of action and stay centered. Rather than trying so hard to change the world, some days the best you can do is to prevent the world from changing you.

Closely aligned with the Law of the Echo is the story of a Native American grandfather who was talking to his grandson about how he felt about a tragedy. He said, "I feel as if I have two wolves fighting in my heart. One wolf is the vengeful, angry one. The other wolf is the loving, compassionate one." The grandson asked him, "Which wolf will win the fight in your heart?" The grandfather answered, "The one I feed."

Keep feeding within you what you most want around you. What you give will come back to you eventually, but not always in your time frame. People are like stained glass windows. They radiate beauty when the sun is out, but when darkness comes, their true magnificence is revealed only if there is a light from within.

It is my belief that we — you as reader and I as the author — have come together by some kind of divine appointment. In every relationship you take a little bit of me from me and I take a little bit of you from you, and in the end, we are both better off. I hope the perspective and insights I have passed along in this book have inspired and supported you to embark more freely and courageously on the journey of living the life you are meant to live. My intention is that by encouraging each other on this transformational voyage, we can continue, together, to make this world a little more civil, human, and serene. No work is more important than the call to bring our own light to this planet. No journey demands more from us than the courage to be authentic in a world that expects, night and day, that we fit in. No expedition requires more from us than the journey to be true to our heart. It hurts a little less — and fulfills us a great deal more — when we know that we are not alone.

May we each find life's most precious presents along the path, and may each of our lives continue to amplify the voices and forces of peace in the world.

* * * *

Appendix

Exercises for Further Reflection and Action

* * * *

FOR THOSE WHO ARE COMMITTED to continuing the journey to authenticity, I have included some suggestions for further reflections and action in each of the key components of authenticity:

* * * *

MY JOURNEY

Take some time to reflect on your own story. Then ask yourself some questions:

- Where are there parallels between the author's experiences and my own?

- What ways do I use to escape from the reality of my life? What are the consequences of these choices?

- What does my soul desire?

- When have I given up my voice in an effort to comply with the expectations of others?

- What is the truth about my life?

- When have I gone astray from my authentic self in order to meet the expectations of this culture?

- What am I being called to do now?

* * * *

FINDING CENTER

- Notice the ways that you use noise and/or activity to drown out the whisper of your inner life and the vital connections in your life.

- Ask yourself, "What can I take out of my day today to make room for what matters most — my authentic self?"

- Reflect upon the actions you could take today to begin to have more quiet in your life, to be away from excessive noise and/or frantic busyness.

- Practice mindfulness, that is, being mindful of what is around you in each moment.

- Take time for prayer or meditation, time to go within.

- Think about a good time each day to begin a habit of daily reflection. What amount of time would fit into your nature, your schedule, and your current demands? Thirty minutes might be too long at first. How about twenty or even ten?

- Think about who might support you in this endeavor. Do you have a prayer group at a church? Do you have a spiritual advisor who could help you get started? Is a class on meditation offered in your community?

- Make a decision to get started, just for today, and maybe just for ten minutes. Turn off the TV and the radio and the computer. Unplug the phone. Sit. Take a deep breath. Practice being with yourself. Notice the discomfort that surfaces. Stay with it and know that it will get easier.

- Create a sanctuary in your world — a place you go to find refuge from the demands of the world, to pray, listen to your own inner wisdom, meditate, or simply relax. Being with a confidant can be a sanctuary, but sometimes a sanctuary is a specific place where you can be alone. And sometimes a sanctuary is simply a reverent place within you that you retreat to.

- Think about where a place for a sanctuary (where you can withdraw from the world's demands) would be in your home. What would your criteria be for this sanctuary? Would it be outdoors or indoors? What unique items would you want in your sanctuary (e.g., books, pictures, religious objects, mementos — reminders that will help bring you back to yourself)? Take time to work up a plan for creating or sustaining a place you call a sanctuary.

- Reflect on the roles that you have in your life and the methods you use to remind yourself that your roles are not the totality of who you are, that there is a deeper, authentic person that lives below the surface of your roles.

- What rituals are meaningful to you? Reflect on the meaning they have for you. Can you be more mindful of using these rituals to connect with your authentic self?

- Reflect on ways you can use these rituals to discover something important about yourself, to see more deeply who you are and how you operate, and on that basis begin to refine yourself through more conscious actions.

- If you feel the need, create new rituals that reflect the answers to: "What places in my life germinate authenticity?" "What kind of music stirs me?" "What kind of landscape brings me back to myself?" "What authentic place or activity awakens me and sustains me?"

- Where do you find your inspiration?

- Take some time to reflect on what gave you roots. Go through old family photographs and ask yourself: "What are my earliest memories?" "Who influenced my early life?" "What are their traditions and beliefs?" "What were some of the traditions and beliefs that were instilled in me at an early age?" "What beliefs have been useful, but are now outdated and need to be discarded, and what beliefs need renewing and sustaining?"

- As you go about your day, be mindful of a "still, small voice" within you that is guiding you, leading you in the direction you are meant to go. Start to notice that synchronicity is a way of life, not a series of random accidents.

- Whenever you are called upon to make a decision, pause for a moment and ask for help in your decision making. Then, have the courage to do as you are prompted to do. Remember, it has taken years of practice to diminish this inner whisper, so be patient with yourself. You will, like any student, make mistakes as you distinguish between your emotions and your deeper inner guide.

- Practice following your intuition in small ways, such as going into a used book store or library and asking your inner guide for assistance in finding a book that you need for a specific concern in your life. Or, ask your inner guide for support in finding a teacher for a specific challenge you are facing. Keep an open mind and have some fun.

- Don't go to bed angry. Carrying resentment or any high emotional state is like turning on your radio with the antenna down. There is just too much interference to make a connection with your intuition.

- Watch what you take into your body. When used to escape the discomfort of life, certain substances, like alcohol, caffeine, and certain foods or drugs, will insulate you from a connection to your inner guide.

- Learn to trust your body. The body knows. The ability to listen to your body is something we are equipped to do, but like a muscle, if we don't use it or otherwise do something to develop it, it will atrophy. The body will tell us all we need to know, just not always what we want to hear. Herein lies the difference between "hearing" and "listening."

- The next time you get a headache or pain of any kind, regardless of the remedy you may choose to alleviate the pain, don't forget to take the time to also ask yourself, "What is this pain trying to tell me?"

- The next time you have an "accident" (e.g., you cut yourself chopping a salad or you trip over a crack in the sidewalk and scrape a knee), take some time to reflect, "Is this just a random mishap, or do I need to learn something from this?"

- Take some time each day for quietness, just to notice your body. Where do you carry tension? In your shoulders? Your stomach? Your back? What parts of your body are more relaxed than others? Have you ever stopped and appreciated your heart? Your lungs? Your internal organs? Your legs? Your fingers? Like so many of the relationships in life, it seems easier to judge our body than to value it.

- Ask yourself, "What is soothing to my body?" Take time on a regular basis to do something nurturing for your body like you would for a good friend.

- Make time for silence in your day. Turn off the radio or the CD in your car every once in a while. Practice driving in silence. Practice coming home at the end of the day and sitting still for a few moments before turning on the television or engaging in the busyness of an evening routine. If you have loved ones in your life that require your attention as soon as you walk in the door, stop the car a few blocks from home or spend five minutes in a park. Allow yourself to be with yourself.

- Step back and get some perspective on yourself. It is necessary to continually challenge motives and choices. Take a good hard inventory of yourself. Muster the courage to ask yourself which human hungers you struggle with. What is the level of manageability in your life regarding these areas?

- Open up with a confidant or with a trusted friend. Remember that you are not alone. Create a community around you that will support you and hold you accountable to face the truth about yourself honestly and to make some of the tough changes in your life.

- If you need more support in the manageability of human hungers, join a recovery group. Twelve-step programs are designed to give you the awareness, the structure, the tools, and the accountability to face yourself and "show up" in life in a balanced way.

- If you are feeling overwhelmed or lacking a sense of peace in your day, try this exercise: take out a sheet of blank paper. Draw a vertical line down the middle of the page so there are two columns in front of you. In the left-hand column list things that are unchangeable, things you need to accept and let go of. In the right-hand column list things that are changeable, things you can take action on. Make a decision to take action on one thing in your right-hand column while you decide to let go of something in your left-hand column.

- Remember that peace and tranquility are both methods of travel as well as results of right action. You can decide to bring peace into your day, but also know that when you search, choose, and act in accordance with your deepest values, when you live a life of integrity, and when you keep promises both to yourself and to others, you can look yourself in the mirror at night and know both self-respect and inner peace.

- Think of ways that help you, in the moment, to come back to yourself. Perhaps a screen-saver on your computer with a quote or a poem, or a note on your bathroom mirror, or a special object that has significance for you at your workplace will remind you to be present.

- Befriend your breath as a way to bring your awareness into the present. Anyone who works with people in trauma knows that the first thing to do with an anxious person is to have them take a deep breath.

- As you practice being present and tuning in to the moment, observe the things that tell you that you are moving away from your authentic self. Being anxious, frustrated, stressed or overwhelmed are reminders to take a deep breath and bring yourself into a place of faith and trust.

- Be open to the people who are closest to you to give you feedback. Think of people in your life who support you in staying "present" so you can walk through your day with more mindfulness. Teachers, guides and confidants can all be useful in bringing ourselves into the moment if we remember to call them.

- The next time you are angry or frustrated, acknowledge those feelings and then decide to bring a little balance to your internal conversation: "And I am also grateful for…"

- You can reflect on gratitude by inquiring if it is time-based. If you are aware of losing your serenity, ask yourself what happened to all the gratitude you felt in the past. Where did it go? Do you believe that gratitude is dependent on feeling good right now? See if you can be aware of gratitude independent of your current feelings.

- Take a daily inventory. Before going to bed or first thing in the morning, list everything you are grateful for, in spite of your mood at the moment. The making of such a list is not meant to make you feel indebted, but it is intended to clarify your understanding of the complete truth of your life.

- Actively practice noticing things you are grateful for throughout your day. For instance, when you are stuck in traffic, be mindful of your gratitude for having a car. Keep doing this. Your motive here is not to pretend to be nice or to not be frustrated, but rather to see more clearly the true situation of your life.

- Next time you read the paper and hear of someone's misfortune, reach within yourself to a place of compassion and an awareness of gratitude.

* * * *

NOURISHING COMMUNITY

- Take some time to think about what community means to you. What do you yearn for? Are you seeking more solitude and reflection in your life or are you wanting a more substantive connection to others?

- Think of ways you can start fostering a community by examining your values, ideals and virtues, grief and pain, dreams and passions — those things that you want to share with others and receive support for. Reflect upon whom you want to reach out to. Start with your geographic area, local churches, community associations, or groups that are working together for a social cause. Pick up the phone and start reaching out.

- Remember, start small. If it feels daunting to think of investing in a community, start with one person you would like to get to know, that you would like to open up with. It is the planting of vulnerability that brings forth the fruit of meaningful connection. Two people can be a community.

- Stop and think about the network of people in your life. Are any of them currently your confidants? Confidants can be life partners, friends, teachers, and colleagues, or they can be professionals, such as therapists, persons with experience in untying inner knots. They might be religious leaders or other spiritual guides or people who help you value another's humanity and who help you become acquainted with a deeper call to unity, inner peace, freedom, and greater self-appreciation. But relationships with confidants are two-way. One day, you might need a confidant; the next day you could be one for that person.

- Reflect momentarily on the value confidants have had in your life, on the people in your life who have been there for you over the years.

- Reflect on times when you have held off from opening up and ways that confidants could better serve you.

- Make a list of people who are confidants in your life right now. Make a point to connect with at least one of them in the next forty-eight hours, expressing your appreciation for what they bring to your life.

- Make a list of people in your life with whom you would like to connect, people you would like to open up with as potential confidants. Make a point to start nurturing these relationships and be more open about your need for support before a crisis hits. Be intentional about investing in relationships and searching for at least one person you can trust.

- If you don't connect easily with nature, find a mentor in your life who can be a guide in helping you feel a part of the natural world.

- Reflect for a moment on what kind of geography appeals to you. What kind of nature soothes you? Do you have an affinity for water? For trees? For mountains? For prairie?

- Spend time, even if it's only five minutes, every day, getting off the concrete and putting your feet on soil.

*   *   *   *

BUILDING CHARACTER

- Take a few moments to look within yourself and reflect upon your own character and conduct. Ask yourself these questions: "Do I pass the mirror test at the end of a day?" That is, when you look in the mirror at night do you have self-respect? "Is there congruence between how I present myself to the world and the choices I make?" "Do strangers and those closest to me see me as the same person?"

- Take some time to reflect upon any current disturbance in your life, a sense of incompleteness or inauthenticity. It will usually surface in your relationships with others, whether love relationships or work relationships. See if you can recognize, tune into, the cause of the disturbance as lying within you. Look past the blame, of others or yourself, and see if you can begin to own the disturbance. Once you own the disturbance, what actions are needed toward a resolution? (Remember, it is an action even if you simply decide to be in a disturbance in a new way.)

- Look at any conflict you are currently experiencing. Ask yourself, "What do I have to learn here? How am I contributing to the tension?"

- Reflect on areas where you are blaming and ask yourself (without blaming yourself), "How have I been a part of creating this?" For example, ask yourself, "Where have I not been clear enough with myself or others? Where have I lacked courage and acted out of fear? Where have I compromised my values and principles?"

- Review and renew your rights and responsibilities as a citizen. Are you doing your part to uphold the responsibility end of the charter?

- Think of how you contribute to your community. Do you spend more time and energy as a consumer or as a citizen?

- Search out a part of yourself that has shown a pattern of causing you pain or uneasiness, either in yourself or in others, by your actions. Seek to understand it. If you find yourself going into a rage for seemingly no reason, stop and pay attention to that. If you find yourself getting overly anxious, overwhelmed or fearful, perhaps in the middle of the night, acknowledge these incidents. Stop and pay attention. If you find you are in a period in your life where you are tired and low in energy, stop and acknowledge it.

- Name your dark side. Put a label on this part of yourself, without judgment. By doing so, you legitimize it. Just as alcoholics name themselves for what they are at AA meetings, so you can do the same: "I have an insecure side to me" or "I have a sensitive nervous system."

- Let yourself experience what you want to avoid. Whether it is anger, fear, lust, grief, depression, insecurity, over-dependence, or self-doubt — sit with it. Talk about it with a confidant. Ask for help. Read about it. Learn from others who have walked this path before.

- Talk to others about your dark side. It requires discipline, attention, sharing, and accountability for new action, or the darker sides start to take over.

- Acknowledge your darker side and reveal it to others in a constructive way, so you can make new choices. If you turn toward your authentic self, the power that you think will destroy you will be diminished. By facing the shadows in your life with an open heart and a focused mind, you cease resisting and begin to accept and heal. It is not the darkness that is your opponent, but your denial of it. It is in facing your difficulties that you have an opportunity to make contact with a hidden strength.

- Connect with a force beyond yourself that you can lean on and trust to lift the burden of the darker aspects of your nature.

* * * *

SEEKING CALLING

- Be aware of your reaction and your own personal perspective on calling by reflecting on the following questions: "What does calling mean to me? What is my own unique search for calling in my life? Have I 'searched' out my calling or has it seemed to just 'come' to me? Am I aware of any inner frustrations, anxiety, or tension around clarifying my 'call' in life or am I trusting and relaxed about it, knowing that the 'hounds of authenticity' will keep tracking me down? Am I truly living my life or have I been caught in the trap of conforming only to the expectations of others?"

- Take some quiet time over the next twenty-four hours and reflect upon your life. Listen to that whisper of your inner voice — a gut feeling, your heart, or your conscience. Be aware of any tension, discomfort, and uneasiness about any aspect of your life. Ask yourself: "Is there any area in my life that needs attention? Do I feel I have a call? Am I living my call? Am I true to myself or am I living someone else's life?"

- Pause and ask yourself the question: "What do I do well that I don't remember learning?" Take some quiet time and listen for the still, small inner voice that is pulling you toward bringing your gifts to life. Pay attention to the small nudges that are calling you to be more than you currently are.

- Stop and reflect on the following questions: "Where in my life do I experience passion? What activities am I doing when I lose all track of time? When and where am I making room for the passions in my life?"

- Stop, listen for, and follow your passion. It will be a great guide and a friend to you. See if you can reach an underlying desire that is the source of your current passion. Passion whispers to you through your heart, beckoning you toward your highest good. Pay attention to what makes you feel energized, connected and stimulated. Do what you love and give it back in the form of contribution.

- Reflect on the losses you have experienced in your life. Stop and take some time to feel the impact of these on your life. See if you can feel where you may have had a loss in your life that has been swept under the carpet and is in need of healing. Ask yourself, "Who can I reach out to and start talking to about this?"

- Think about the service you render in your life. Reflect upon your motives. What is the truth about your service? Where in your life can you be less self-centered and where can you be more aware of giving rather than taking?

- Take some time to reflect on calling and see how the following statements fit in your life: Calling is a lifelong journey, not a destination. Calling is, by nature, increasingly complex, and yet simple. When you are there, you know it. You know you are living your calling by your energy level, your sense of inner peace, and your connection to yourself and to those around you. You will not tire on the inside. In its truest sense, calling is irresistible. Calling is not about ego; it is not about feeling happy, joyous and free all the time; but it is a deep and sustaining inner contentment of knowing that you are doing what you are meant to be doing.

* * * *

References

* * * *

Barks, Coleman. *The Essential Rumi*. San Francisco: Harper, 1995.

Bellman, Geoff M. *The Consultant's Calling: Bringing Who You Are to What You Do*. San Francisco: Jossey-Bass, 1990.

Blake, William. *The Marriage of Heaven and Hell*, 1793.

Block, Peter. *The Answer to How Is Yes: Acting on What Matters*. San Francisco: Berrett-Koehler, 2002.

Bly, Robert, James Hillman, and Michael Meade (eds.). *The Rag and Bone Shop of the Heart: Poems for Men*. New York: HarperPerennial, 1992.

Brehony, Kathleen A. *Awakening at Midlife: Realizing Your Potential for Growth and Change*. New York: Riverhead Books, 1996.

Campbell, Joseph. *The Hero With a Thousand Faces*. New York: MJF Books, 1949.

Campbell, Joseph with Bill Moyers. *The Power of Myth*. New York: Doubleday, 1988.

Canfield, Jack and Mark Victor Hansen. *Chicken Soup for the Soul*. Deerfield Beach, FL: Health Communications, 1993.

Covey, Stephen R. *Seven Habits of Highly Effective People*. New York: Simon & Schuster, 1990.

_____. *Seven Habits of Highly Effective Families*. Provo, UT: Covey Leadership Center, 2001.

_____. *The Divine Center: Why We Need a Life Centered on God and Christ and How to Attain It*. Salt Lake City, UT: Bookcraft, 1982.

de Mello, Anthony. *The Heart of the Enlightened: A Book of Story Meditations*. New York: Doubleday, 1989.

de Tocqueville, Alexis. *Democracy in America*. J. P. Mayer, ed.; George Lawrence, translator. New York: Doubleday Anchor Books, 1969.

Fox, Matthew. *The Reinvention of Work: A New Vision of Livelihood for Our Time*. San Francisco: Harper, 1995.

Guiness, Og. *The Call: Finding and Fulfilling the Central Purpose of Your Life*. Nashville, TN: Word Publishing, 1998.

Heifetz, Ronald A. *Leadership Without Easy Answers*. Cambridge, MA: Belknap Press/Harvard University Press, 1994.

Henderson, Nancy I. *Learners Learning Inc. Newsletter*, 7th edition (January 1999). Toronto, ON, Canada.

Jaworski, Joseph. *Synchronicity: The Inner Path of Leadership*. San Francisco: Berrett-Koehler, 1996.

Kabat-Zinn, Jon. *Wherever You Go There You Are: Mindfulness Meditation in Everyday Life*. New York: Hyperion, 1994.

Khan, Hazrat Inayat. *The Art of Being and Becoming*. New Lebanon, NY: Omega, 1982.

Koesenbaum, Peter and Peter Block. *Freedom and Accountability at Work: Applying Philosophical Insight to the Real World*. San Francisco: Jossey-Bass/Pfeiffer, 2001.

Kornfield, Jack and Christina Feldman. *Soul Food: Stories That Nourish the Spirit and the Heart*. San Francisco: Harper, 1996.

McKnight, John. *The Careless Society: Community and Its Counterfeits*. San Francisco: Harper Collins, 1997.

Meade, Michael. *Men and the Water of Life: Initiation and the Tempering of Men*. San Francisco: Harper, 1993.

Moffitt, Phillip. "Selfless Gratitude." *The Yoga Journal* (July/August 2002). Berkley, CA.

Moore, Thomas. *Care of the Soul: A Guide for Cultivating Depth and Sacredness in Everyday Life*. New York: HarperPerennial, 1992.

Nachmanovitch, Stephen. *Free Play: Improvisation in Life and Art.* New York: Jeremy P. Tarcher/Putman, 1990.

Oliva, Father Max, S.J. *The Masculine Spirit, Resources for Reflective Living*. Notre Dame, IN: Ave Maria Press, 1997.

_____. *God of Many Loves*. Notre Dame, IN: Ave Maria Press, 2001.

Palmer, Parker. *Let Your Life Speak: Listening to the Voice of Vocation*. San Francisco: Jossey-Bass, 2000.

Rechtschaffen, Stephan. *Time Shifting: Creating More Time to Enjoy Your Life*. New York: Doubleday, 1996.

Rilke, Rainer Maria. *Letters to a Young Poet*. New York: W. W. Norton, 1963.

Robertson, Joel and Tom Monte. *Natural Prozac: Learning to Release Your Body's Own Anti-Depressants*. San Francisco: Harper, 1998.

Satir, Virginia. *The New PeopleMaking*. Mountainview, CA: Science and Behavior Books, 1988.

Savory, Allan with Jody Butterfield. *Holistic Management: A New Framework for Decision Making*. Washington, D.C.: Island Press, 1999.

Scherer, John. *Work and the Human Spirit*. Spokane, WA: JS&A, 1993.

Schiffmann, Erich. Yoga: *The Spirit and Practice of Moving into Stillness*. New York: Pocket Books, 1996.

Schor, Juliet. *The Overworked American*. New York: Basic Books, 1997.

Shain, Merle. *Hearts That We Broke Long Ago*. New York: Bantam Books, 1983.

Teilhard de Chardin, Pierre. "The Evolution of Chastity" in *Toward the Future*. Translated by René Hague. London: Collins; New York: Harcourt Brace Jovanovich, 1975.

Terry, Robert. *Authentic Leadership: Courage in Action*. San Francisco: Jossey-Bass, 1993.

_____. *Seven Zones for Leadership: Acting Authentically in Stability and Chaos*. Palo Alto, CA: Davies-Black, 2001.

Zukav, Gary. *Seat of the Soul*. New York: Simon & Schuster, 1989.

* * * *

I am indebted to Fred Kofman, former teacher at the University of California and MIT and a colleague of Peter Senge, who has been a mentor and has also been very influential to me in the area of integrity and consciousness in the workplace. Fred has an audio cassette series entitled *Conscious Business* (Sounds True Audio Cassette), as well as a book by the same title, also published by Sounds True Publications, that I highly recommend.

Thanks to Father Max Oliva, friend and colleague, for his insights on integrity.

Over the years I have been greatly influenced by the work of Allan Savory, a former wildlife biologist, farmer, and politician and co-founder of the Center for Holistic Management, based in Albuquerque, New Mexico. I attribute much of my material on quality of life to Allan's work, specifically his book entitled *Holistic Management: A New Framework for Decision Making* (1999, Island Press, Washington, D.C.).

I am grateful to Ralph Stacey for giving me the inspiration for "shadow" in the context of organizations.

I am also grateful to Dan Sullivan for giving me the concept of "free days." Dan directs a program called *The Strategic Coach*.

* * * *

Notes

* * * *

INTRODUCTION

p. xxix   Hazrat Inayat Khan, *The Art of Being and Becoming* (1982, p. xiii, Omega, New Lebanon, NY).

p. xxxv   The analogy of finding an internal thermostat comes from Og Guiness, *The Call: Finding and Fulfilling the Central Purpose of Your Life* (1998, pp. 75–76, Word Publishing, Nashville, TN).

MY JOURNEY

p. xxxix   Michelangelo's quote; as cited in Kathleen A. Brehony, *Awakening at Midlife: Realizing Your Potential for Growth and Change* (1996, Riverhead Books, New York). Brehony does a superb job of reframing and guiding one through the midlife process.

p. 1   The notion of depression being a result of an imbalance is adapted from Joel Robertson and Tom Monte, *Natural Prozac: Learning to Release Your Body's Own Anti-Depressants* (1998, Harper, San Francisco).

CHAPTER 1: FINDING CENTER

p. 1   For many years I have been inspired by the daily readings in Jonathon Lazear's *Meditations for Men Who Do Too Much* (1992, Simon & Schuster, New York). This is an extremely helpful book for men who are committed to shifting their center from their work to a deeper, more sustaining core. For women, there is a companion book by Dr. Anne Wilson Schaef, *Meditations for Women Who Do Too Much* (2000, Harper, San Francisco).

p. 2–3   The notion of "finding your center" was introduced to me by Stephen R. Covey, *The Divine Center: Why We Need a Life Centered on God and Christ and How to Attain It* (1982, Bookcraft, Salt Lake City).

p. 5   "... following the counsel St. Paul gave..." was cited in John Scherer, *Work and the Human Spirit* (1993, p. 34, JS&A, Spokane, WA).

p. 20   The concept of transitional rituals comes from Ronald A. Heifetz, *Leadership Without Easy Answers* (1994, Belknap Press/Harvard University Press, Cambridge, MA).

p. 24   One of the most listened to audio cassette programs in my car library is still Earl Nightingale's *The Strangest Secret* (Nightingale Conant Corp., Niles, IL).

p. 27   "Inspiration, and inspired living..." and the concept of a "five-sensory culture" comes from Gary Zukav, *Seat of the Soul* (1989, Simon & Schuster, New York).

p. 29   The metaphor of the "aerial perspective" was inspired by Erich Schiffmann's *Yoga: The Spirit and Practice of Moving into Stillness* (1996, p. 329, Pocket Books, New York).

p. 32   Carl Jung's notion of synchronicity, as cited in Joseph Jaworski, *Synchronicity: The Inner Path of Leadership* (1996, Berrett-Koehler, San Francisco). Jaworski's book is a must-read for anyone wanting to deepen his or her skills as a leader — in any capacity.

p. 33   Improvisation as "intuition in action" comes from Stephen Nachmanovitch, *Free Play, Improvisation in Life and Art* (1990, Jeremy Tarcher/Putman, New York).

p. 36   This section on listening to your body was inspired by conversations with Pat Copping.

p. 40   This section and the notion of "managing human hungers" benefited greatly from Ronald A. Heifetz, *Leadership Without Easy Answers* (1994, Belknap Press/ Harvard University Press, Cambridge, MA).

p. 44   The story of Socrates in the marketplace is retold by Anthony de Mello in *The Heart of the Enlightened: A Book of Story Meditations* (1989, p. 27, Doubleday, New York).

p. 46   "... compulsive work habits" correlated with "watching television" is cited in Matthew Fox, *The Reinvention of Work: A New Vision of Livelihood for Our Time* (1994, p. 35, Harper, San Francisco). This is a thoughtful book that reframes the place of work in life and how to bring forth work from a deeper part of yourself.

p. 50   For a more extensive study in the practice of mindfulness, I refer you to Jon Kabat-Zinn, *Wherever You Go There You Are: Mindfulness Meditation in Everyday Life* (1994, Hyperion, New York).

p. 51   "If there is light in the soul..." was quoted in Jack Canfield and Mark Victor Hansen, *Chicken Soup for the Soul* (1993, p. vii, Health Communications, Deerfield Beach, FL).

p. 51–52   The St. Francis prayer is found in *The Twelve Steps and Twelve Traditions of Alcoholics Anonymous* (1998, AA World Services, Inc., New York).

p. 52   This section on practicing gratitude and generosity benefited greatly from an article by Phillip Moffitt entitled "Selfless Gratitude" in the July/August 2002 issue of *The Yoga Journal*.

p. 54   David Irvine, *Simple Living in a Complex World: Balancing Life's Achievements* (2004, Wiley & Sons Canada, Toronto).

p. 55   "The Guest House" poem can be found in *The Essential Rumi*, translated by Coleman Barks with John Moyne (1995, p. 109, Harper, San Francisco).

p. 57   The definition of "abundance mentality" was inspired by a conversation with Don Campbell. (See also pp. 95–96 of chapter 2.)

CHAPTER 2: NOURISHING COMMUNITY

p. 61   Pierre Teilhard de Chardin, "The Evolution of Chastity" in *Toward the Future*. Translated by René Hague. London: Collins; New York: Harcourt Brace Jovanovich, 1975.

p. 61   This entire chapter on nourishing authentic community was enriched by the influence of John McKnight, *The Careless Society: Community and Its Counterfeits* (1997, Harper Collins, San Francisco).

p. 62   Alexis de Tocqueville, *Democracy in America* (J. P. Mayer, ed.; George Lawrence, translator; 1969, p. 287, Doubleday Anchor, New York); cited in M. Scott Peck, *The Different Drum: Community Making and Peace* (1987, Simon & Schuster, New York). I recommend all of Scott Peck's books, including *The Road Less Traveled* (1978,

Simon & Schuster, New York) and *A World Waiting To Be Born* (1993, Bantam Books, New York).

p. 68   Michael Meade, *Men and the Water of Life: Initiation and the Tempering of Men* (1993, p. 19, Harper, San Francisco).

p. 70   This section on confidants benefited from Ronald A. Heifetz, *Leadership Without Easy Answers* (1994, Belknap Press/Harvard University Press, Cambridge, MA).

p. 75   The notion of a "leg-up person" came from a lecture given by Sid Simon in Calgary, AB, Canada (November 12, 1991).

p. 78   Robert Terry, *Authentic Leadership: Courage in Action* (1993, Jossey-Bass, San Francisco) and *Seven Zones for Leadership: Acting Authentically in Stability and Chaos* (2001, Davies-Black, Palo Alto, CA). These are in-depth and useful texts that explore the work of authenticity in a leader.

p. 78–79   Father Max Oliva, S.J., *The Masculine Spirit, Resources for Reflective Living* (1997, Ave Maria Press, Notre Dame, IN) and *God of Many Loves* (2001, Ave Maria Press, Notre Dame, IN). These are practical, useful books for deepening your spiritual connection written by a Jesuit priest.

p. 80   Parker Palmer, *Let Your Life Speak: Listening to the Voice of Vocation* (2000, Jossey-Bass, San Francisco). Any of Parker's books are well worth reading, especially *The Courage to Teach: Exploring the Inner Landscape of a Teacher's Life* (1998, Jossey-Bass, San Francisco). Although written for teachers, this is a wonderful book for those who wish to amplify their impact in the world.

p. 82   No teacher shifted my perceptions on human development more than the late Virginia Satir. Virginia's philosophy is eloquently outlined in her book, *The New*

PeopleMaking (1988, Science and Behavior Books, Mountainview, CA).

p. 90   The concepts of Descartes' mechanistic model emerged from conversations with Ian West.

p. 95–96   The Oxford College story is cited in Stephan Rechtschaffen, *Time Shifting: Creating More Time to Enjoy Your Life* (1996, Doubleday, New York). This is a very thoughtful and practical book on time management and beyond.

CHAPTER 3: BUILDING CHARACTER

p. 99   This entire chapter benefited greatly from Jim Rohn's audio tape, *Unshakable Character*, produced by Nightingale Conant Corp., Niles, IL. I am also grateful for the impact of my conversations with Don Campbell. For a practical application of building character and accountability in organizations, see Bruce Klatt, Shaun Murphy, and David Irvine, *Accountability: Getting a Grip on Results* (2004, Bow River Publishing, Calgary, AB, Canada). For application of building character in schools, see Kevin Ryan and Karen Bohlin, *Building Character in Schools: Practical Ways to Bring Moral Instructions to Life* (1999, Jossey-Bass, San Francisco).

p. 101   "Chiseling away your character" is cited in Jim Rohn's audio tape, *Unshakable Character*, produced by Nightingale Conant Corp., Niles, IL.

p. 109   For a more extensive study of "the hero's journey," see Joseph Campbell's classic work, *The Hero With a Thousand Faces* (1949, MJF Books, New York).

p. 111   Carl Jung's note that "disobedience is the first step towards consciousness" is cited in Peter Block, *The Answer to How Is Yes: Acting on What Matters* (2002, p. 115, Berrett-Koehler, San Francisco).

p. 112 This section on citizenship was enriched by Peter Koesenbaum and Peter Block, *Freedom and Accountability at Work: Applying Philosophical Insight to the Real World* (2001, Jossey-Bass/Pfeiffer, San Francisco).

p. 112 "... from full service to lip service..." is from another major contributor to this section, Peter Block, *The Answer to How Is Yes: Acting on What Matters* (2002, p. 84, pp. 116–120, Berrett-Koehler, San Francisco).

p. 115–120 This section on integrity, and specifically the notion of integrity related to keeping promises, comes from Fred Kofman. I highly recommend his audio cassette series entitled *Conscious Business*, Sounds True Audio Cassette, Boulder, CO. This section also benefited from the teachings of Max Oliva.

p. 120 The concept of clearing was inspired by Nancy I. Henderson, *Learners Learning Inc. Newsletter*, 7th edition (January 1999). Toronto, ON, Canada.

p. 126 This section on the concept of "shadow" benefited from the contribution of Ralph Stacey.

p. 129 "... responsibility to... responsibility for..." is from Og Guiness, *The Call: Finding and Fulfilling the Central Purpose of Your Life* (1998, p. 91, Word Publishing, Nashville, TN).

p. 130 The story of the rich industrialist is cited in Jack Kornfield and Christina Feldman, *Soul Food: Stories That Nourish the Spirit and the Heart* (1996, Harper, San Francisco).

p. 131 Allan Savory with Jody Butterfield, *Holistic Management: A New Framework for Decision Making* (1999, pp. 67–83, Island Press, Washington, D.C.).

CHAPTER 4: SEEKING CALLING

p. 141   This chapter benefited from several sources: David Spangler, *The Call* (1996, Riverhead Books, New York); Janet Amare, *Soul Purpose: A Practical Guide for Creating a Life You Love* (2001, Life On Purpose Publishing, Campbellville, ON); Og Guiness, *The Call: Finding and Fulfilling the Central Purpose of Your Life* (1998, Word Publishing, Nashville, TN); Gary Zukav, *Seat of the Soul* (1989, Simon & Schuster, New York); Po Bronson, *What Should I Do With My Life? The True Story of People Who Answer the Ultimate Question* (2002, Random House, New York); Laurie Beth Jones, *The Path: Creating Your Mission Statement for Work and for Life* (1996, Hyperion, New York); Laura S., *12 Steps on Buddha's Path: A Spiritual Journey of Recovery* (2006, Wisdom Publications, Boston).

p. 145   "When the deepest part of you becomes engaged in what you are doing..." comes from Gary Zukav, *Seat of the Soul* (1989, Simon & Schuster, New York).

p. 157   The concept of "life force" was inspired by Thomas Moore, *Care of the Soul: A Guide for Cultivating Depth and Sacredness in Everyday Life* (1992, HarperPerennial, New York).

p. 156   The question "What do you do well that you don't remember learning?" was given to me in a conversation with John Scherer (June 21, 2000, Vernon, BC, Canada).

p. 161   "... sixty billion U.S. dollars is spent annually by businesses in North America to pay for depression claims by employees..." (Juliet Schor, Harvard University Economics professor, in *The Overworked American*, 1997, Basic Books, New York).

p. 171   Rainer Maria Rilke, *Letters to a Young Poet* (1963, p. 35, W. W. Norton, New York).

p. 172   This Hasidic legend can be found in Merle Shain, *Hearts That We Broke Long Ago* (1983, p. 21, Bantam Books, New York).

CHAPTER 5: THE CHALLENGE

p. 193–194   The "Miracle of the Chinese Bamboo Tree" is cited in Stephen R. Covey's book, *Seven Habits of Highly Effective Families* (1997, pp. 22–23, Covey Leadership Center, Provo, UT). I also recommend Stephen Covey's *Seven Habits of Highly Effective People: Powerful Lessons in Personal Change* (1990, Simon & Schuster, New York).

p. 194   This Antonio Machado poem can be found in Robert Bly, James Hillman, and Michael Meade (eds.), *The Rag and Bone Shop of the Heart: Poems for Men* (1992, pp. 372–373, HarperPerennial, New York).

APPENDIX

p. 212   The questions related to facing your "dark side" were inspired by Geoff Bellman, *The Consultant's Calling: Bringing Who You Are to What You Do* (1990, Jossey-Bass, San Francisco).

p. 213   "… hounds of authenticity…" is adapted from Francis Thompson's famous picture, as cited in Og Guiness, *The Call: Finding and Fulfilling the Central Purpose of Your Life* (1998, p. 14, Word Publishing, Nashville, TN).

Additional Reading

* * * *

Although not specifically referenced above, the following books can support you on your journey to authenticity:

James Hillman. *The Soul's Code: In Search of Character and Calling.* New York, NY: Random House, 1996. Hillman provides an in-depth examination of passion, uniqueness, and destiny.

David Irvine. *Simple Living in a Complex World: Balancing Life's Achievements.* Toronto, ON: Wiley & Sons Canada, 2004. This is a simple, reflective book on how to live authentically through simplicity.

David Irvine and Jim Reger. *The Authentic Leader: It's About PRESENCE, Not Position.* Sanford, FL: DC Press, 2006. This book applies the notion of authenticity to the work of leadership. Whether you are a CEO, an elementary school principal, a community volunteer, a frontline nurse, a manager in a government agency, or a parent, opportunities are available for authentic leadership.

John Izzo. *The Five Secrets You Must Discover Before You Die.* San Francisco, CA: Berret-Koehler, 2008. My friend, John Izzo, interviewed over 200 people, ages 60–106, and shares the wisdom gleaned from these conversations.

Lew Losoncy. *If It Weren't for You, We Could Get Along! How to Stop Blaming and Start Living.* Sanford, FL: DC Press, 2000. Anything written by Lew Losoncy is worth reading.

Philip Simmons. *Learning to Fall: The Blessings of an Imperfect Life.* New York, NY: Bantam Books, 2000. Philip Simmons is a gifted journalist who shares his story of living with — and eventually dying from — ALS (Lou Gehrig's disease).

Jean Vanier. *Becoming Human.* Toronto, ON: Anansi, 1998. Jean Vanier is an authentic, compassionate human being whose influence permeates every chapter in this book and in my life.

Margery Williams. *The Velveteen Rabbit or How Toys Become Real.* Philadelphia, PA: Running Press, 1998. This is a wonderful children's story that is an inspiration for all of us who want to courageously take the authentic journey.

David Whyte. *Crossing the Unknown Sea: Work as a Pilgrimage of Identity.* New York, NY: Riverhead Books, 2001. For those interested in exploring work as an opportunity to discover and express your authentic self, you will find this book full of wisdom. Anything by David Whyte is worth reading.

Zondervan NIV Study Bible. Grand Rapids, MI: Zondervan Publishing House, 2005.

About the Author

* * * *

D AVID IRVINE is among North America's most sought-after corporate speakers and mentors. He has more than twenty-five years of experience as a family therapist, consultant, professional speaker, workshop facilitator and executive coach. His unique, personal approach to human dynamics has inspired hundreds of leaders to transform their organizations, build more accountable, authentic, productive workplaces, and find meaning and contentment in their lives. He now speaks to thousands of people every year, from large corporations to small entrepreneurial ventures, from community associations to all levels of government, education, and health care. David has taught at three universities and the Banff School of Management. He is the author of three other bestselling books: *The Authentic Leader: It's About PRESENCE, Not Position; Simple Living in a Complex World;* and *Accountability: Getting a Grip on Results.* David lives with his wife and daughters in the foothills of the Rocky Mountains in western Canada.

* * * *

For Additional Information

* * * *

I F THIS BOOK HAS INSPIRED YOU, or if you would like to receive information on presentations, programs, or coaching I offer on authentic living and leading, I invite you to contact me:

David Irvine
The Leader's Navigator
Box 358
Cochrane, Alberta,
Canada
T4C 1A6
Email: david@davidirvine.com
Website: www.davidirvine.com
www.newportinstitute.com